CW01465923

CONTEMPORARY SOCI

General Editor: ANTHONY GIDDENS

This series aims to create a forum for debate between different theoretical and philosophical traditions in the social sciences. As well as covering broad schools of thought, the series will also concentrate upon the work of particular thinkers whose ideas have had a major impact on social science (these books appear under the sub-series title of 'Theoretical Traditions in the Social Sciences'). The series is not limited to abstract theoretical discussion – it will also include more substantive works on contemporary capitalism, the state, politics and other subject areas.

CONTEMPORARY SOCIAL THEORY

General Editor: ANTHONY GIDDENS

Theoretical Traditions in the Social Sciences

This series introduces the work of major figures in social science to students beyond their immediate specialisms.

Published titles
Barry Barnes, *T. S. Kuhn and Social Science*
Ted Benton, *The Rise and Fall of Structural Marxism*
David Bloor, *Wittgenstein: A Social Theory of Knowledge*
Christopher G. A. Bryant, *Positivism in Social Theory and Research*
Mark Cousins and Athar Hussain, *Michel Foucault*
Bob Jessop, *Nicos Poulantzas: Marxist Theory and Political Strategy*
Julian Roberts, *Walter Benjamin*
Rick Roderick, *Habermas and the Foundations of Critical Theory*
Dennis Smith, *Barrington Moore: Violence, Morality and Political Change*
James Schmidt, *Maurice Merleau-Ponty: Between Phenomenology and Structuralism*
Piotr Sztompka, *Robert K. Merton: An Intellectual Profile*

Forthcoming titles
Ira Cohen, *Structuration Theory*
John Forrester, *Jacques Lacan*
William Outhwaite, *Realist Philosophy in the Social Sciences*
Dennis Smith, *The Chicago School*
Robin Williams, *Erving Goffman*

Habermas and the Foundations of Critical Theory

Rick Roderick

M

MACMILLAN

First published 1986

Published by
Higher and Further Education Divison
MACMILLAN PUBLISHERS LTD
Houndmills, Basingstoke, Hampshire RG21 2XS
and London
Companies and representatives
throughout the world

Printed in Hong Kong

British Library Cataloguing in Publication Data
Roderick, Rick
Habermas and the foundations of critical theory.
1. Habermas, Jürgen
I. Title
193   B3258.H324
ISBN 0–333–39655–3
ISBN 0–333–39656–1 Pbk

*This book is dedicated to my wife, Irene,
without whom it would not have been possible*

Contents

Acknowledgements

I would like to thank Douglas Kellner, Paul Woodruff, Louis Mackey, Harry Cleaver and Charles Guignon for many improvements in this manuscript. Douglas Kellner, in particular, has provided not only help along this line, but also encouragement and support for the entire undertaking. Finally, I would like to thank those members of my generation who continue to think that 'things might be otherwise'. Several of these are my friends: Tom and Frank Zigal, Turner and Holt Williamson, Joan and Tom Burditt, and Jim Bogard. Without the lessons I have learned from them, I would not have undertaken this work.

I would also like to thank Suhrkamp/Insel Publishers Boston, Inc. for permission to reprint from Habermas's *Theorie des kommunikativen Handelns*.

Department of Philosophy
Duke University

RICK RODERICK

Preface

In conformity with the aim of this series of books on theoretical and philosophical traditions in the social sciences, I have attempted to introduce the reader to the work of Habermas from its earliest formulations to its most recent in order to further debate and discussion, and not to present as a finished product a body of work that is still developing. The complexity of Habermas's project, as well as the multiplicity of theoretical currents upon which he draws, demanded that I select a focus for my account which would highlight its fundamental claims without losing the reader in a mass of inessential detail. To this end, I began with two problems that appear and reappear throughout his work: the problem of developing a justification for the normative dimension of critical social theory; and the problem of establishing a connection between the theory and political practice. Both problems can be traced back to Marx and followed throughout the subsequent development of the Marxist tradition, although they appear in particularly acute form in the elaboration of his social theory developed by the Frankfurt school. The first involves what is to count as a rational criticism of society, while the second is directed at how such criticisms are to aid in the construction of a society that is actually more rational. At attempt to answer them thus requires an account of rationality developed at, at least, two levels: a formal account of the concept; and an account of its social and historical embodiment in institutions, modes of production, and ways of life. Harbermas attempts to supply such an account explicitly in his latest work and it is implicit in his early work. This theme serves as the guiding-thread of my account and it is primarily in this context that I place the work of Habermas. To proceed in this way requires that I address philosophical, sociological and political issues: a combination of concerns that are a leading feature of Habermas's own work and one which generates much of the interest in it.

Through his account of rationality, Habermas hopes to respond to what he sees as the deep and manifold problems not only of the Marxist tradition but also of the modern project of enlightened, rational thought in general. What E. P. Thompson calls exterminism (the rationally planned, technologically secured, institutionally empowered nuclear arms race) is the most spectacular example, although others abound – threatened ecological systems, mass starvation, genocidal wars, and so on. Viewed in this light, the historical and theoretical developments I examine under the heading of the 'problematic of rationality' are central not only for Habermas and the Marxist tradition but also for any project of modern social theory that hopes to do more than ratify the existing state of affairs. Although very sophisticated theoretically, Habermas's response is too weak on the politics of these concrete embodiments of 'rationality'. My discussion of Habermas in the context of the Marxist tradition is thus not intended simply as a philosophical introduction, but rather as a preparation for a fundamental critique of his project. This critique is itself developed from a (somewhat unorthodox) Marxist perspective, a perspective that I am well aware requires more defence than I provide in the present volume. I hope to make up for this deficiency at a later time. For the present, I attempt to contrast Habermas's communication theory of society with Marx's social theory based on production. My purpose is to expose the limitations of the communication paradigm not only in Habermas's formulation, but indirectly for the general shift in this direction taken by critical social theory. It is my view that the resources of Marx's production paradigm are far from exhausted, a point I argue for briefly at the conclusion of this work. Whether or not I am right in this, I hope to have at least raised the important questions.

Department of Philosophy   RICK RODERICK
Duke University
May 1985

1
Reading Habermas

'Philosophy remains true to its classic tradition by renouncing it.'—Jürgen Habermas

The task of introducing the work of Jürgen Habermas to the English-speaking world is well under way. Thomas McCarthy's excellent study has clarified and systematised Habermas's work by shaping it into a coherent whole, capable of addressing a wide range of current problems in philosophy of language, social and political theory, ethics and theory of knowledge. David Held's work has succeeded in situating Habermas in the tradition of the critical theory of the Frankfurt School, as well as raising a series of compelling objections both to the work of Habermas and to critical theory as a whole. Raymond Geuss's study of Habermas analyses central contentions in his position, making it more accessible to Anglo-American philosophers, while Garbis Kortian's study locates Habermas in the German philosophical tradition from Kant through Hegel to Marx. Richard Bernsteins' work clarifies Habermas's contribution to social theory and explicates connections between Habermas and the classical philosophical tradition.[1] In addition to these major studies, an extensive and ever increasing number of reviews and articles devoted to extending, improving, defending or simply explicating Habermas's position mark the most recent phase in the reception of his work in the English-speaking world.[2] This secondary literature, while not for the most part uncritical, basically represents what Habermas has called 'a co-operative effort to advance the argument'.[3] Although coming from a wide spectrum of perspectives and academic disciplines, these friendly critics seek to clarify, extend, revise or apply Habermas's position so as to further the basic intentions of his project.

All this positive interest in Habermas is curious in several respects. First, his works are difficult and demanding, drawing on a bewildering variety of seemingly disparate approaches and perspectives. He presents key elements of his position in the form of open-ended research programmes and provisional argument sketches. And, in the process of developing his position in response to criticisms, substantive changes have appeared from one stage to the next. This makes a sequential reading of his works important and greatly complicates either attacking or defending any one element in his position. Secondly, his works are written in a dense and technical style, offering the reader few of the intrinsic rewards provided by the dramatic language of predecessors such as Benjamin and Adorno. Their highly polemical style is dropped in favour of a more open and conciliatory approach towards competing views and traditions. Because of this shift, Habermas tends to adopt the idioms of the positions whose strenghts he wishes to incorporate into his own systematic approach. This frequently appears to distort not only the positions he attempts to assimilate, but his own as well. Finally, through this process of assimilating competing and seemingly incompatible approaches, Habermas risks offending everyone while pleasing no one. And in fact his work has been attacked by Marxists, critical theorists, conservatives, liberals, mainstream sociologists, linguists and philosophers from both the European and Anglo-American traditions.

Unlike those engaged in 'advancing the argument', these hostile critics present cases for rejecting all, or almost all, of it. Their criticisms of Habermas's position are developed in a body of work almost as large and varied as the 'co-operative' approach to his project. From an orthodox Marxist perspective, Goran Therborn has attacked Habermas for deviating from the 'path of true science' by developing a purely 'speculative' theory which rejects key Marxist concepts. Axel van den Berg, an American sociologist, rejects Habermas's position because of its hostility to 'empirical research and ordinary logic' and its dangerous political implications. Philosophers associated with the analytic tradition like Karl Popper, Y. Bar-Hillel and Quentin Skinner have attacked Habermas for his lack of 'clarity', his 'confusion' and his lack of theoretical 'rigour'. From the independent Left, Murray Bookchin rejects Habermas's work, along with the 'Habermas Industry', for its 'reified jargon' and political irrelevance. European philosophers such as Rudiger Bubner accuse Habermas of being vulnerable to 'the sophistic danger', with all the political dangers associated with it, and thus of failing to do justice to the concerns of classical philosophy.[4] The increasing number of these dismissive criticisms also indicates the significant impact of Habersmas's work.

My reading of Habermas will be carried out within the context of these ongoing debates. This is not only because of the intrinsic merits of the debates themselves, but also because Habermas's texts have been produced in close connection with them. In relation to these previous readings, I will certainly attempt to 'advance the argument' in a 'co-operative' way and with a willingness to read charitably. I will, however, reserve the right to question and attack fundamental elements of Habermas's position which underlie the polemic that it has generated.

In my view, previous readings of Habermas (both by friendly and hostile critics) are flawed in several different and important ways. Some obscure the real tensions in his work generated by the Kantian, Hegelian and Marxian poles in his thought. This is especially true of friendly critics influenced by the analytic tradition (like Geuss) who wish to make Habermas's position more plausible by removing its ambiguities. Although such readings are undertaken to 'clarify' Habermas's position, they generally end up by distorting it or, what is worse, draining it of its really interesting features. This is because all these poles are in fact a part of Habermas's project, as I hope to show. The tensions they generate are real. Further, they may prove to be productive and useful. One need only think of the tensions in Freud and Marx to see that powerful and important theories are not always the product of simple and rigorously self-consistent viewpoints. Therefore, an initial principle of my reading will be to do justice to the real tensions in Habermas's texts.

Some readings of Habermas ignore the complex development of his position and the important changes it has undergone from one stage to the next. This is the case with hostile critics like van den Berg and Skinner. Again, such readings distort Habermas and lead to misguided polemics over positions that have been modified or, in some cases, abandoned. Other readings sever the connection between Habermas's project and the tradition of the critical theory of the Frankfurt School. This hides the ties to the Marxian tradition without which his project cannot be understood at all. Without the attempt to not only understand social practice, but to criticise and change it, without the emancipatory practical intention of the theory, Habermas's work would be of little interest or relevance. This also means that the value of his work cannot be measured in terms of 'pure theory' alone, it must also be measured politically in terms of the practical intention the theory claims as its own. Therefore, a second principle of my reading will be to place the texts within the context of the complex and discontinuous development of Habermas's project without obscuring the practical, political core running through all the stages of his attempt to develop a critical social theory.

Finally, some readings of Habermas attempt to reduce his project, and the widespread positive interest in it, to the class 'interests' of a certain strata of intellectuals or to other 'ideological' motivations. It is ironic that this kind of reading has been carried out more often by non-Marxist critics like Disco, van den Berg and Skinner than by Marxists such as Therborn. Of course, the interest in Habermas's work cannot be completely severed from the interests of the radical strata of what Gouldner calls 'the new class' of intellectuals or from the struggle for social change within and outside the universities.[5] A consistent Marxian recognition of this does not, however, license a reductive reading of the relevant texts or a dismissal of the serious arguments developed within them. These arguments deserve attention in their own right since they have something to contribute to important current philosophical developments. Therefore, a third principle of my reading will be to place texts within their social contexts without reducing them to mere 'reflections' of their social context. This means I will take Habermas's arguments seriously.

My alternative to these readings will be developed in the first four chapters. In Chapter 1, I attempt to show the significance of Habermas's work for current philosophical developments and to establish a broad philosophical framework for my detailed elaboration of his position. In Chapter 2, I locate Habermas's project in the context of the development of the critical theory of society from Marx through the later Frankfurt School. I argue that Habermas's work represents a response to the two fundamental problems for critical theory: the problem of justifying the normative dimension of the theory and the problem of the relation of the theory to practice. Further, I try to show how both these problems are rooted in the articulation of the concept of rationality. I trace Habermas's response to these problems in Chapter 3, from his early work to his latest – *The Theory of Communicative Action*. I discuss this latest work at length in Chapter 4. In the fifth and final chapter, I use my reading of Habermas to develop a critique of what I call the 'paradigm shift' in radical social theory from production to communication. Through this critique, I attempt to clarify both the strengths and weaknesses of Habermas's position. I conclude by suggesting a direction for contemporary radical social theory more in line with Marx's original project. While I cannot hope to settle all accounts with a project as complex as Habermas's, I do hope that I at least succeed in raising the fundamental theoretical and practical questions to which it gives rise in a new and fruitful way. I will now begin by outlining two of the major contributions which Habermas can make to developments in contemporary philosophy as they have emerged in recent discussions of his work.

Habermas and contemporary philosophy: social practice as explanandum

The central position occupied by a concern with language in twentieth-century philosophy is commonly recognised. In Anglo-American philosophy in particular, the 'linguistic turn' met with great success through its criticisms of the traditional analysis of the ideas of the individual consciousness.[6] The abstract and one-sided character of the Cartesian concern with the accomplishments of the isolated thinking subject became apparent through investigations into the intersubjectively shared structure of language. Attempts to solve or dissolve traditional philosophical problems were carried out with the aid of formidable new logical and linguistic techniques. Partly because of the apparent success of these attempts, the 'linguistic turn' continues to dominate the philosophical scene in England and the United States. Within the analytic tradition itself, however, recent developments have begun to expose the limitations under which it always suffered.

The general direction of these developments may be discerned in a number of recent studies. Frederick Will has argued that the Cartesian problem of the justification of knowledge claims, which has been a central obsession of analytic philosophers, cannot be solved unless one takes into account 'the material conditions of life' and begins to view language as a complex 'social institution'.[7] Richard Rorty has extended this argument by suggesting that 'either all justification, whether in matters of knowledge or morals, appeals to social practices or to illusory foundations'.[8] Both point out how the search for a solution to the problem of justification, of finding secure 'foundations' for our knowledge, through the use of linguistic analysis (ideal or ordinary) is distorted by abstracting from the social dimension of our shared linguistic practices.

Of course, speech-act theorists, and others influenced by the work of the later Wittgenstein, have always recognised this social dimension of language. A theory of social action which would give substance to this recognition, however, remains a desideratum still very far from being carried out, as John Searle has remarked.[9] Further, it may reasonably be doubted whether it can be carried out at all within the confines of the analytic tradition. In spite of the recognition of the importance of the social dimension of language, analytic philosophers continue to appeal to 'social practices' and to talk of 'social action' in abstraction from the larger context of institutions, of economic structures, of political relations and cultural traditions within which these 'practices' and 'actions' are embedded and which shape and constrain them. What counts as 'giving a command' or 'issuing a report', as well as the conditions under which we are expected to 'be relevant' or ' be perspicuous', obviously depend on this larger and unthematised context. And, of course, what counts as 'justified belief' or 'moral' also depends upon it.

The complex developments, only hinted at above, point out clearly a crucial limitation of the analytic tradition – it never reached an adequate understanding of the social dimension of knowing or doing.[10] For all its vaunted clarity and thoroughness it left the social dimension unanalysed beyond appeals to vague concepts like 'forms of life' or 'social practices'. This is the first contribution which the work of Habermas, and the tradition to which he belongs, can make to current philosophical developments. The undeniable gains in conceptual clarity achieved as a result of the 'linguistic turn' do not justify a neglect of Hegel and Marx. The revival of interest in their work in the English-speaking world already shows this awareness. But it is not enough. If one wants to know what a 'social practice' *is* and not simply treat it as a self-evident end to inquiry, then one should take seriously those who have considered the question with theoretical rigour. Philosophers cannot continue to appeal to 'social practices' while ignoring the great tradition of social theorists represented by Simmel, Weber, Durkheim, Lukács and the Frankfurt School. If a concentration on the acts and achievements of the isolated, individual consciousness appears abstract and one-sided in the light of a consideration of our shared linguistic practices, then a concentration on these practices appears equally abstract in the light of a consideration of the larger social context within which they are embedded. Thus, the 'linguistic turn' leads to the necessity for taking a 'socal turn'. The work of Habermas not only presents a strong case for this additional 'turn', it also begins the difficult work of appropriating that tradition without which such a 'turn' would be in danger of remaining abstract and one-sided.

For Habermas, 'social practice' is not viewed as the seemingly self-evident end to inquiry that it is for many philosophers; rather, it is viewed as the starting point of inquiry. 'Social practice' requires explanation, it cannot itself serve as the basis for explanation of moral justification or knowledge claims. 'Social practice' is the explanandum and not the explanans. Habermas *begins* with an account of 'social practice' distinguished into two categories: *labour* (purposive–rational action) and *interaction* (communicative action). Broadly speaking, *labour* is the sphere in which human beings produce and reproduce their lives through transforming nature with the aid of technical rules and procedures, whereas *interaction* is the sphere in which human beings produce and reproduce their lives through communication of needs and interests in the context of rule-governed institutions. By breaking down the complex of 'social practice' into these two parts, Habermas is able to incorporate important sociological insights drawn from Weber, Durkheim and Marx into his account, thus overcoming the one-sided notion of 'social practice' dominant in the analytic tradition. From this Habermasian perspective, to abstract from the social conditions and functions of philosophical concepts and knowledge claims is just as distorted and mistaken as to abstract these concepts and claims from common or constructed linguistic practices. Because an understanding of 'social practice' as constituted both in labour and language is central, for Habermas, the epistemological and systematic claims of philosophy can only be carried out as social theory. Further, such a social theory cannot ignore the fact that the autonomous dialogue philosophy claims to be, is, and always has been, distorted by socal constraints and forms of social domination. This is one sense in which, for Habermas, social theory must be 'critical'. A 'critical' social theory not only describes social reality, but also criticises it and attempts to change it. Thus, it is a theory with a 'practical intent'.[11]

Habermas and anti-foundationalism

Habermas's second contribution to recent philosophical debate is an outcome of his attempt to provide a 'foundation' for such a critical social theory. This attempt directly counters the current vogue of 'anti-foundationalism'.[12] The anti-foundationalist argues that the problem of justifying our knowledge claims by providing a secure 'foundation' for them is fundamentally misconceived, whether in such cognitively respectable domains as science, or in morality or art. From this perspective, foundationalists (whether from the continental tradition or the analytic tradition) are those who want to do for knowledge what the tradition from Descartes through Kant wanted to do for it – namely, provide it with a justification where possible, and a critique where none is possible, in order to rest all our knowledge on a firm, indubitable, unshakable basis. For foundationalists epistemology is the central, if not the only, philosophical discipline. Its task is to tell us in a timelessly true way what can and cannot be counted on in the edifice of human knowledge.

According to anti-foundationalists this is an impossible dream, as the developments within analytic philosophy already outlined suggest. The move from the indubitable ideas of the individual thinking subject to the intersubjectively shared practices of actual language use seems to leave us with no 'foundations' outside or beyond the changing and contingent social practices within which such linguistic practices are actually to be found. Based on this insight, anti-foundationalists have assembled an impressive array of arguments against the traditional foundationalist view. They have argued that there are no theory-neutral set of 'facts', no absolutely unblurrable distinctions, no unmediated 'given', no timeless structure of reason, no absolutely neutral standpoint for inquiry outside the ongoing interpretations, values and interests of the actual community of inquirers at work in our current social practices. From this perspective, inquiry cannot be underwritten with anything more lasting than the rather humble and socially variable constraints of 'conversation'. Epistemology understood as the search for a way to end conversation by developing methods for presenting the final and unmediated truth is thus misconceived, whether it is carried out by an analysis of 'forms', 'ideas', 'eidetic essences' or 'language'.[13]

On the other hand, the foundationalist is likely to see all this as simply a new form of attack by various old adversaries (real or imagined), such as the sceptic or the relativist in one or another of their extremely various guises. He sees the anti-foundationalist as one who encourages irrationalism by denying the existence of *real* constraints on what can be said, constraints found either in the very nature of *reality itself* or in the *timeless* structure of consciousness, and not just in human practices. Just as Plato worried about the verbal excesses and the accompanying moral excesses of the sophists who used words without attention to the timelessly true, so the foundationalist worries that both cognitive and moral disaster will follow from the excesses of the anti-foundationalist. The dispute between the two camps thus takes on a peculiar moral fervour usually missing from current philosophical debate. Anti-foundationalists like Rorty try to defuse the moral worries by offerring their allegiance to the Socratic virtues (willingness to talk, to listen, to reflect, and so on) and redrawing the battle lines so as to skirt the dangerous implications of 'relativism'. Thus Rorty: 'the real issue is not between people who think one view as good as another and people who do not. It is between those who think our culture, our purpose, our intuitions cannot be supported except conversationally, and people who still hope for other sorts of support'.[14] But is allegiance to the Socratic virtues enough if, as Rorty does, one admits that they are merely a cultural preference finally undefendable by rigorous argument? At this point it seems it is not only the foundationalist who balks.

I have only sketched this impasse above. Its lines of argument run in many directions, from the various issues involving relativism (historical, cultural, ethical, aesthetic, and so on) to the debate over the status of the human sciences. 'Anti-foundationalism', in the wide sense I have given it, cuts across the fateful analytic–continental divide; it seems to join the later Wittgenstein, Heidegger, Gadamer, Derrida and Rorty against Husserl, Frege, Russell, Dummett and Popper. In this context I do not wish to trace these various issues or these various alignments and Habermas's complex responses to them. Here I want only to argue that Habermas's general approach suggests a way out of this impasse. Although sometimes accused of a hyperrationalism which overestimates the power and potential of human reason by ignoring its limited and conditioned character, Habermas clearly accepts the basic upshot of the critique of foundationalism. For him also there is no uninterpreted 'given', no theory-neutral 'facts', no timeless and absolutely neutral standpoints for inquiry. In agreement with the anti-foundationalists, Habermas holds that 'the unsettled ground of rationally motivated agreement among participants in argumentation is our only foundation – in questions of physics no less than in those of morality'.[15] Habermas, however, rejects the moral drawn from this critique by many anti-foundationalists. All search for justification and theoretical grounding should not be abandoned. All theory of knowledge is not pointless. Within the fallible context of human inquiry, 'foundations' in an attenuated sense can be found within the intersubjective workings of the community of inquirers themselves, once properly understood and adequately reconstructed. While the search for ultimate foundations undertaken by what Horkheimer called 'traditional theory' must be abandoned (a position held by the critical theorists long before the current dispute), 'theoretical justifications' can still be offered for ethical and cognitive positions.

For Habermas, these 'foundations' can be located by examining the presuppositions of communication. The necessary and unavoidable presuppositions of communication reveal a rational dimension within the 'conversation' itself which Habermas attempts to reconstruct by connecting up with Kant's transcendental mode of posing questions. In analogy with Kant, Habermas attempts to answer the question 'What are the conditions for the possibility of reaching an understanding in ordinary language?' It is largely this Kantian dimension in Habermas's thought that has brought upon him charges of hyperrationalism from the anti-foundationalists. Recent statements of Habermas's position show that these charges are misconceived. Whitebook explains as follows:

Habermas seems concerned to avoid two equally unacceptable alternatives. He does not want to accept that the validity of fundamental norms can be demonstrated with the rigor sought by 'traditional theory'. Yet he is equally opposed to the sceptical contention that these concepts are arbitrary, in the sense of either being the mere products of convention or of biological adaptation in any simple sense. While the validity of these principles may not be demonstrable in a completely compelling fashion, there are nevertheless 'good reasons' for their acceptance.[16]

This basic intention has been pursued by Habermas in both his early work, *Knowledge and Human Interest*, and in his later work on communication theory. His adoption of a kind of transcendental standpoint does not entail either an acceptance of the mode of procedure or the expected results of traditional Kantian transcendental philosophy. Again quoting Whitebook:

> It is somewhat ironic that Habermas, who is often accused of hyperrationalism . . .requires so large an element of judgement at the very base of his scheme. The way in which one 'comes to terms' with the transcendental standpoint ulimately bears a closer resemblance to aesthetic taste or Aristotelian phronesis than to emphatic philosophic proof. While Habermas' transcendental scheme is meant to serve a theoretical function of grounding our knowledge. . .the scheme itself is not grounded in as emphatic a fashion as one generally finds in first philosophy.[17]

Habermas's latest work attempts to develop an account of 'communicative rationality' (a concept I will examine in detail later) which would serve as a basis for critique capable of providing a 'normative foundation' for critical theory in the above sense. This is the second sense in which social theory must be critical – it must reconstruct the fundamental norms which guide the theory. Habermas attempts to develop this account in a series of investigations of universal pragmatics, communicative competence and communicative action.[18] Among the strengths of Habermas's approach is a possible answer to the question of what constitutes a 'rational' consensus. If agreement *within* the conversation counts and not agreement with the 'facts', how do we know such an agreement is *itself* rational? For Habermas, a rational consensus is one that is arrived at in free and equal discussion within the framework of what he calls the 'ideal speech situation' (a concept I will also discuss in detail later). Since only a rational consensus can ultimately serve as the ground for truth claims, his argument (at least in its earlier formulations) yields a series of mutual implications between the concepts of truth, freedom and justice. These concepts, in particular the concept of truth, are presupposed when we enter discussion. If we do not intend truth, then rational discussion itself is called into question. And, if we intend truth, then we must also intend freedom and justice as well, since without the latter we cannot arrive at the former. By presupposing these concepts in discussion, we at the same time anticipate a 'form of life' free from unnecessary domination in all its forms. Using these arguments, Habermas attempts to explicate the basis of legitimate authority. Such legitimacy rests upon the claim that it can be vindicated in a 'rational consensus'. The appearance that political decisions represent such a consensus when, in fact, they do not becomes a Habermasian version of the Marxian concept of 'socially necessary illusion'. Habermas's critical theory thus attempts to draw on both the Marxian and the Kantian sense of 'critique'.

In part, because of his Marxian emphasis on the constraints to be found in 'social practices', Habermas is eager to overcome the appearance of an abstract linguistic utopianism by connecting these arguments with an evolutionary account that indicates the growing objective possibilities for embodying communtive rationality in social structures and increasing its scope in concrete forms of life. Habermas attempts to develop this account through an investigation of processes of rationalisation. Habermas's account of communicative rationality is an original and important attempt to overcome the aporias of a theory of society with a practical intent. Here lies much of the importance of Habermas's approach for the Marxist tradition, a point I shall return to later.

Habermas's position is not without problems which I can only briefly indicate here. The theory of communication is, in part, intended to answer the hermeneutic challenge raised by Gadamer: 'how can critical theory claim to be free of the distortion it locates in others without raising itself above the role of a partner in dialogue?' Since Habermas rejects ultimate foundations of the philosophical or critical kind, as well as a purely negative response in the manner of Adorno, what positive answer can he give? The theory of communication provides such an answer: the basic categories of critical theory are presupposed in communication.

This theory, however, may not finally meet the hermeneutic challenge. The theory of communication, particularly as developed in Habermas's work on universal pragmatics, does not eliminate the context dependency of critical theory. As McCarthy has argued, the gap between Habermas's 'universal-pragmatic framework' and the 'concrete expressions of sociocultural life' can only be filled by the employment of hermeneutic procedures. The necessity for interpretation and the absence of a final and total perspective from which to interpret remain. Thus, 'even armed with this theory the critical theorist can claim no monopoly on truth'.[19] Further, to overcome the charge that the theory of communication is unredeemably abstract and ahistorical, Habermas must convincingly connect it with a theory of social evolution which reconstructs the successive developmental stages of social structures conceived in terms of speech and action. As I will argue later, throughout Habermas's project a tension exists between its transcendental dimension (the synchronic account of the structure of communication) and its historical dimension (the diachronic account of the development of these structures). This tension shows the difficulties inherent in Habermas's attempt to provide a 'normative foundation' for critical theory capable of meeting the hermeneutic challenge even in an attenuated sense of 'foundation'.

The anti-foundationalism present in current philosophical debate seems to find support from Gadamer's hermeneutics in so far as it emphasises the socially and historically rooted condition of human knowledge, although both Habermas and Gadamer are opposed to what they see as the destructive and irrational moral drawn from this perspective by some anti-fondationalists. While Gadamer is content to meet this challenge by looking backward to the positive function of tradition, Habermas hopes to meet it by looking forward to the possibility of embodying concrete structures of communicative rationality in a transformed society.[20] For Habermas, meeting the hermeneutic challenge means providing a theoretical justification for this prospective and normative dimension without falling back into the kind of ahistorical hyperrationalism so effectively criticised by Gadamer and the anti-foundationalists. This attempt to find a middle way is the second contribution Habermas's work can make to current philosophical debate. Whether this attempt finally succeeds or fails is a question that I will turn to only after my detailed elaboration of Habermas's position.

Habermas and the continental tradition

A focus upon the influences on Habermas's thought may help to clarify these contributions and further specify the context for a reading of his work. The interest in Habermas is also, at least partially, to be found in the way he reconstructs significant strands in the continental tradition. Initially, the relationship between Hegel and Habermas deserves attention. A brief consideration of this topic may also aid us in clarifying the tension between the transcendental and historical dimensions in Habermas's work.

Hegelian themes

Habermas has recently commented on the relationship between his work and Hegel in a way that illuminates this issue, distinguishing four enterprises pursued by Hegel as aspects of a single process:

1. the rational reconstruction of universal presuppositions of paradigmatic types of cognition and communication;. . .the Kantian enterprise of transcendental analysis (as) integrated into, Hegel's philosophy;
2. the rational reconstruction of developmental patterns for the genesis of transcendental universals; this is Hegel's genuine enterprise of discovering developmental logics:
3. the phenomenological analysis of the experience of those involved in processes of self-reflection. . .which step by step critically destroys the objective delusions arising from different modes   and   levels   of   false   consciousness. . .(the) enterprise. . .which, after Hegel, is continued by Feuerbach, Marx, and Freud;
4. the construction of a rational history, which can explain the observational and the narrative evidence of empirical regularities. . .in terms of the internal genesis of basic conceptual structures. . .the enterprise that Hegel attempted in his *Realphilosophien*.[21]

Although Habermas recognises that today we cannot be certain that these 'four types of analysis will reveal only different aspects of one unified process', his project may be veiwed as an attempt to reconstruct as much as possible of the Hegelian enterprise. In my view, only after writing *Knowledge and Human Interests* did Habermas work out the distinction between (1) and (3) in terms of an opposition between 'rational reconstruction' (that is, explications of general rules of human competency in a given area such as communication or cognition based on the contemporary model of Chomsky's rational reconstruction of grammatical competence) and 'self-reflection' (that is, reflection which makes unconscious elements conscious in a way that has practical, emancipatory consequences based on the Marxian critique of ideology and Freudian psychoanalysis). Since drawing this distinction, Habermas has pursued (1) in the form of a theory of universal pragmatics while paying less attention to (3) in his post–1970 work. From both (1) and (3), Habermas now distinguishes (2) 'developmental logic' (that is, the rational reconstruction of the various stages in the development of the human competency to speak and act based on the contemporary model of Piaget's developmental psychology) and (4) 'rational history' (that is, an explication of actual historical development in terms of the account produced by develomental logical reconstruction – a type of theory for which no adequate contemporary example exists, although debates in the philosophy of science deriving from Kuhn suggest avenues of approach). Recently, Habermas has pursued (2) in his theories of ego development and the moral consciousness as well as in his latest work on the development of rationality structures and worldviews. He has pursued (4) in his theory of social evolution, the reconstruction of historical materialism and, again in his latest work, the theories of modernity and rationalisation.[22] (1) represents the transcendental dimension in Habermas's project, while (2), (3) and (4) represent its historical dimension. In regard to both (2) and (4), Habermas attempts to update and defend what he sees as the central elements of Hegel's project.

I will examine these distinctions, and the work that is based upon them, in detail later. For now, I want only to suggest the connection between these disinctions and the direction taken by Habermas's project. The general picture of Habermas's development projected in the English-language literature moves from an early Hegelian–Marxism towards a Kantian position when, in fact, many of the basically Hegelian–Marxian themes have not been abandoned, but rather refined and developed. Many interpreters fail to emphasise adequately the continuing dependence of Habermas on the Hegelian tradition. On the other hand, those who stress Habermas's Hegelianism fail to understand the importance of the rational reconstructive side of his project.[23] Consequently, the one-sidedness of previous interpretations can be overcome by recognising the dependence of Habermas on the Hegelian tradition, as well as his attempt to rebuild as much of this tradition as possible in the light of his commitment to Marxism and significant contemporary developments in the types of analysis distinguished above.

A revealing exchange between Richard Bernstein, Kenley Dove and Habermas on 'The Relationship of Habermas's view to Hegel' further clarifies the relationship between his thought and Hegel's. Bernstein and Dove, following interpretations by Rudiger Bubner and Dieter Henrich, show how Habermas has utilised the dialectical strategy of argumentation employed by Hegel in such works as *Knowledge and Human Interests, Zur Logik der Sozialwissenschaften* and *Theorie der Gesellschaft oder Sozialtechnologie*.[24] Like Hegel, Habermas explicates positions or arguments, reveals their contradictions or aporia, and passes beyond the given position to another synthetic position which overcomes the contraditions, or deficiencies, while preserving the truth of the 'sublated' (*aufgehoben*) position. In turn, Habermas immerses himself in the new position, examines it form within, probes its strengths and weaknesses, and moves on to another position. In this way, Habermas builds an ever more complete synthesis and increasingly comprehensive theories.

Although Habermas utilises this Hegelian strategy, he rejects the Hegelian claim to bring together logic and history in a total and final system comprehended by a unified, absolute and universal *Vernunft* (substantial reason). Habermas sees no way to lead theory back from the differentiation of reason into its three aspects, as divided out by Kant's three critiques (science, morality, art) towards Hegel's concept of substantial reason. For Habermas, this differentiation is characteristic of modernity, and thus cannot simply be overcome or abolished by a return to the concepts of the philosophical tradition. Habermas's distinctions between the four types of analysis pursued by Hegel signals his acceptance of this differentiation and creates tensions in his own attempt to produce an increasingly synthetic theory. In particular, the tension between the transcendental dimension represented by the theory of universal pragmatics and the historical dimension represented by the theory of social evolution is an outcome of these distinctions. They signal the decisive abandonment, not only of the presupposition of the identity of logic and history in Hegel, but also of Hegelian–Marxist attempts to relocate the logic of history in the agency of the proletariat. By separating logic and history, Habermas is left with the problem of agency – the missing link between theory and practice without which the practical intention of the theory to aid in the rational transformation of society remains in doubt. To help overcome the tension between the transcendental and the historical dimension, Habermas believes that it is necessary to continue to develop each of the enterprises already cited in order to advance an understanding of social action that might pave the way towards a solution to the problem.

Before such a solution can be convincingly attempted, Habermas locates three theoretical problems that must be overcome: (i) the development of a 'concept of rationality sufficiently comprehensive to cover not only cognitive but communicative processes and their embodiment in social interaction'; (ii) the explication of 'developmental patterns of rationality which can be identified in cognitive and moral belief systems, in law, and in the basic institutions of social integration'; and (iii) the linking of 'rational reconstructions to all these internal structures with empirical assumptions about the conditions under which societies can and do learn by incorporating available cognitive structures into evolutionary new institutions and mechanisms'.[25] He tackles all three problems in his latest work on communicative action. The attempt to solve problems (2) and (3) reveal the Hegelian pole in his thought, his historical side. His rejection, however, of Hegel's holistic concept of substantial reason, and the 'emphatic concept of truth' it entails, reveals his break with Hegel. Habermas's attempt to solve problem (1), as well as his modern reworking of the Hegelian tradition in regard to (2) and (3), require a brief account of the Kantian pole in his thought, his transcendental side.

Kantian themes

The transcendental dimension in Habermas's project, his reworking of the Kantian tradition, is evident in several important strands of his theoretical programme. His theories of universal pragmatics and communicative competence, which raise the question of 'the condition for the possibility' of understanding and communicating, stand in a direct line with Kant's central question concerning 'the conditions for the possibility' of human knowledge and experience. His accounts of the possibility of knowledge and action stand in this same line. Further, his important argument for the 'ideal speech situation' which rests upon the universal and formal conditions for all speech acts also depends upon a Kantian style of argumentation.

Perhaps even more important than the above is Habermas's acceptance, as I have already suggested, of the Kantian division between science, morality and art. This point has been missed by many.[26] Habermas's attempt to construct a comprehensive theory of rationality is not to be understood as a modern justification of Hegel's concept of substantial reason. Rather, it is an attempt to defend the cognitive status of each against the usurpation of a single branch, the scientific–technological. This is not to confuse 'is' with 'ought' or with the judgement of beauty. For Habermas, all these modern value spheres appeal ultimately to the context of argumentation and the community of inquirers for justification. Each has an equal right within its own sphere. Each can be supported by its own procedures of argument that, while formal, can generate claims with 'good reasons' for their acceptance. Habermas's defence of a Kantian 'procedural' communicative ethics along cognitivist lines is to be understood in this light. The Habermasian critique of scientific–technological rationality is also to be understood in this context, and not in the Hegelian context of the Frankfurt School's attack on instrumental reason.

It is precisely here, the concept of reason, where Habermas parts company with anti-foundationalists like Rorty, as well as hermeneuticists like Gadamer. Both the latter want to remove the Kantian grid and the differentiation of reason – Gadamer by looking back before its implacement in our culture, Rorty by looking beyond it towards its obsolescence. Habermas also parts company here with the older generation of the Frankfurt School, each of whom attempted to overcome what they saw as the alienation and the dissection of reason by an explicit or implicit appeal to a concept of substantial reason and its historical possibilities. For Habermas the differentiation of reason into its aspects as theorised by Kant, and worked out in a line of thought running through Weber, is characteristic of modernity, and cannot be simply discarded without abandoning the project of modernity: to enlighten and free humanity. From this perspective, only at the cost of the 're-enchantment' of the world can we move beyond it.

In spite of the importance of this Kantian strand in his though, it also can be overemphasised. Habermas rejects Kant's transcendental ego and, with Hegel, holds to the view that knowledge, language, action and society must be comprehended in their development. This is especially prominent in his interest in social development, social rationalisation and learning processes. Further, Habermas accepts the limitations of the individual theorists' own fallibility and rejects both the procedure and the results of traditional transcendental philosophy. This, coupled with his rejection of the Hegelian concept of substantial reason, calls for a new model of theory construction. While making use of Hegelian argumentation strategies, this model of theory construction can obviously no longer rely on the philosophical tradition's concept of truth or of ultimate foundations. Habermas explains:

> The renunciation of ultimate foundations, be they of a traditional or of a critical sort, exacts a price that from time to time brings upon me the reproach of eclecticism. I am referring to the necessity of linking up with various, reconstructive approaches and corresponding lines of empirical research, with the aim of ascertaining whether the results of the specialised sciences fit together within the overlapping theoretical prespectives that interest me. ....The coherence theory of truth is certainly too weak to explain the concept of propositional truth; but it comes into its own at another level, the metatheoretical, where we put together the individual pieces of theory like a puzzle.[27]

By making use of theories (both empirical and *a priori*) developed in different and insulated areas, Habermans is able to check them for coherence against each other. He can then discard and select, and as the theory grows ever more synthetic, more coherence tests can be made. In this way, the theory can become more and more encompassing and powerful. This is the theoretical advantage of his synthetic approach to theory construction which owes more to Hegel than to Kant. Its disadvantage seem to be that the connection with social practice which is the guiding insight of the theory becomes ever more remote. This brings us to the Marxian pole in Habermas's thought.

Marxian themes

Habermas follows Marx in his emphasis on material conditions, social practice, the importance of the critique of ideology and other

Marxian themes that appear throughout his work. In *Legitimation Crisis*, Habermas attempts to reconstruct the Marxist crisis theory and, in several studies, to reconstruct historical materialism itself. Thus Bernstein's claim that 'the Marxist elements are more and more muted, and soften, in his most recent work' needs qualification.[28] Habermas is constantly relating his work to Marxism, and in many of his recent articles and inteviews Marxian themes predominate. Moreover, from the mid-1970s there is an increased tendency to criticise capitalism and to direct his inquiries to political questions and struggles of the day. On the crucial question for the early Frankfurt School of the relation of theory to practice, however, Habermas's position has certainly softened since his earlier works *(Knowledge and Human Interests, Theory and Practice)*. In Habermas's view, both our confidence in revolutionary struggle and our theoretical self-certainty have lapsed as result of historical and theoretical developments. Without theoretical certainty to guide practice, their distance must grow, although Habrmas has *not* totally given up developing a new approach to this old Frankfurt problem. Only within the context of a whole series of Frankfurt School views can his approach be adequately understood: the deterioration of orthodox Marxism into a 'legitimation science', the inability of the modern proletariat to fill the role originally assigned to it by Marx, and the worldwide advance of technological and bureaucratic modes of domination.

Thus, Habermas is best read in the tradition of critical theory which likewise in various ways utilises Kant and Hegel as well as Weber, Freud and others, to revitalise Marxism by developing a critical theory of society with practical intent. Consequently, Habermas's relation to Horkheimer, Adorno, Marcuse and Benjamin is important in interpreting his thought. Even McCarthy does not adequately situate Habermas within the tradition of critical theory, although others are recognising the importance of doing so. In spite of Habermas's roots in critical theory he is more affirmative towards the classical philosophical tradition, and particularly the tradition of the Enlightenment, than his predecessors. Habermas's most recent work is focused on the 'dialectic of modernity' which will explicate those features of 'enlightenment' and 'emancipation' produced by modernity in contrast to elements of oppression and inhumantity.[29] Whereas Adorno and Horkheimer saw the 'dialectic of enlightenment' producing domination and lack of freedom,

Habermas believes that its 'cultural differentiation' (that is the separation of the 'value spheres' of science, morality, art) has brought about gains in freedom, autonomy and social rationality. Habermas is currently exploring ways in which the 'unfulfilled project of modernity' can be realised through institutionalisation of emancipatory learning processes which will make possible a more rational society. This project is theoretically underpinned by his attempt to construct a comprehensive theory of rationality.

In a sense, Habermas's project of developing a more comprehensive concept of reason is a return to the 1930s' problematic of critical theory. He wants to use empirical sciences to work out and to confirm the existence of developmental patterns of rationality in the economy, morality, culture and social life generally. He is aware of threats to social rationality in all these domains, but he also wants to defend the positive advancements of enlightenment, modernity and Western rationality. Here he decisively breaks with the historical pessimism of the later Adorno and Horkheimer who saw the development of Western rationality as the totalisation of reification, domination and repression.

Habermas attempts to carry through these tasks in his most recent work on modernity, evolutionary theory, communicative rationality and communicative action. In this work, he also explores how social movements might provide new agents for social transformation, although this more affirmative connection with social practice is admittedly tentative. Consequently, Habermas continues his fundamentally Hegelian–Marxist attempt to defend concepts of critical reason and emancipation from conservative atacks, as well as from what he sees as the nihilistic relativism of the destructive anti-foundationalists. Finally, Habermas at once reconstructs important themes in the philosophical tradition and continues, under changed historical circumstances, the emancipatory project inherited from critical theory: the project of saving the potential for liberation remaining in the Marxist tradition.

2

Habermas and the Heritage of Critical Theory

'What today separates us from Marx are evident historical truths, for example, that in the developed capitalist societies there is no identifiable class, no clearly circumscribed social group which could be singled out as the representative of a general interest that has been violated . . . Both revolutionary self-confidence and theoretical self-certainty are gone.' — Jürgen Habermas

The overview of Habermas's project presented in Chapter 1 marks out its general theoretical terrain and suggests the primary focus for my reading. In brief, I read Habermas as engaged in the continuation of the project of the Frankfurt School to develop a critical social theory capable of maintaining the 'practical intentions' of establishing a good and just society which he believes are central to Marx's theory. The basic question, for Habermas, is whether a critical theory of society in the contemporary age that shares the practical intention of Marx's theory is still at all possible. Habermas faces this question squarely, courageously, and across a wide range of theoretical and political issues. His attempt to provide an answer generates much of the interest in his project (both positive and negative) and makes its stakes extremely high.

Habermas's attempt to articulate and defend a comprehensive concept of rationality that does not exclude practical questions of values, norms, interests and commitments is central to this attempt. Both the 'social turn' in philosophy that Habermas argues for, and the construction of a theoretical justification for critical social theory that he attempts, depend upon a comprehensive concept of rationality. Only the successful development of such an expanded concept of rationality can address two fundamental problems encountered throughout the work of the Frankfurt School.

The first problem arises from the special theoretical status claimed for the critical theory of society. Critical theory cannot be identified with a 'pure' scientific theory (the status claimed by so-called 'orthodox Marxism') or with 'pure' philosophy in the sense of the philosophical tradition. Critical theory is located, in Habermas's phrase, 'between philosophy and science'.[1] From this difficult position, critical theory sets out not only to describe, but also radically to criticise and qualitatively transform social reality without recourse to either the fundamental concepts of traditional philosophy (that is, reason, freedom, truth) or the value-free model of science. Philosophy and science understood as 'traditional theory' are equally criticised for obscuring the fundamental human interests and material contitions of life that underlie their 'pure' pursuit of knowledge, for their merely 'contemplative' status which tacitly accepts the status quo, and for their failure to recognise their own social and historical contextuality. Thus, critical theory locates a general and systematic distortion in prevailing modes of thought under the heading of ideology which it attempts to make the subject of a radical critique. This critique locates the conditions for the possibility of these modes of thought as well as their necessary limits (critique in the Kantian sense), and also attempts to uncover their 'hidden core' of material social conditioning as a guide for overthrowing those very material social conditions (critique in the Marxian sense).

But how can critical theory locate the distortions in other modes of thought, and condemn them as ideology, unless it itself is free from the distortions? To what can it appeal to justify its own fundamental critical norms and practical commitments once the contextuality of modes of thought is recognised? These problems are parallel to the current worries over 'relativism' already discussed. But the problem is particularly acute for critical theory owing to its special theoretical status which requires that a basis for critique be found which, as David Held says, 'is both part of historical reality and yet not identifiable with the status quo'.[2] Such a basis cannot be dispensed with, since to locate the distortions in the thought of others implies the mastery of the distinction between distorted and undistorted thought which entails criteria of knowledge and truth as well. Only a comprehensive theory of rationality can, in the last analysis, solve this fundamental theoretical problem – the problem of justifying the normative basis of critique.

The second fundamental problem Habermas hopes to address

by developing a comprehensive concept of rationality involves the relationship of critical theory to practice. How can critical theory hope to further a revolutionary social transformation in line with the practical intention it shares with Marx when, by its own account, it is developed in and for a period without a central revolutionary agent? How can critical theory establish the linkage with practice which is a requirement of the theory if it is not to be merely 'contemplative', if the theory itself suggests the impossibility of such a linkage? For Marx, rationality must be located as socially and historically embodied reason characterising real historical agents. The worker's movement, the proletariat, in the generality of their interests, could serve Marx both as a basis for critique and as the link between theory and practice in so far as the proletariat was both a part of historical reality and yet not identifiable with the status quo. What is to replace Marx's reliance on the agency of the proletariat, if the proletariat is no longer viewed as the embodiment of social and historical rationality or political opposition? Again, the problem of agency cannot be bypassed without critical theory taking on the purely 'contemplative' character it criticises in other modes of thought and in other theories of the 'traditional' kind. Thus, contemporary critical theory also faces the problem of the relation of the theory to the practice it attempts to further, and upon which it finally depends.

Both these problems raise questions concerning the very possibility of a critical theory of society. Neither problem, in Habermas's view, can be addressed adequately apart from a consideration of the concept of rationality. Such a consideration cannot proceed on philosophical grounds alone, it must also draw on the history of the problem of rationality worked up by the sociological tradition in its attempts to locate the distinctive features of Western rationality and explain the development of modern forms of bureaucratice-technological rationality. I hope to clarify this programme by tracing the development of a theory of rationality from Habermas's early work to the later formulations. Before this can be accomplished, however, it will be necessary to reconstruct the development of the concept of rationality, and the problems raised in connection with it, from Marx through the Frankfurt School.

Social rationality in Marx

Marx developed his critical theory of society by drawing on three of the most advanced theoretical currents of the nineteenth century:

German classical idealism, British political economy, and French revolutionary socialism. He attempted to bring each of these theoretical traditions to completion in a theory capable of explaining the totality of human interaction with the world in terms of social relations and production. Through this attempt, Marx made use of a concept of social rationality which he never explicitly developed or systematised. In the light of the practical and revolutionary nature of his project, he was more concerned with analysing and abolishing the embodiments of unreason (that is, social conditions of oppression and domination). As Habermas has noted, however, Marx's critique never 'forfeited the power of an appeal to reason'; otherwise, 'it would have been reduced to a lament or to sheer agitation'. Instead, Marx's theoretical approach was always 'guided by the intention of recovering a potential for reason encapsulated in the very forms of social reproduction'.[3] In what follows, I will develop an interpretation of Marx which makes his concept of social rationality more explicit. I will also discuss some of its far-reaching implications and consequences.

As Gyorgy Márkus has argued, Marx's critical theory of society in general, and in particular his concept of social rationality, rests on an encompassing and underlying presupposition – 'that of the paradigmatic character of material production for the understanding of all the manifestations of human social life'.[4] For Marx, 'religion, family, state, law, morality, science, art, etc. are only particular modes of production, and fall under its general law'.[5] And again: 'As individuals express their life, so they are. What they are, therefore, coincides with their production, both with what they produce and with how they produce. The nature of individuals thus depends on the material conditions determining their production.'[6] And finally, from the *locus classicus* of Marxism:

> In the social production of their existence, men inevitably enter into definite relations, which are independent of their will, namely relations of production appropriate to a given stage in the development of their material forces of production. The totality of these relations of production constitutes the economic structure of society, the real foundation, on which arises a legal and political superstructure and to which correspond definite forms of social consciousness. The mode of production of material life conditions the general process of social, political, and intellectual life.[7]

Marx's 'paradigm of production' (that is, his thesis of the primacy of material production for an understanding of human social life developed under the heading 'materialism') was not an attempt to answer the philosophical problems of the relation of mind to body or the question of the ontological status of matter. Rather, Marx's 'materialism' involved a critique of 'philosophy as a whole' in the name of those 'material conditions of social life' which had set the limits of its reflection while themselves remaining unreflected. It represented a ruthless critique of the privileging of 'ideas' as absolutely independent social forces, and a denial of their autonomy and independent power. 'Ideas' are not, for Marx, representations of facts or autonomous active agents, but *expressions* of the real material life-processes of human beings. 'Expression' does not refer here to a passive 'reflection' or to an 'epi-phenomenon', but to the active articulation of these life processes in communication and self-understanding.[8] 'Consciousness' is always, in the last analysis, consciousness of the prevailing social practices which philosophical thought both conceals (as domination) and reveals.

On the other hand, Marx's 'materialism' does not represent a strictly economic theory of social reality in the narrow sense of a separate scientific discipline. Marx also developed a 'critique of political economy' in the name of the realisation of those philosophical ideals distorted and crushed by the prevailing 'material conditions' only described and justified as 'natural laws' by the political economists. Thus, Marx's 'materialism' was primarily of a practical and revolutionary character. It was conditioned and, to a large extent, determined by a concern with overcoming the social problems of the time. This is true not only in terms of the motivation of the theory, but also in terms of its constitution. Marx posits 'the material conditions of life' not as a philosophical construct or as the central thesis of an economic science, but rather as the very battleground upon which the crucial struggles will be waged. These 'material conditions' are not simply an object of contemplation, but a field of action. In short, Marx's 'materialism' is important not as a philosophical or economic doctrine, but only in the light of a possible socialist transformation of the existing society. It is to this practical context that the theory appeals for justification in its claim to be the expression of those social forces capable of such a transformation.

Marx's social theory thus develops a critique of philosophy

and of political economy linked by the practical commitment to revolutionary socalism. But to what standards of rationality can such a theory appeal once both philosophical and scientific standards are made dependent on the 'paradigm of production'? The answer to this question seems to require a new standard of rationality, and indeed this is what Marx attempted to supply by overcoming the limitations of the philosophical concept of reason in German classical idealism. Marx's concept of social rationality grounded in the 'paradigm of production' cannot be understood apart from a consideration of this background.

The development of German classical idealism from Kant through Hegel may itself be characterised as a search for a new principle of rationality capable of overcoming the problems raised by the Enlightenment conception of reason. Kant's critical philosophy was already a response to the challanges laid down by Hume and Rousseau. Hume's attack on the power of reason and his virtual dissolution of the isolated self called into question the basic Enlightenment belief in the reasoning subject as the pivotal point for the theoretical and moral understanding of the world. Rousseau's indictment of an unfree and alienated social life raised doubts about the Enlightenment project of establishing a society based on reason, freedom and the common interest. This origin of the search for a new principle of rationality in Kant, capable of meeting these two challenges, sets the agenda for the later development of German idealism in its attempt to find a middle way between the reduction of reason to its mere empirical employment and the Romantic ideal of an organic expressive immediacy beyond reason.[9] Both failed to do justice to the Enlightenment view, brilliantly expressed by Kant, of the rational subject as an autonomous and self-dependent agent who was to examine and judge everything in independence from authority and tradition by means of reason courageously employed.[10] This view of the rational subject included the idea of freedom to act in accord with reason's insight.

Hegel expanded this concept of reason as freedom to its limits. An extension of reason is always an extension of the area in which we can exercise responsibility, and freedom cannot be extended without increasing our knowledge. Thus, he joins the two concepts so as to reveal freedom as the essence of human beings, 'not something which they have, as humans, but which they are'.[11] Hegel was perhaps the first to grasp clearly the conditions which the new conception of rationality must meet: (i) it had to respect the principle of autonomous rational subjectivity; (ii) it had to allow for the substantive freedom for humans to express their lives in a community of common interest. Expressed another way, the new concept of reason had to mediate the claims of the individual (as rational subjectivity) and the claims of the universal (as species life in a community).

This new principle of rationality is expressed in the two moves carried out in the course of the development of German idealism – the transition from the primacy of the theoretical to the primacy of the practical, and the transition from the individual empirical consciousness to superindividual consciousness (species or transcendental consciousness). The problems with this construction, however, cannot be solved within the context of philosophy alone. The fundamental assumption of German idealism equates the concrete and practical intersubjectivity of human thought, speech and action with reason in itself as superindividual subject. This assumption remains no matter how the relation of superindividual reason to the individual empirical employment of reason is understood – whether the first is viewed as the abstract framework for the second as in Kant, or whether the first is viewed as the actual historically unfolding embodiment of the second as in Hegel. And this assumption is not just an excess of 'idealism', but rather a conceptual requirement in order to mediate between the individual and the universal in the necessary way.

Through the 'paradigm of production', Marx rejects this entire construction. He rejects the inner split between the subject as a representative of the universal and the bearer of an isolated egoistic individuality as an expression of the real split between the labourer, his product and his fellow labourers. The radical foundation of this criticism is that the material, concrete, living persons are the only knowing subjects or historical actors. Human beings cannot be understood in terms of the rational subjectivity of the Enlightenment with its illusions of absolute autonomy. Humans are natural beings and, thus, finite: 'a suffering, conditioned and limited being . . . which . . . has its nature outside itself'.[12] This 'outside' is the natural world as constantly transformed through human labour; it is actually a social and historical product, 'the product of industry and the state of society'.[13] Thus, the 'essence of human beings' is, in reality, 'the ensemble of social relations'.[14]

Marx critically destroys the idea of the superindividual subject by transforming it into the notion of human social intersubjectivity through the use of his 'paradigm of production'. Hegel's 'substantial spirit' becomes the 'sum of productive forces, capital funds and social forms of intercourse, which every individual and generation finds in existence as something given'.[15] Intersubjectivity is understood as conditioned by social life in general. 'Conditioned' does not mean here 'causally determined' since Marx's emphasis on the empirical, living individuals also contains the idea that they make their own history, although under definite objective social conditions. These social conditions are the historical result of human activities which only become 'objective' through their appropriation by human beings engaged in reproducing and changing them. Human beings interact with the human powers thus objectified by transforming them into new needs, abilities and functions of actual living human beings as social actors. This can only take place in the social interaction of the concrete individuals themselves.

This, of course, changes the very meaning of 'subject'. Autonomy, creativity, self-expression and freedom as characteristics of the concept of the rational subject are no longer understood as metaphysical properties, but as historical possibilities to be redefined concretely in terms of the limits of nature and the present, socially conditioned, needs and interests of the human individuals themselves. Autonomy, creativity, self-expression and freedom can only relate to real possibilities whose realisation depends on the individuals' control over their social life processes, their ability to structure consciously their own life activities.

This notion of the subject is the key to Marx's overcoming of the philosophical concept of reason through the concept of social rationality. The famous antitheses between subject and object, human existence and essence, the individual and the universal are not viewed as 'problems of language', nor as eternal metaphysical categories; rather they are regarded as expressions of an historical situation that can be overcome under definite conditions by the collective practical activity of individuals. Social rationality is not reason standing abstractly *above* history, and it is not reason *in* history to be comprehended by the individual in a supreme act of dialectical reflection over its own process of formation. It is simply historical reason 'embodied' in the worker's movement, in that 'practical activity of the association of the socially determined (class-)

individuals, which concretely abolishes the contradictions of their immediate material existence, making it possible for them to give (and not to find) a meaning to their own lives'.[16] Only the success this actual movement finds in pushing back the social limitation on the autonomy, creativity, self-expression and freedom of individuals can finally justify and ground Marx's concept of social rationality. The struggle to overcome these socially created limits is rational. But even rationality itself is not transcendentally above or metaphysically in history; rather it is socially and historically embodied reason which depends upon the struggles of human beings.

Against the 'idealism' of the philosophical tradition, including its 'crude materialism' (even that of Feuerbach), Marx holds that 'the constitution of the common and meaningful world of human experiences appears . . . not as the achievement of the (individual or transcendental) consciousness, but as the social-historical result of material practical activities'.[17] By moving beyond the philosophical concept of reason towards the concept of social rationality, Marx can show how the constitution of our knowledge, the structure of our needs and interests, our actions and creations depend upon and are limited by the level of our 'material practical activity' which is itself a result of historical development. 'Social practices' are not accepted as merely given, but are understood as an historical result. Marx offers an explanation of this historical development through the 'dialectic' of the 'relations of production' (those relations which constitute the power to control the forces of productions, the institutional framework of society, especially property relations) and the 'forces of production' (anything that 'is or can be used to make a material use-value', anything that satisfies a human need, the technical and productive capacity of a society).[18] This dialectic develops as the relations of production (fetters on the development of rationality) are threatened by developments in the forces production, opening up the objective possibility for a more rational social arrangement.

Unlike Hegel's 'dialectic', which views historical development as the development of 'ideas' through 'contradictions' that are both 'real' and 'logical', Marx's 'dialectic' is limited to the historical mode. Marx rejects 'ideas' as the principle of historical development, and thus he focuses only upon the 'real contradictions' found in the struggle between classes. Hegel identifies 'real contradictions' with 'logical contradictions', while Marx rejects 'logical' development, along with the primacy of 'ideas', in favour of the 'real contradictions' embodied in human social relations. These 'contradictions' are not a matter of 'logical' analysis or philososphical speculation, but rather of concrete historical investigation. In Hegel, 'contradictions' are simply determined (determined by a single factor), with one thesis negating one antithesis. In Marx, 'contradictions' are complexly determined, with many factors of uneven weight entering into the process of development.[19] Thus, for Marx, history is not a metaphysical construct following strict 'logical' laws because it is not 'ideas' and their logical relations but human beings and their productive relations which are primary. Ideas, modes of reasoning, logic and philosophical speculation itself are historical phenomena which depend, for Marx, upon the 'material practical activities' of human beings. Unlike Hegel's progressional 'dialectic' which is inherently finalistic as it ends in Absolute knowledge, Marx's 'dialectic', while progressional, is not necessarily completable since, at the very least, human history faces the uneliminable contingencies of actual social struggle, as well as the ever receding limits of nature. Marx's concept of social rationality is thus essentially and concretely historical.

As Marcuse argues, the transition from Hegel to Marx is 'a transition to an essentially different order of truth, not to be interpreted in terms of philosophy'. The transition is from philosophy to social theory: 'all the philosophical categories in Marxian theory are social and economic categories, whereas Hegel's social and economic categories are all philosophical concepts'.[20] For Hegel, the truth is the whole which must be present in each of its moments. If a single material fact cannot be reconciled by reason, then the truth of the whole is destroyed. For Marx, the existence of the proletariat is the material fact which contradicts the alleged reality of reason in bourgeois society and, consequently, falsifies Hegel's philosophy in so far as it reconciles itself with that society. For Hegel, as well as for Marx, human beings realise themselves through productive activity. If the mode of production destroys and debases its members, then the entire social order stands condemned. Marcuse draws the revolutionary consequences of the transition from Hegel's philosophical concept of reason to Marx's concept of social rationality: 'the existence of the proletariat thus gives living witness to the fact that the truth has not been realised. History and social reality themselves thus "negate" philosophy. The critique of society cannot be carried through by philosophical doctrine, but becomes the task of socio-historical practice'.[21]

Thus, Marx's concept of social rationality grounded in his 'paradigm of production' is not only, and cannot be, a theoretical tool for understanding and explaining human action and social life, it is also a weapon designed for those capable of radically transforming social life. This is the basic Marxian meaning of critique. The problems of philosophy from this perspective can only be solved through the practical struggle to realise the highest concepts of which philosophy is capable – reason as freedom, autonomy, self-expression, creativity. This is a task that speculation cannot accomplish alone because it cannot abstractly overleap the material conditions of which it is the expression; it cannot overleap history. It is thus a task for revolutionary practice. Only the historical outcome of this practice can, in the last analysis, speak for (or against) the truth of the theory. The question of truth is, for Marx, 'not a question of theory but is a practical question'. Finally, Marx summarised his critique of philosophy in the justly famous eleventh thesis on Feuerbach: 'the philosophers have only interpreted the world, in various ways: the point, however, is to change it'.[22]

Social rationality from Weber to the Frankfurt School

Marx's theory of society contained conceptual tensions from the beginning. Although developed as an essentially 'critical' theory, as I have argued, Marx continued to appeal to the scientific criteria of the time for justification as well. Between the appeal for revolutionary freedom to abrogate 'the iron laws of the economy' and the deterministic thesis that these 'laws' themselves would automatically generate revolution, a tension remains which Marx was never able to settle. His understanding of his own theory as a science and the critical and political character of his concrete social investigations and political writings reflects this tension.

From the time of the Second International, this tension was resolved in 'orthodox' Marxism in favour of the the scientific side, later codified as a universal superscience in 'Diamat'. The failure of the Second International culminating in the First World War, coupled with the defeat of revolutionary upsurges in Hungary, France and Italy, raised deep problems for the 'orthodox' interpretation. According to the 'orthodox' Marxists, objective economic conditions themselves would generate revolution as a more or less 'automatic' outcome of the crisis dynamics of capitalism. They neglected the 'subjective conditions' for revolution: will and consciousness. The revolutionary failures of the period seemed not to lack the objective conditions, but rather these 'subjective conditions'. The forerunners of the Frankfurt School, the so-called 'Western Marxists' (Lukács, Korsch, Gramsci) attempted to explain these failures in terms of failures of 'revolutionary consciousness' that could only be overcome by concentrating on the formation of revolutionary subjects capable of establishing true socialism, a process that could no longer be viewed by them as 'automatic'.[23] To carry out this task each of these theorists felt it necessary to rethink the relationship between philosophy (in particular, the philosophy of Hegel) and Marxism.

The Frankfurt School (here we will consider primarily Marcuse, Horkheimer and Adorno) took over this problematic faced with continued revolutionary failures and, later, the rise of Fascism and the emergence of Marxism itself as a 'legitimation science' used to justify the crimes of Stalin.[24] Building on the work of their 'Western Marxist' forerunners, they attempted to rejuvenate Marxism by emphasising its role as a critical theory of society, not reducible to an economic science or to a philosophical system. The attempt to explain the theory's failures again came to the fore. And again, the concentration on subjective conditions for revolution and the role of philosophy in Marx was important. The Frankfurt School, beginning with Horkheimer, was concerned with the problem of what I call social rationality.[25] They located both theoretical errors and practical failures in the tendency, common to 'orthodox' Marxism and 'positivism', to reduce what I have called Marx's concept of social rationality to scientific – technological rationality limited to its purely instrumental functions. Fundamental to the critical theory of the Frankfurt School is an articulation of the concept of social rationality as both historically embodied and objective, and yet capable of self-transcendence (that is, capable of overcoming its own limitations).[26] The development of the Frankfurt School goes from an attempt to articulate such a concept towards a despair over its very possibility. It will be necessary to trace this trajectory in order to understand the problematic addressed by Habermas's attempt to construct a comprehensive concept of rationality. We will begin with a challenge posed to Marxism by Max Weber which is of decisive importance for the Frankfurt School and Habermas.

The work of Max Weber concerning the progressive rationalisation of modern life had a decisive impact on Lukács and many other 'Western Marxists'.[27] Weber's concept of rationalisation attempted to comprehend a whole series of tendencies related to technological and scientific progress in their effects on the institutional and cultural structure of traditional society. Among these effects were the progress of industrialisation, the urbanisation of social life, the increase in the areas of social life subject to rational decision procedures such as private law, economic activities, and bureaucratic control, the bureaucratisation of administration and the expansion of bureaucratic authority, the radical devaluation of tradition and the destruction of traditional forms of life, the rise of cultural secularisation and the consequent 'disenchantment' of the world.[28] Weber distinguished 'formal' rationality (the degree to which action is oriented by rationally calculable rules) and 'substantive' rationality (the application of rational calculation to further definite goals or values). The relationship of the spread of formal rationality to substantive rationality was, for Weber, highly problematic. On the one hand, capitalist rationalisation was a substantive success in productivity and efficiency. On the other hand, traditional values were being lost. Weber's analysis of this rationalisation process led him to regard it as fundamentally irreversible; it would inevitably lead to a loss of freedom (*Freiheitsverlust*) and a loss of meaning (*Sinnverlust*). The differentiation of culture into different value spheres (science, religion, morality, art) which Weber called 'cultural rationalism' lead to irreconcilable conflicts between each of them and placed the burden of creating meaning squarely on the modern individual. With growing 'social rationalisation' (the social process of the increase of formal, calculable reasoning in the economy and the state), however, the modern individual became increasingly unable to create autonomous meaning to replace the meaning content of devalued tradition. Collective social life becomes a rationalised hierarchical apparatus of experts, limited in their skills, and trained to obey. Modern man was 'fated' to live in an 'iron cage' – in particular, a socialist revolution could not overcome the process of rationalisation. Instead, in Weber's view, it would only accelerate it, especially through the extension of bureaucratic control to the economy.

Weber's analysis of rationalisation was opposed to Marx's theory in so far as Weber saw no possibility of escape from the 'iron cage' of modern society.[29] Lukács attempted to meet this challenge by incorporating Weber's analysis of rationalisation into Marx's critique of political economy. Lukács connected rationalisation with reification (*verdinglichung*) – a phenomenon in which a 'definite social relationship between human beings' appears in the form of a 'relation between things". Through reification, concrete social relations took on the appearance of a 'second nature' in which what Weber called 'rationalisation' appeared as a nature-like process beyond human control. Drawing out the implication of Marx's analysis in volume one of *Capital*, Lukács argued that reification was rooted in the 'commodity fetishism' and was thus a consequence of the universalisation of the commodity form in capitalist society.[30] Weber's pessimism was thus unjustified since the breakdown of capitalism would present the 'objective possibility' of overcoming reification and a chance to break out of the 'iron cage'.

Against Weber's analysis of rationalisation which proceeds by privileging the logic of 'formal rationality', Lukács returns to Marx's broader concept of a historically developing social rationality. Formal rationality, for Weber, dealt with questions answerable by science, by an appeal to the facts, while substantive rationality dealt with questions which science could clarify, but not finally decide, since they included values. This separation of fact and value both Marx and Lukács regarded as itself an expression of capitalist society, and thus not 'ultimate'. Placing at the centre of his interpretation of Marx the notion of 'the social totality', Lukács argued that it is only from the perspective of the proletariat as a potential universal class that the truth of the society can be revealed. Further, Lukács identified the proletariat as the identical subject – object of history (that 'object' of the historical process which can become aware of itself as 'subject' in its role of realising the meaning of history through establishing a truly rational society); a move he would later call 'the attempt to out-Hegel Hegel'.[31] From this perspective, Lukács contrasted Weber's account of the rationalisation of social subsystems with 'the relative irrationality of the whole'.[32] The irrationality of the unplanned economy would inevitably lead to crises which in turn, through their catastrophic consequences for society, would call into question the rationality of the social whole and create the 'objective possibility' for revolution. Finally, Lukács followed

Marx in emphasising the historical role of the concrete social agents themselves, the proletariat, as providing the real embodiment of reason that justifies the concept of social rationality in whose light Weber's 'rationalisation' appears as itself irrational.

Although Lukács' analysis of 'reification' as a characteristic of capitalist society was shared by members of the Frankfurt School, their confidence in the breakdown of capitalism was less. They began to question the idea that the internal development of capitalism would create not only the objective but also the subjective conditions for a radical social transformation. Although still accepting the basic validity of Marx's critique of politcal economy, they attempted to strenghten the link between it and the theory of revolution by including the social and cultural dimension neglected by 'orthodox' Marxists. In the meantime, the 'rationalisation' process Weber analysed in its emergence from traditional society had continued to expand to all areas of social life. Weber's analysis was directed at the emergence of modern society, while the Frankfurt School anaylsed the developed and stabilised result of the process. 'Instrumental reason', for the Frankfurt School, referred to the almost total political and administrative domination of social life through the increasingly efficient and predictable téchniques developed and stabilised by institutions such as the military, the bureaucracy, the schools, business and, in particular, 'the culture industry'.[33] In all these areas, the ever-expanding application of science and technology (grown increasingly interdependent) made possible the domination not only of external nature, but of society and the inner nature of individuals as well. In this situation, the historical role of the proletariat (upon which Lukács still depended) became increasingly questionable as their integration into the system increased. This general movement from the liberal capitalism of Marx's time to 'state capitalism' (in Pollock's usage) and the 'authoritarian state' (in Horkheimer's usage) called for a fundamental rethinking of Marx's social theory, and , in particular, his concept of social rationality.

McCarthy has clearly expressed a central revision in Marx's social theory called for by Horkheimer and Adorno: 'For Marx, the overcoming of philosophy as philosophy was the precondition for establishing critique as scientific. For Horkheimer and Adorno, in contrast, the overcoming of scientism was the precondition for restoring Marxist theory as critique.'[34] The idealism of the philosophical tradition that Marx attacked at least contained a concept of reason which included the critical ideals of freedom and autonomy, even if in an abstract and distorted form. Under the conditions of modern society, these ideals were more likely to be irretrievably lost than 'realised'. Thus, the 'critique of instrumental reason' (that is, scientific – technological, formal rationality instantiated in social rationalisation processes and philosphically expressed in positivism) replaced the critique of philosophical idealism as the central opponent of critical theory.

'Reason,' Marcuse said, 'is the fundamental concept of philosophical thought, the only one by means of which it has bound itself to human destiny . . . (it) is not only a category of bourgeois philosophy, but a concern of mankind'.[35] Thus, the Frankfurt School position in the 1930s took a more affirmative attitude to the philosophical tradition, drawing on it for richer concept of reason with which to counter its reduction to instrumental reason. They attempted to develop a concept of 'critical reason' (substantive reason): a form of thought with access to universal concepts, values, potentialities and objective critical standards that could be used to critique the one-sidedness of a merely formal rationality. This distinction (formal versus substantive reason) was based on the Hegelian distinction between *Verstand* (analytical understanding) and *Vernunft* (substantive reason).

In a programatic essay, Horkheimer argued for a critical theory that would release the critical potentials in philosophical thought by unmasking their present social distortions. Recognising the social and historical contextuality of thought, the method was to be immanent critique which confronts 'the existent, in its historical context with the claim of its conceptual principles, in order to criticise the relationship between the two and thus transcend them'.[36] Following Marx, Horkheimer's model of critical theory would locate the contradiction between bourgeois ideals (justice, equality, freedom) and social reality. For this purpose, critical theory would make use of the findings of the separate scientific disciplines to approach the 'social totality', as well as a concept of critical reason to locate and critique their one-sidedness and partiality. Following Lukács, Horkheimer emphasised the practical and revolutionary character of Marx's theory by retaining the appeal to 'class-subjects' as the addressees of the theory. For Horkheimer, critical theory is the 'unfolding of a single existential judgement' condeming the irrationality of capitalist 'rationalisation', the crisis-ridden course of the commodity economy and the loss of freedom and autonomy produced by this process. Critical theory is an expression of this 'bitter reality'.[37] The concepts of critical theory address social subjects dominated by this 'bitter reality' and are linked to their struggles. The possible convergence of reason and freedom is immanent in human beings and their historical struggles. The 'objective conditions' for such a convergence are present, only the 'subjective conditions' lag behind. The critique of instrumental reason is directed at overcoming the subjective barriers (that is, the reification of consciousness) to the creation of a truly rational society. In the final analysis, the truth of the theory depends on its ability to enlighten its addressees about their real condition and their historical role so as to further such a transformation.

By the 1940s, this formulation of the theory, which depended upon a positive and substantive concept of a historically developing social rationality drawing on both Marx and the philosophical tradition, was abandoned. The failures of the labour movement, Fascism and Stalinism, and the post-war stabilisation of capitalism lessened the Frankfurt School's confidence that the forces of production still contained an explosive force for liberation. The subsequent advance of instrumental reason in the administered societies of East and West called Marx's theory of history into even deeper question. The Frankfurt School positon shifted, under the influence of Adorno, from the attempt to articulate a positive concept of reason and Horkheimer's method of immanent critique towards Adorno's very different method.

For both Horkheimer and Adorno, critique could not be transcendentally or metaphysically grounded. Thus, for both, critique had to be immanent. For Horkheimer, this meant using the social sciences in conjunction with critical reason in order to confront bourgeois ideals with social reality. On this formulation, philosophy as a separate discipline disappears. For Adorno, on the other hand, immanent critique meant an internal investigation of the logic of philosophy itself. Social contradictions appeared within philosophy in a mediated form and must be overcome philosophically by pressing them to the point where 'idealism' could be overcome. As Susan Buck-Morss summarises it, 'this argumentation from within, on the basis of philosophy's own inherent, historically developed logic, in order to break out of bourgeois idealism and into revolutionary materialism, was Adorno's meaning of immanent critique'.[38] Such critique proceeds by a reciprocal criticism of the universal and the particular which shows 'whether the concept does justice to what it covers, and whether the particular fulfills its concept'.[39] Concepts continue to be an expression of social reality, and yet they have a relative autonomy which resists identification with social reality. Immanent criticism requires no 'foundation', it recognises that it must work with historically and socially rooted concepts; and yet is can proceed to criticise a given period and a given society for failure to do justice to its own concepts, to live up to its own values. The method does not involved a pure historical relativism because the potentials in the concepts still depend upon objective historical developments to be realised. And this still means an at least implicit reliance on a Marxist theory of history. Without this reliance the results of such critique become totally negative. They are capable only of exposing the historical embodiments of unreason. For the later Frankfurt School, this meant a ruthless criticism of instrumental reason since it serves to legitimate an irrational reality. It is to the specifics of this critique that I will now turn.

According to the Frankfurt School, the epistemological illusion generated by instrumental reason is that the more efficient, scientific and immediate domination becomes, the more impersonal and anonymous it appears. Although Horkheimer, Adorno and Marcuse continue to link rationalisation with reification in Lukács' sense, they change the emphasis. Lukács emphasises the 'phantom objectivity' of the social world which hides its character as a product of the concrete social actors themselves, while the Frankfurt School theorists emphasise the 'totalising anonymity' of domination which thus ceases to appear as domination at all.[40] The consequences of instrumental reason, and the processes of rationalisation and reification, are a loss of freedom and autonomy. Weber had distinguished between the social process of rationalisation and modern cultural rationalism per se.[41] Under their increasingly pessimistic (or realistic) premises, Horkheimer, Adorno and (to a lesser extent) Marcuse increasingly tended to identify both as an expression of the very structure of Western reason itself. At this final stage critique becomes total and entirely negative. It marks the Frankfurt School's abandonment of their last vestiges of faith in Marx's theory of history and social rationality in the face of the 'totally administered society'.

The critique of instrumental reason is carried out to this extreme consequence in Horkheimer's and Adorno's *Dialectic of Enlightenment*. Instrumental reason is no longer identified with a particular class, society or historical period. The analysis of rationalisation moves from a socio-historically specific to a global level, applying not only to historically situated agents but to the human species in general. Here the critique of instrumental reason and the rationalisation of social life expands into a critique of the very structure of Western reason. Horkheimer and Adorno argue that the Enlightenment project of liberating humanity from myth and the unknown has, by becoming an end in itself, turned into its opposite – a new and more powerful force of domination. The old terror before the unknown becomes a new terror: the fear of anything that cannot be calculated, standardised, manipulated or instrumentalised. Enlightenment progress in scientific-technological knowledge (= power), while creating the objective possibility for a truly free society, leads to the domination of external nature, society and inner nature. What Lukács analysed as the reification of consciousness was the price the potential subjects of liberation paid for the progressive overcoming of material necessity. Throughout the course of Western civilisation, the rationality of myth, as well as the Enlightenment which replaced it as reason only to become a myth itself, exposes Western reason as a destructive force. Reason abstracts, conceptualises, and seeks to reduce the concrete and the non-identical to identity, to destroy the otherness of the other. Horkheimer and Adorno locate the irrationality of what Weber analysed as rationalisation at its deepest source – the identity logic which is the fundamental structure of Western reason. Human liberation could be conceived, if at all, only as a complete break with mere formal rationality and instrumental reason.

Although convinced of the link between enlightened thought and a free society, Horkheimer and Adorno hoped to warn the Enlightenment about itself. Unlike the critics of progress, they wanted to save the Enlightenment from itself and preserve its goal of human liberation. In the same spirit, Marcuse also attacks the prevailing forms of scientific–technological rationality and instrumental reason. Marcuse focuses on the concrete political implications of what he calls 'one-dimensional thought'.[42] As 'technical reason' it has specific substantive outcomes; its very structure limits it to relations of possible control:

The very form of technical reason is perhaps ideological. Not only the application of technology but technology itself is domination (of nature and man) – methodical, scientific, calculated, calculating control. Specific purposes and interests of domination. . . enter the very construction of the technical apparatus. Technology is always a historical–social project: in it is projected what a society and its ruling interests intend to do with men and things. Such a 'purpose' of domination. . . belongs to the very structure of technical reason.[43]

For Marcuse, what Weber called 'rationalisation' realises, in Habermas's words, 'not rationality as such, but rather, in the name of rationality, a specific form of unacknowledged domination'.[44] It remains 'unacknowledged' because, as Marcuse argues, the growth in the forces of production fuelled by scientific and technological progress becomes the basic and crucial legitimation of the social system. The relations of production appear as subject to the technical necessities and imperatives of a totally 'rationalised' society. Freedom and autonomy of the individual begin to appear as 'technically' impossible. Reason is reduced to a mere instrumental residue. Thus, reason loses its function as a critical standard against which the present society can be measured, instead it merely describes what is the case – and thus legitimates it. For Marcuse as well, human liberation can only be conceived as a radical break with 'one-dimensional thought'.

The early Habermas and critical theory

Habermas is centrally concerned with articulating a response to the complex developments of the problem of rationality outlined above. The critique of instrumental reason developed to its extreme by the later Frankfurt School is especially important in so far as it represents a challenge to Habermas's attempt to separate the distortions of the Enlightenment from its real advances, so as to save its goal of human liberation. For Habermas, the permanent achievement of this critique (particularly as developed in *Dialectic of Enlightenment*) is a justified suspicion of 'enlightenment' and a warning concerning the extreme difficulties of saving the achievements and goals of the Enlightenment by developing a positive and comprehensive account of reason. The theoretical necessity for such an account only gradually became clear to Habermas through difficulties encountered in his own early work.

Habermas's first book, *Structural Transformation of the Public Sphere* (*Struckturwandel der Offenlichkeit*, 1962) is a detailed historical study of structural changes in the bourgeois public sphere from its emergence in the eighteenth century to the present.[45] Although written as a *Habilitationsschrift* for a small circle of scholars, it soon became an important work which helped to shape the political consciousness of the emerging New Left in the 1960s. The book remained influential even after 1968 when many student leftists broke with Habermas.

In *Structural Transformation of the Public Sphere*, Habermas used a method of immanent critique influenced by the Frankfurt School to compare the concept of the 'public sphere" with its limited and distorted historical embodiments. The concept of the 'public sphere' refers to a realm of social life in which 'public opinion' can be formed. Citizens meet as a part of the public sphere when they come together not as subjects of the state or as private economic actors concerned with matters of individual interest, but rather as a free and open public body to discuss matters of general interest. Public opinion refers to the tasks of criticism, influence, oversight and control which such a public body practices over the state, usually informally except for periodic elections. The central principle of the public sphere Habermas calls 'discursive will-formation' – equal, open and constraint-free discussion. Within the public sphere, the 'reasoning public' was to attempt to acheive a consensus on political questions under conditions of the open and free discussion of all issues without dogmatic appeal to authority or tradition. Under such conditions, 'public opinion' would possess legitimate authority as an expression of 'the rule of reason' and, thus, be capable in principle of truly articulating the general interest.

As Habermas's historical account revealed, however, the social basis of the public sphere which effectively limited the 'reasoning public' to the bourgeoisie meant that the commitment to 'rational formation of the public will' was never actualised. Further, with the development of the capitalist economy, the distance between the concept and its social and historical embodiment continued to grow. The commercialisation of the public media, the increase in state intervention in the economy, the increase in large economic enterprises and the expanding influence of science and technology all furthered the process of the 'depoliticalisation of the public sphere'. Public opinion became increasingly a matter of the technically sophisticated manipulation of the public which forecloses its practical and political function. Although Habermas located countertendencies in contemporary society (such as the demand for open information on all public matters), he concluded that under the influence of 'technocratic consciousness', and the institutions which support it, a 'repoliticisation' of the public sphere is unlikely.

This argument is important both for its central idea of communicatively generated rationality (a concern that runs through all of Habermas's work) and for its use of a method of immanent critique influenced by the early Frankfurt School. In the essays collected in *Theory and Practice* (*Theoria und Praxis*, 1963), Habermas continued to use this method to compare bourgeois ideals with their social and historical embodiments, as in his analysis of the concept of 'natural right' in 'Naturrecht und Revolution'.[46] His initial contribution to the positivist dispute in German sociology ('Analytische Wissenschaftstheorie und Dialektik', 1963) presented a defence of the method which appealed explicitly to Hegelian-Marxist 'dialectics' with Habermas's interpretation of Marx's 'philosophy of history with a practical intent' as its basis.[47] His uneasiness with this appeal is already apparent in his second contribution to the debate ('Gegen einen positivistisch halbierten Rationalismus', 1964) where Habermas attempts to explain his position using arguments drawn from American pragmatism and the analytic philosophy of language.[48] This uneasiness was conditioned by what Habermas came to see as the relativistic implications of immanent critique. It could only appeal to truths or values which are internal to a given society in a given historical period. Immanent critique can escape relativism only if it, however tacitly, relies on a theory of history which can objectively distinguish between 'what men and things could be and what they actually are'.[49] The method loses its critical thrust if a society refuses to recognise those truths and values as their own and the theory of history offers no objective assurance that they ever will. In Habermas's view, the method of immanent critique of the early Frankfurt School thus depended upon Marx's theory of history for its theoretical justification. In order to determine if this dependence was itself justified, Habermas returned to the origin of the critical theory of society in Marx. A discussion of his crucial confrontation with Marx and the Frankfurt School legacy will pave the way for an account of the early Habermas's reformulation of critical theory in *Knowledge and Human Interests* (*Erkenntnis und Interesse*. 1968).[50]

Habermas first engaged the work of Marx in a survey of 'The Philosophical Discussion of Marx and Marxism' (*Philosopische Rundschau*. 1957).[51] Here he argued that the whole discussion was misdirected since Marx was not, strictly speaking, a philosopher; instead he was a social theorist who sought to 'abolish philosophy' by 'realising' it. Traditional philosophy was to be replaced by a 'philosophy of history' that was no longer strictly philosophical because it did not rest on ontological or metaphysical foundations. Marx's theory of history could best be understood as a 'critical prologue to praxis'. Habermas summarised by calling it 'a philosophy of history with a practical intent'.[52] This interpretation of Marx remained within the framework of the interpretations given by Lukács and the early Frankfurt School. Habermas's next engagement with Marx moved decisively beyond this framework by bringing Marx into contact with contemporary social reality.

In 'Zwischen Philosophie und Wissenschaft. Marxismus als Kritik' Habermas argued that modern society presented 'four facts against Marx' which showed that 'the philosophy of history with a practical intent' could no longer rely on the basic soundness of Marx's theoretical framework.[53] These 'four facts' are: (i) unlike liberal capitalism, in advanced capitalism the state and the economy are inextricably interlocked and politically mediated – they no longer stand in a simple relation of economic base to political superstructure; (ii) unlike liberal capitalism, in advanced capitalism the real rise in the standard of living for broad strata of society means that human liberation can no longer be articulated in directly economic terms; (iii) under the above conditions, 'the proletariat as proletariat, has been dissolved' – it is no longer plausible in the role of the central revolutionary agent; and (iv) the degeneration of Marxism in Russia in to a 'legitimation science'.[54] Although Marx's theory was appropriate for liberal capitalism, it must now be reformulated for advanced capitalism. Thus, Habermas believes it is necessary, if the 'practical intentions' of the theory are to be saved, to reformulate the 'philosophy of history with a practical intent' on a new basis.

Such a reformulation could no longer unproblematically rely on the method of immanent critique practised by the early Frankfurt School, since the addressees of this version of critical theory had failed to recognise its truths and values as their own. Under the influence of 'scientism' and 'technocratic consciousness', earlier truths and values seemed outdated, technically obsolete, impossible to realise. In a phrase Habermas was to use later, 'bourgeois consciousness has become cynical'.[55] In this situation (and with the loss of confidence in Marx's theory of a socially and historically developing rationality), immanent critique became 'total critique'. But the stage of 'total critique' reached by the later Frankfurt School is even more unsatisfactory, both theoretically and practically. Theoretically, how can a critique of the totality of Western reason proceed except through the use of that very reason, a move which, by their own account, could only reproduce domination? Under the direct identification of Western reason with domination, even the method of immanent critique is, in Adorno's phrase, 'dragged into the abyss by its object'. As McCarthy was to argue later, no positive justification for this critical enterprise is possible since 'under the presupposition of universal distortion, any such positive specification would itself be suspect. The radical critic, like the radical skeptic, appears to be condemned to silence'.[56] Further, 'total critique' is practically and politically impotent. It must forego even the possibility of activating social classes capable of transforming the dominate social reality. It is left appealing to the 'wholly other' and discovering traces of liberated thought in esoteric art.

Marcuse, to a lesser extent than Horkheimer and Adorno, remains caught in the web of 'total critique'. In 'Technology and Science as "Ideology"', Habermas argues that by interpreting the modern 'fusion of technology and domination, rationality and oppression' as a 'world project', Marcuse cannot even conceive social emancipation 'without a complemetary revolutionary transformation of science and technology themselves'.[57] Marcuse does envision a New Science in which techincal control would be replaced by a project of 'preserving, fostering, and releasing the potentialities of nature'. To this Habermas objects 'that modern science can be interpreted as a historically unique project only if at least one alternative project is thinkable'. Further, a New Science would require a New Technology – but 'technology, if based at all on a project, can only be traced back to a "project" of the human species as a whole, and not to one that could be historically surpassed'. For Habermas, as long as the human species achieves self-preservation through labour, 'it is impossible to envisage how... we could renounce technology, more particularly our technology, in favour of a qualitatively different one'.[58] These arguments directed explicitly against Marcuse (and implicitly against the whole later Frankfurt School position) point to a central feature of Habermas's thought to which I will soon turn – the construction of a more differentiated and comprehensive account of reason.

In Habermas's view, the stage of 'total critique' leaves critical theory without a normative justification and without an answer to the practical problem of agency. Benhabib has cogently summed up the dilemma facing the later Frankfurt School: 'Either the empirical diagnosis of the one-dimensionality of social and cultural rationalisation processes must be revised, or critical theory must admit the conditions of its own historical impossiblity.'[59] In the face of his growing awareness of this dilemma, the early Habermas attempted to supply a new basis for 'the philosophy of history with a practical intent' which marked the beginning of his return to the effort of the Frankfurt School of the 1930s to develop a positive concept of reason. Habermas takes up this attempt in *Knowledge and Human Interests* which represents his initial reformulation of the basis of critical theory. And again, he returns to the origin of the critical theory of society in Marx.

In *Knowledge and Human Interests*, Habermas turns to the basic unresolved tension in Marx's work, the tension between 'science' and 'critique', at its source – the concept of historical and social rationality as rooted in social practice (what I have called Marx's 'paradigm of production'). Through a reconsideration of Marx's account of social practice, Habermas hopes to explain this tension in Marx, both the problems it has generated and how they can be overcome. He begins with a distinction between Marx's concrete historical and empirical analyses and his theoretical understanding of their significance. Marx's concrete social inquiries incorporate both an analysis of the way human beings produce and reproduce the material conditions of their lives and an analysis of the ways in which they interpret and transform their institutions in historical struggles. Habermas argues that Marx's concrete analyses view the history of the species 'under categories of material activity and the critical abolition of ideologies, of instrumental action and revolutionary practice, of labour and reflection'.[60] Marx distinguishes two related dimensions: (i) the forces of production – the realm of scientific–technical progress; (ii); the relations of production – the realm of social control and class struggles. For Marx, the self-formation of the human species takes place in these two dimensions: in confrontation with nature through production and in transforming societies through class struggle. Thus, Habermas argues, Marx's concrete investigations take into account both technical and practical activity.

According to Habermas, Marx's theoretical self-understanding is not consistent with the above viewpoint. Instead, Marx tends to reduce the self-formation of the human species to labour alone. Marx thus reduces the practical to the technical. This generates the following problems: (i) Marx tends to view his critique of ideology as a natural science, thus concealing the 'practical intentions' of his theory beneath a logic of progressive technical development; (ii) Marx comes close to the view (particularly in the *Grundrisse*) that progressive technical development will lead directly to human liberation; (iii) Marx is thus unable to demonstrate theoretically his major thesis that class struggle is the central dynamic of history because he cannot show how social actors become conscious and change society.[61] Finally, the concentration on the logic of progressive technical development led historically to the theory falling apart in two different directions. On the one hand, 'orthodox' Marxism (especially in Russia) optimistically turned progressive technical development into the major, if not the only, social goal which, if met, would lead to human liberation. In the meantime, Marx's theory becomes a tool in the hands of the social engineers who understand its 'scientific necessity'. On the other hand, the later Frankfurt School (especially Horkheimer and Adorno) pessimistically turned progressive technical development into an unconditional evil. Marx's theory becomes a totally negative critique of culture and society without the possibility of transforming social reality.

For Habermas, the reduction of the practical to the technical is fundamental not only in Marx and the Frankfurt School, but also for modern scientific rationalised thought in general. In *Theory and Practice* he traces the history of this reduction in its impact on political thought.[62] Habermas returns to the origins of 'practical philosophy' in Aristotle. For Aristotle, politics was a necessary continuation of ethics that concerned itself with forming and cultivating habits of virtue (*arete*) in the citizen. The type of knowledge aimed at was *phronesis* (that is, 'a prudent understanding of the situation'). Since the social object domain of politics is changing and variable, politics cannot achieve the status of the theoretical sciences which seek certain knowledge (*episteme*) through contemplating objects which seldom or never change.

For Habermas, the emergence of the modern social sciences from the classical doctrine of politics may be understood in terms of the change in the relationship between the categories of *praxis* (human action directed to a goal), *poesis* (the production of beautiful or useful objects) and *theoria* (the contemplation of the unchanging cosmos). For Aristotle, a good action (*eupraxis*) cannot be viewed as an object we contemplate (like a star or a mountain) nor as an object we make with workman like skill (*techne*) for future use (like a bowl or a chair). Instead, it is an action performed by one who had formed a character for which virtue is a habit. The cultivation of such habits in the members of the *polis* define the 'practical intentions' central to the classical doctrine of politics – guidance in the formation of a good and just society.

The distinction between *theoria* and *poesis* was challenged at the beginning of the early modern period when it was argued that theoretical knowledge could be attained by means of technical fabrication. The model of the world as a great machine which could be technically understood and mastered was an important theme in that movement analysed by Weber as cultural rationalism which effectively undercut Aristotle's distinctions.[63] Habermas accepts the basic idea that we know best what we make ourselves, an idea Marx took over from Vico, as long as it remains directed at nature. For Habermas, in agreement with modern cultural rationalism, nature can only be understood in a theoretically fruitful way as an object of possible technical manipulation. When this view is applied to society (as it was first in Hobbes), however, problems arise.

Habermas approaches these problems through a discussion of 'the scientisation of politics' that was concomitant with the rise of cultural rationalism, the process of social 'rationalisation' and the modern differentiation of reason which Weber placed at the center of modernity.[64] On the theoretical level, the move from practical philosophy to the modern social sciences (understood as value-free enterprises) generates fundamental problems. First, the scientific approach to society must ignore the social values built into their basic categories and descriptions. The social scientist must, at least tacitly, draw on the unproblematically assumed knowledge of the social actors themselves. Further, he is himself such a social actor. He cannot get 'outside' his object domain in order merely to contemplate it like a star. His own social values and interests, as well as the socially assumed background of values and interests, cannot be totally filtered out. Finally, and crucially, the conceptualisation of the interaction of citizens cannot be completely carried out through a monological language appropriate to the designation of objects (for example, an observation language capable, in principle, of being mastered by a single subject, what Wittgenstein might call a 'private language') because language is also used dialogically by social actors to achieve consensus. This is implicit even in Hobbes' account of the social contract. Stated another way, modern social science cannot fully succeed in the attempt to suppress the communicative dimension of social life. The very attempt betrays what is itself a value, an implicit judgement in favour of technical solutions to social problems which might otherwise be addressed practically through the formation of a rational consensus. Thus, on the practical political level, the problems generated by the scientisation of politics centre on the extent to which decisions which require the consent of citizens are presented as technical problems for experts. The loss of the theoretical distinction between the practical and the technical finds here its concrete political parallel in our technocratic society with its administered way of life.

For Habermas, the move from 'practical philosophy' to the separate social sciences is, in some important respects, an advance. The rigorous scientific analysis of social problems is a progress in enlightenment (even Marx absolutely required the careful reports of the factory inspectors). It is, however, a progress with a cost, namely, the eclipsing of those 'practical intentions' which were at the very centre of the classical doctrine of politics. As Habermas sees it, the task is to develop a social theory which retains 'the rigour of scientific knowledge' without relinquishing the 'practical intentions' of classical politics.[65] To the extent that Marx's theory abetted in the scientisation of politics by reducing the practical to the technical, it is precisely these 'practical intentions' of forming a good and just society which Marx had hoped to save that are lost.

In terms of my earlier discussion, Habermas's central claim is that the 'paradigm of production' is too narrow a base for Marx's concept of a historically developing social rationality. Habermas agrees with Marx that social practice is the appropriate object of investigation, thus following the move emphasised by Marcuse from philosophy to social theory. Habermas, however, claims that Marx needs a distinction between humans as tool-making animals and as language-using animals, if his 'brilliant insight' into the relationship between the forces and the relations of production is not to be lost (with the negative theoretical and practical consequences already discussed). Habermas's critique of Marx leads him to formulate a distinction (first introduced in his essay on Hegel's Jena *Philosophy of Spirit*) which is central to his entire project – the distinction between labour (instrumental action) and interaction (communicative action).[66]

In *Knowledge and Human Interests*, Habermas draws this distinction at three levels. At the sociological level, the distinction is an analytic tool for locating (in empirical situations where both are mixed) the degree to which institutions further 'technical control' or 'social integration'. At the methodological level, the distinction is between 'empirical–analytical inquiry' and 'hermeneutic or critical inquiry'. At what Habermas calls the 'quasi-transcendental' level, the distinction is between the 'technical interest' in the prediction and control of objectified processes and the 'practical interest' in undistorted communication in ordinary language.[67] Based on this distinction, Habermas conceives the self-formation of the human species through social practice not only in terms of growth of the technical power of production, but also in terms of growth in the practical dimension of law, morality and worldviews.

This multilayered distinction is central to Habermas's early attempt in *Knowledge and Human Interests* to formulate a concept of reason capable of a more differentiated critique of instrumental reason and of providing a more satisfatory normative justification for the critical theory of society. The critique of instrumental reason is reformulated as a critique of 'scientism'. For Habermas, 'Scientism means. . . that we no longer understand science as one form of possible knowledge, but rather identify knowledge with science'.[68] Habermas focuses on the relation between scientism and positivism, which provides scientism with its sophisticated philosophical defense. Positivism itself began as a critique of ideology (metaphysics, religion, dogmas and tradition) only to become a central element in technocratic consciousness and thus a key feature of modern ideology. *Knowledge and Human Interests* investigates the 'dissolution of epistemology' effected by positivism. Habermas argues that, since Kant, epistemology as a critique of knowledge has progressively been undermined. The rise of scientism resulted in a turn away from the traditional concerns of the critique of knowledge. Inquiry into the conditions for the possiblity of knowledge, as well as the meaning of knowledge itself, gave away to an exclusive concern with the methodology of the sciences. In this process, the fundamental importance of the role of the knowing subject and of reflection by the subject on its own activities was effaced. Philosophy, through its own development, became unable to take a critical approach to knowledge. It could not question the meaning or validity of science because it recognised no form of knowledge besides science. Thus, 'the meaning of knowledge itself became irrational – in the name of rigorous knowledge'. The rehabilitation of the importance of reflection is crucial for Habermas, since 'positivism is the denial of reflection'.[69]

With Horkheimer, Habermas holds that knowledge is historically and socially rooted and interest bound. Unlike Horkheimer, Habermas locates these interests as anthropologically deep-seated interests of the human species. He develops the theory of 'cognitive interests' (or knowledge-constitutive interests) in order to explain the relationship of knowledge to human activity. The theory is concerned with uncovering the conditions for the possibility of knowledge. As with Kant, knowledge is understood as the result of the constituting activity of the subject. Habermas, however, rejects locating such activity in an ahistorical, transcendental subject. As with Marx, history, society and nature (as known) are products of the constituting labour of the human species. Thus, knowledge must be viewed in terms of the problems humans encounter in producing and reproducing their social and material existence. For Habermas, it is these historical–material conditions in which the species developed that conditon the constitution of knowledge.

Habermas's method of argument in *Knowledge and Human Interests* is characterised as a 'materialistically transformed phenomenological reflection' which attempts to reconstruct internally 'a history of ideas with a systematic intent'.[70] Thus, Habermas still makes use of internal critique. This method (unlike Horkheimer's method of immanent critique) does not emphasise the gap between bourgeois ideals and their social embodiments, but rather attempts an internal investigation of philosophy itself (like Adorno's method of immanent critique). Unlike Adorno, however, Habermas uses the method to build up a positive theory by examining earlier positions from within, exposing their limitations, building on their strengths, moving on to later positions and repeating the process in order to arrive at a more comprehensive and satisfactory position. Habermas first used this method of internal critique in an important contribution to the *Philosophische Rundshau* on the logic of the social sciences (*Zur Logik der Sozialwissenschaften*, 1967) to develop a criticism of the contemporary social sciences that could lead to a more comprehensive approach to social theory.[71] The justification for this method, however, shifts in *Knowledge and Human Interests* (1968) from an implicit reliance on Hegelian–Marxist 'dialectics' to a 'materialistically transformed transcendental reflection' which links 'critique' in the Marxist sense with 'critique' in the Kantian sense. The standard for critique can no longer be Hegel's philosophical concept of Absolute truth nor Marx's concept of the historically embodied 'truth' of the worker's movement; rather the standard is claimed to be implicit in the very structure of communication and rooted in fundamental human interests. It is to the specifics of this argument that I now turn.

Habermas's central contention is that the human species organises its experience in terms of cognitive interests that constitute our knowledge *a priori*, although they arose contingently in the natural development of the species. These knowledge-guiding interests 'have a transcendental function but arise from actual structures of human life', thus Habermas calls them 'quasi-transcendental'.[72] The 'basis of interests' follows, Habermas argues, from an understanding of humans as both tool-making and language-using animals. Humans must produce what is required for their material existence in confrontation with nature through the manipulation and control of objects. Humans must also communicate with each other through the use of intersubjectively understood symbols within communities. The species thus has an interest in the creation of knowledge which enables it to control objects and to communicate. From this it follows, in Habermas's account, that there must be a third fundamental human interest, namely, the interest in the reflective appropriation of human life without which the interest bound character of knowledge could not itself be understood. This interest is based in the human capacity to act rationally, to be self-reflective and self-determining. The species thus also has an interest in the creation of knowledge which furthers autonomy and responsibility (*Mundigkeit*). It is an emancipatory interest.

Habermas's model of the way in which reality is constituted and acted upon may be summarised as follows. The human species has three cognitve interests: the technical, the practical and the emancipatory. These develop in three social media: labour, interaction and power (relations of domination and constraint). They are the conditions for the possibility of three sciences: the empirical–analytic, the hermeneutic and the critical. The role of these three sciences is to systematise and formalise the procedures required for basic human activities (controlling external conditions, communicating and reflecting) necessary for the functioning of the human species. Thus, Habermas replaces Horkheimer's distinction between traditional theory and critical theory with a trichotomous division between the natural sciences, the cultural sciences and critical science.

Using an interpretation of Peirce as a guide, Habermas argues that the natural sciences are fundamentally and structurally oriented towards the production of technically useful knowledge. They are a reflected form (*Reflexionform*) of basic learning processes already present in the structure of instrumental action (action directed at the control of the external conditions of existence). Thus, they are bound to an interest in the prediction and control of objectified processes – the technical interest. Positivism presents scientific knowledge as 'pure' and therefore neglects its connection to the human interest in technical control which remains as an implicit value in their own accounts of science. Positivism, by equating rationality with technical rationality, must treat practical questions as beyond rational settlement. As in Weber, they are ultimately abandoned to the decisions and commitments of the individual who is left with no means of rational justification. The ideological effect on social consciousness this produces is a systematic pattern of framing social problems that encourages technical (rather than practical) solutions, which then extends the 'rationalised' sphere of technocratic control.

By attempting to grasp all knowledge within the framework of a single unified science, positivism must either presuppose as unproblematic the availability of an intersubjectively constituted language or adopt a position of 'methodical solipsism'. But this assumes, as Karl-Otto Apel has pointed out, that 'objective knowledge is possible without intersubjective understanding through communication being presupposed'.[73] In either case, positivism is unable to account for the very language upon which it depends, the non-objectified intersubjective language of the scientific community itself. Here Habermas draws an important distinction. The interaction between a subject and an object which can be regarded as another subject must be distinguished from the interaction between a subject and an object which cannot be regarded as another subject. The former is a case of communicative interaction (it is 'dialogic'), while the latter is a case of instrumental action (it is 'monologic'). Habermas argues that the attempt by positivism to reduce the former to the latter cannot succeed.

Natural science is not the only viewpoint from which reality may be disclosed. Another such viewpoint is that of the historical–hermeneutic sciences (the cultural or human sciences). Unlike the monological viewpoint of the natural sciences, which 'grasp reality with regard to technical control that, under specified conditions, is possible everywhere and at all times', the dialogical viewpoint of the cultural sciences 'grasps interpretations of reality with regard to possible intersubjectivity of action-orienting mutual understanding specific to a given hermeneutic starting point'.[74] The objective knowledge produced by the natural sciences is impossible without knowledge in the form of intersubjective understanding. The natural sciences assume a shared framework of intersubjectively valid pre-scientific ordinary language. The cultural sciences concern themselves with this framework in its extension to the whole cultural life-context (*lebenszusammenhang*) of which scientific practice is but one element. Habermas's distinction is an epistemological one concerning not different 'worlds', but different orientations to the one 'world'. From one perspective, we encounter objects in motion, events and processes capable of being causally explained; from the other, we encounter communicating subjects, speech and action capable of being understood.

Using an interpretation of Dilthey as a guide, Habermas argues that the culture sciences are fundamentally and structurally oriented towards the production of mutual understanding and agreement. On Habermas's reading, Dilthey postulated the 'community of life unities' as the objective framework of the cultural sciences. The 'community of life unities' is marked for Habermas by the process of self-formation and ego-identity and the dialogic relation between subjects who reciprocally recognise each other as intentional subjects sharing meanings. Individual life histories are thus constituted in the cumulative experiences of individuals over time (the diachronic dimension) and through intersubjectively shared communicaton with other individuals (the synchronic dimension). The 'community of life unities' is formed in the complex interaction of these two dimensions. Its explication is the task of the cultural sciences.

The cultural sciences are also 'interest bound'. They seek to further mutual understanding and agreement which overcomes conflicts of interpretation and misunderstandings that arise first of all in practical life. The successful functioning of human beings as a social species requires that communication be maintained by overcoming misunderstanding. This is the practical interest. Thus, the cultural sciences are also a reflected form of basic learning processes already present in the structure of communicative action (action directed at mutual understanding and agreement in communication). Unlike the natural sciences that operate within the 'transcendental framework' of instrumental action (a framework shared by the cultural sciences), the cultural sciences are 'directed toward the transcendental structure of various actual forms of life'. Not simply communicative action, but rather 'the grammar of ordinary language' plays the role of transcendental framework here since it provides 'schemata for world interpretation' as soon as an individual is socialised into a language community.[75] The hermeneutic inquirer can interpret only from this starting point. The 'texts' interpreted, however, are at once both symbols and facts. Inquiry proceeds both empirically and conceptually. Thus, interpretation is directed towards a world constituted through ordinary language and towards the linguistic rules that constitute this world.

For Habermas, historicism plays the role of positivism in these sciences by blocking critical reflection. Historicism, intoxicated by the panorama of workdviews and the multiplicity of cultural objects, reduces their meanings to those given to them by the subjects being studied. It can say nothing about the truth content or the possible distortions expressed by the subjects. Discussion centres on description, questions of logical consistency and problematic areas of interpretation. To move beyond the limitations of both positivism and historicism requires a critical science – the critical theory of society.

Habermas's account of the technical and practical interests and their link to the natural and cultural sciences could proceed in a

Kantian manner by addressing already existing bodies of knowledge. The case is different for the emancipatory interest because what is in question is the very possibility of a critical theory. The two primary purported examples (the theories of Marx and Freud) were both subject to 'scientistic misunderstanding'. Thus, an adequate model of critical theory is lacking. This Habermas attempts to supply through the idea of a critical social theory with practical intentions incorporating an emancipatory interest. This basic idea brings us to the very centre of Habermas's early attempt to provide a normative justification for critical theory.

Besides the technical and the practical interest, Habermas argues for a third interest, namely the emancipatory interest in securing freedom from self-imposed constraints, hypostatised forces and conditions of distorted communication. Again, this interest is based in the human capacity to act rationally, to be self-determining and self-reflective. The process of self-formation of the human species is, at least potentially, a process in which history can be made with 'will and consciousness'. But it is apparent that history embodies unreason in the form domination, repression and ideological constraints on thought and action. Thus, it is also apparent that human self-understanding is limited by systematically unacknowledged conditions. If the rational capacity of humans is to function truly, if their rational potential is to be fulfilled, a particular type of knowledge becomes necessary to overcome and abolish these constraining conditions. This form of knowledge is self-reflection:

> Self-reflection brings to consciousness those determinates of a self-formative process of cultivation and self-formation (*bildung*) which ideologically determine a contemporary practice and conception of the world... (leading) to insight due to the fact that what has previously been unconscious is made conscious in a manner rich in consequences: analytic insights intervene in life.[76]

Thus, self-reflection can, by revealing the structure of distortions, aid human beings in overcoming them.

The human capacity to reflect on our own development, and thus to act with greater consciousness and autonomy, is the basis upon which the emancipatory interest can be revealed. This interest is an interest in reason:

In self-reflection, knowledge for the sake of knowledge comes to coincide with the interest in autonomy and responsibility (*mundigkeit*). For the pursuit of reflection knows itself as a moment of emancipation. Reason is at the same time subject to the interest in reason ... it obeys an emancipatory cognitive interest.[77]

In both the natural and cultural sciences, the act of knowing is not immediately connected with the utilisation of knowledge, the theory and the practice to which it is directed are separated. But, Habermas argues, theory and practice are linked in the process of self-reflection; our act of knowing coincides with our release from previously unacknowledged forces. Further, it is only through reflection on the self-formative process of the species that human beings can grasp the connection between knowledge and interest. Compared to the two other interests, however, the emancipatory interest has a 'derivative status'. It is not rooted in (perhaps invariant) structures of experience and action which are the basic elements of social systems, but only arises through their distortions. Thus, it is able to reveal 'the connection between theoretical knowledge and ... practical life which comes into existence as a result of systematically distorted communication and thinly legitimised repression'.[78]

The emancipatory interest is the guiding interest of critical theory and of all systematic reflection, including philosophy. The goal of the critical sciences is to further processes of self-reflection and to dissolve barriers to the self-conscious developement of the human species. The critical sciences are required for an adequate understanding of all social activity (including science). Through revealing systematic distortions in communication and action, they attempt to aid human beings in coming to awareness so that they can make history with 'will and consciousness'. Habermas turns to Frued for a 'tangible example' of a critical science which incorporates 'methodical self-reflection'.[79]

Although Freud (like Marx) tended to misunderstand his own enterprise by ascribing to it the status of a natural science, Habermas argues that psychoanalysis reveals important methodological guidelines for the construction of a critical theory of society. For Habermas, psychoanalysis is concerned with interpretation. But unlike the hermeneutic sciences, plausible interpretations can only be constructed with the aid of explanations involving causal connections. Further, such explanations can only be constructed with reference to a general theory. Habermas distinguishes three levels in Freud's theory: (i) the metapsychological level containing the basic categories and concepts of the theory, consisting of basic assumptions concerning the connection between distorted language and pathological behaviour, for example, the theory of instincts and the id-ego-superego model; (ii) the level of general interpretation of psychodynamic development in the form of a systematically generalised narrative constructed with the aid of the metapsychology, but drawing on empirically substantive data and clinical experiences; and (iii) the level of the application of the interpretive framework to the reconstruction of individual life histories. These applications may be viewed as hypotheses generated by the theory. Verification, however, is not what it is for the natural sciences (establishing agreement concerning the results of observation and experiments in the light of predictions) or the cultural sciences (reaching a consensus about an interpretation); rather it means acceptance by the individual being analysed, acceptance incorporating self-reflection that is able to overcome symptoms. Ultimately, the assessment of emancipatory reflection is a matter of practice: 'Only the context of the self-formative process as a whole has confirming or falsifying power.'[80]

Habermas transfers this model to the realm of social theory, suggesting a reforumlation of Marx's theory as a critical theory of society which incorporates the psychoanalytic insight into the role of self-reflection. For Habermas, the critiques developed by Marx and Freud contain 'an interest in emancipation going beyond the technical and the practical interest of knowledge'.[81] Based on this emancipatory interest, Marx's theory is reformulated as a critique of ideologies (understood as systematically distorted communication) with a practical intent. Such a critical science is not directed primarily at the 'causality of nature', but at the 'causality of fate' – the process set in motion by repressed life and the struggles to overcome such repression. A critical theory of society constructed on this model begins with a questionable or unclear situation. It proceeds to employ hermeneutic procedures as a means of exploring possible interpretations. But it moves beyond traditional interpretative techniques to explanations with empirical content constructed with reference to a general theory. Finally, it tests the general theory through the reconstruction of the historical situation of specific societies. Ultimate verification of the entire enterprise depends upon practice, that is, upon the actual eradication of barriers to self-reflection and human autonomy, and the overcoming of social structures that support such barriers.

The three levels of critical theory of the Freudian model (meta-theory, general interpretation and specific application) correspond to the following levels of Habermas's project: (i) the theory of cognitive interests; (ii) the theory of history; and (iii) the analysis of advanced capitalism with the intent of identifying crisis points, their ideological supports and groups capable of taking part in processes of enlightenment. As conceived in the early work of Habermas, the critical theorist is thus the 'psychoanalyst of the working class'.[82]

The dialectic of social rationality: a brief recapitulation

The dialectic of social rationality I have traced begins with Marx's transformation of Hegel's dialectic. Hegel claimed both logical necessity and real necessity for his dialectic. The dialectic of history is determined by the dialectic of ideas. Marx's concept of social rationality rejects the determining power of ideas through the 'paradigm of production', while retaining the dialectic of history. But any dialectic must claim some form of necessity to function. The connections between ideas (or between social forces) must be rigorous. Marx finds the real necessity that powers his dialectic in the historically embodied movement of the working class. Marx's concept of social rationality, which attempts to 'abolish' philosophy by 'realising' its highest concept, reason as freedom, is held together by the linchpin of the proletariat. The mature Marx attempted to demonstrate the 'real necessity' of the proletariat's role (as histor-ically embodied reason, as potentially universal class) through a critique of political economy that at the same time captured and denounced the embodiments of unreason.

Weber, from a later historical vantage point, called into serious question the possibility of any class realising freedom. Reason, for Weber, was identified with the social process of 'rationalisation'. The 'real necessity' of the dialectic was an inevitable loss of autonomy, meaning and freedom,. The separation between fact and value which Marx hoped to overcome historically is accepted by

Weber as an undeniable feature of modern cultural rationalism. Values are left to the no longer even possibly autonomous individual as irrational decisions and commitments. Weber stoically delivers us up to the 'puralism of value systems, gods and demons'.[83]

Lukács attempts to incorporate Weber's 'rationalisation' within Marx's critique of political economy. Under the heading 'reification", Lukács attempts to demonstrate that 'rationalisation' is a feature of the universalisation of the commodity form, and can thus be overcome by overcoming capitalism. The role of the proletariat, once their 'reified consciousness' has been enlightened, is precisely to bring about this transformation. The standpoint of the proletariat as universal class with a veiw of the social totality coincides with reason; and its oppression under capitalism shows, at the same time, its irrationality as a socity. But even Lukács has lost some faith in the 'real necessity' of the historical dialectic. For him, all that can be claimed is the 'objective possiblity' of a true socialist transformation.

Horkeimer's early formulation of the critical theory of society continued to appeal to a class-subject potentially capable of being the historical embodiment of reason. The critical theory of the 1930s attempted to retain a positive concept of reason linked to the philosophical tradition that was comprehensive enough to adopt a totalising approach to the study of social reality. The 'real necessity' claimed for the theory was made dependent on its ability to activate its class–subject addressees. With the expansion of what Weber called 'rationalisation' and the increasing 'reification of consciousness' Lukács diagnosed (and with the rise of Fascism and Stalinism), the appeal to class–subjects receded. The linchpin of Marx's theory had been pulled. Even Adorno's fall-back position, immanent critique, was 'dragged into the abyss' of a 'rationalised' world gone mad.

To a large extent, the later Frankfurt School joined in both Weber's analysis and his pessimism. They launched a full-scale attack, however, on what for Weber was the cultural embodiment of reason. The critique of instrumental reason as developed in *Dialectic of Enlightenment* identified Western reason itself as the problem. Without any remaining faith in Marx's concept of social rationality, the dialectic turns negative. It becomes a total critique admitting the conditions of its own historical impossibility. In this form, the 'practical intentions' of the theory fall away.

The early Habermas picks up the pieces of this dialectic. He traces the tragedy of the Enlightenment to an antinomy within the progress of modernity, the confusion of the technical and the practical, which can be resolved without falling behind the real achievements of the Enlightenment or falling forward into a new barbarism. Habermas further rejects the contention that the triumph of scientific–technical rationality has foreclosed all possibilities of resistance and truly rational change. If the dialectic is to be saved from self-destruction, however, Marx's concept of social rationality must be rebuilt on a broader and firmer base than the one provided by the 'paradigm of production' alone. Habermas's first attempt to provide such a base, a base capable of justifying the premises of critique, took the form of a materialist epistemology. The 'missing agent' became the species as a whole, since today it is the species as a whole that is threatened. The justification rested on the power of self-reflection contained in the emancipatory interest of the human species – an interest in reason. The criticisms of this solution, and Habermas's attempt to meet them in the theory of communication, form the next stage in his attempt to save the 'practical intentions' of critical theory in the face of the problematic of rationality.

3

Habermas and the Reconstruction of Critical Theory

'The human interest in autonomy and responsibility is not mere fancy, for it can be apprehended a priori. What raises us out of nature is... language. Through its structure, autonomy and responsibility are posited for us. Our first sentence expresses unequivocally the intention of universal and unconstrained consensus... Reason also means the will to reason.' — Jürgen Habermas

Habermas's initial formulation of the basis of critical theory in *Knowledge and Human Interests* became the object of extensive discussion and detailed criticisms.[1] Habermas responded by critically rethinking his position. This process was carried forward in debates with leading exponents of critical rationalism (Albert), systems theory (Luhmann) and philosophical hermeneutics (Gadamer).[2] These discussions and debates tended to focus on Habermas's concept of reason and the attempt to justify critical theory and link it to practice that depended upon it. A brief discussion of the central criticisms raised against the early Habermas on these issues will clarify some of the basic reasons for the major revisions in his later work. This discussion will also serve as an introduction to the later Habermas's reformulation of the basis of critical theory in a concept of 'communicative rationality' developed through various stages of his communication theory.

Critical theory criticised

The notion of self-reflection is central to the argument of *Knowledge and Human Interests*, but it contains a fundamental ambiguity. First, 'self-reflection' refers to the Kantian idea of a critique of knowledge which involves reflection on the subjective conditions that make knowledge possible (that is, 'the synthetic achievements of the knowing subject'). Second, 'self-reflection' refers to the Marxian idea of a critique of ideology which involves reflection capable of freeing the subject from 'hidden constraints' in the structures of social action and speech. These two are obviously not identical. In the first case, we have a transcendental account of the a priori conditions of knowing for *any* subject. In the second case, we have a critical and practical account of the formative history of a specific individual, class or species subject. Habermas's concept of reason posits an inherent link between the two – the 'identity of reason with the will to reason'. As Kortian has argued, Fichte and Hegel supply the necessary link between Kantian and Marxian critique.[3] Fichte provides the idea of a practical interest in autonomy operative within reason itself. Hegel provides a phenomenological reflection on the self-formative process of the super-individual subject. Hegel's account maintains the link between the practical interest in autonomy and reason since it includes both reflection on the conditions of knowledge and the critical destruction of dogmatic forms of thought and action.

As several critics have pointed out, linking the two senses of critique (Kantain and Marxian) directly by means of German idealism is unsatisfactory. As I argued earlier, Marx broke with this tradition through his concept of social rationality. The critical–revolutionary practice central to this concept cannot be reduced to 'self-reflection'. Thus, Karl-Otto Apel criticises the 'simple identification of reflection and practical engagement' entailed by Habermas's construction.[4] Reflection, in the philosophical sense, as a thorough examination of all claims to truth or rightness may be said to pursue an interest in emancipation from dogmatism in all its forms. But this interest is pursued in all genuine theoretical reflection, and thus cannot be confused with that interest Marx pursued in claiming (against all philosophy) that the world was not merely to be interpreted but changed. This interest involves specific (and sometimes dangerous) political and practical engagement. To identify the two interests is 'an idealist illusion'.[5] Habermas goes from an interest in knowing for the sake of knowing (in general) to knowing for the sake of action (in a specific and concrete situation). The latter is the emancipatory interest pursued by Marx and developed further by the Frankfurt School. The very generality of Habermas's 'quasi-transcendental' basis for the critique of systematically distorted communication makes it unsuitable as a guide for specific and situated practice aimed at transforming concrete social conditions.

This crucial criticism calls into question not only the link Habermas hoped to establish between theory and practice, but also the normative justification for critical theory as well. A central claim of *Knowledge and Human Interests* is that a radicalised critique of knowledge can only be carried out as a social theory capable of the critique of ideology. As long as 'self-reflection' includes both senses (reflection on the transcendental conditions of knowledge and reflection on the 'hidden constraints' on speech and social action), Habermas can argue that 'the heritage of philosophy passes over to the critique of ideology'.[6] This argument is based on an interpretation of the movement of thought from Kant through Hegel to Marx as a radicalisation of the critique of knowledge, an epistemological version of Marcuse's interpretation of the move from philosophy to social theory already discussed.

Unlike Marcuse, who saw Marx as overcoming philosophy, Habermas argues that Marx lost the chance to truly overcome philosophy because of his reduction of interaction to labour. In Habermas's view, the process of the self-formation of the species cannot be reconstructed solely as the 'history of industry' which is, for Marx, the 'open book' of the development of the powers of human beings.[7] It must also be reconstructed in terms of insights gained through the revolutionary activity of classes, including the self-reflective, critical activity of unmasking ideological constraints. *Knowledge and Human Interests* attempts to explicate this dialectic of class consciousness in its manifestations in terms of both labour and interaction. Through this explication directed at the practical self-understanding of social groups, Habermas attempts to raise the consciousness of the species to the point where it 'has attained the level of critique and freed itself from all ideological delusion'.[8] From this perspective, reflection on the subjective conditions of knowledge necessarily leads to a critique of ideology. And once again Habermas's argument depends upon the conflation of Kantian and Marxian critique.

To what critical standards can Habermas's 'materialist phenomenology' appeal in unmasking 'ideological delusion', once philosophical standards (such as Hegel's concept of absolute truth) are rejected under the Marxian thesis of the general distortion of philosophical consciousness in capitalist society? On the one hand, Habermas shares with Marx and the Frankfurt School the thesis of the social and historical contextuality of modes of thought. On the other hand, he rejects both the 'orthodox" Marxist claim to justify critique with scientific standards and Adorno's claim that critique requires no systematic justification. To what critical standards can he then appeal? Habermas's response in *Knowledge and Human Interests* is that the critical 'standards of self-reflection are exempted from the singular state of suspension . . . of all other cognitive processes' because the emancipatory interest upon which they are based (the interest in 'autonomy and responsibility') is implicit in the very structure of communication and can thus be 'apprehended a priori' with 'theoretical certainty'.[9]

As several critics have argued, this response is inadequate.[10] How can we be certain that the emancipatory interest is not just a particular socially and historically relative interest? How can we be certain that it is not itself subject to the same distortions critical theory locates in other modes of thought? It is difficult to see how the appeal to 'a priori' insight can be reconciled with a consistent recognition of the social and historical contextuality of modes of thought. Further, precisely how does *Knowledge and Human Interests* differ from the philosophical efforts of 'traditional theory' to discover 'ultimate grounds' for human knowledge? It seems that Habermas's theory of human interests is itself an attempt to provide such 'grounds', at least in the sense of limits beyond which thought cannot go. The tension between the Kantian and Marxian moments in the argument reappears. The Kantian appeal to 'a priori' insight cannot justify the situated and concrete political action required by Marx's theory. The Marxian thesis of socially and historically rooted modes of thought distorted by 'hidden constraints' in the system of social labour cannot be (in any simple way) reconciled with Kantian apriorism. Finally, 'the attempt to ground practice in the transcendental conditions of theory does justice to neither'.[11]

This brings us to the second crucial criticism raised against Habermas's early formulation of critical theory. This criticism concerns the very idea of a 'quasi-transcendental' theory of knowledge. The attempt to combine a Kantian 'transcendental' approach with a Marxian 'naturalistic' approach to the subjective conditions of knowledge generates the following dilemma: 'either nature has the transcendental status of a constituted objectivity and cannot, therefore, be the ground of the constituting subject; or nature is the ground of subjectivity and cannot, therefore, be simply a constituted objectivity'.[12] Habermas's use of the term 'quasi-transcendental' to describe the fundamental human interests which are the 'fixed framework' of inquiry expresses his desire to hold on to both horns of the dilemma. He treats the subject of knowledge both as a 'community that constitutes the world from a transcendental perspective' and as an empirical 'species (that) emerged in natural history'.[13] From the first (Kantian) perspective, Habermas argues that the objectivity of experience is constituted by the subject within a 'fixed framework' determined by deeply rooted structures of human action. From the second (Marxian) perspective, Habermas argues that, although the 'transcendental framework within which nature appears objectively to these subjects does not change', the particular and specific categories of human objectification (synthesis through social labour) 'belong to the historically alterable inventory of societies'.[14] Thus, nature is an objectification of the knowing subject constituted under both the general conditions of instrumental action (labour) and the specific conditions of historically variable social systems.

From the Kantian component of the argument, it follows that nature cannot be consistently appealed to as the ground of subjectivity because to do so would be to ground 'transcendental' conditions in a phenomenal realm which exists only in relation to these conditions. Consistent with the Marxian component of the argument, however, Habermas holds that the objective structures of human life that give rise to the orientations of inquiry (labour and interaction) can only be explained by a theory of evolution. From this it follows that nature is, after all, the ground of subjectivity. How then can it also be a constituted objectivity? Once again the tension between the Kantian and Marxian perspectives returns. And here the two are simply not compatible.

Michael Theunissen, in an influential critique, locates the basis of this dilemma in the very idea of a critical theory.[15] Horkheimer's original formulation of critical theory distinguished between an approach that grants priority to nature, as a whole within which history is to be included (traditional theory); and an approach that grants priority to the historical human world, as a whole within which interpretations of nature appear as human constructions (critical theory). For Habermas, as for Horkheimer and the Frankfurt School generally, approaches that grant priority to nature are rejected. According to Theunissen, however, Habermas fails to abide by this rejection consistently and tends to fall back behind Kant to the 'objectivism' of a simple naturalism or, at least, to an approach that grants nature priority over history. Theunissen locates the basis of the relapse in an 'overburdening' of the empirical subject inherited from German idealism:

Looked at from the point of view of the history of philosophy, all the representatives of critical theory once again repeat for themselves the post-Hegelian repetition of Kant – attempted above all by the left Hegelians – on the basis of history prepared by Hegel. Viewed systematically, the overburdening of empirical subjects arises from transferring the powers with which Kant outfitted 'consciousness in general' to the human species (whose real unity is as yet only anticipated).[16]

Once this move is made (from 'transcendental' to 'species' subjects) the nature that appears in history must, paradoxically, serve as the origin and ground of history. As Habermas was later to recognise, at least part of the problem is generated by the concept of 'species subject' in its relation to the real, concrete human individuals. How is this relation to be understood once Marx's idea of a class-subject with universalisable interests is abandoned?

The first criticism relates to Habermas's confusion of the two senses of reflection, the second calls into question the very idea of a 'quasi-transcendental' theory of knowledge. The third important criticism of Habermas's early formulation of critical theory to be considered here relates to his use of psychoanalysis as a model for a critical social theory that systematically includes 'self-reflection'. Gadamer, in particular, attacks 'the analogy between psychoanalytic and sociological theory' drawn by Habermas.[17] Psychoanalysis gains its legitimacy because it is entered into voluntarily and on the basis of mutual agreement within a given social order. The given society also sets the limits to its therapeutic practice in the form of codes of conduct, commonly accepted professional norms, legal sanctions, and so on. Habermas's attempt to extend psychoanalytic techniques to the whole social order transcends these limits and thus forfeits this socially based legitimacy. The extension of the therapist–patient relation to the social order as a whole contains the danger of an uncontrolled exercise of force on the part of self-appointed élites, who dogmatically claim a privileged insight into the delusions of others and the truth of their own viewpoint. For Gadamer, truth (certainly political and social truth) is the result of an openness to other viewpoints and a willingness to reach agreement in dialogue which does not foreclose the possibility that the convictions of others could be right.

From another perspective, Marxists have called Habermas's psychoanalytic model of critical theory into question. Hans-Joachim Giegel has argued that important features of psychoanalytic therapy make it unsuitable as a model for the kind of critical–revolutionary practice central to Marx's theory. In particular, Giegel argues, it does not take into account the conditions under which class struggle is carried out:

> The revolutionary struggle is by no means a psychoanalytic treatment on a large scale. The difference between these two forms of emancipatory practice is a result of the fact that the patient is helped to free himself from compulsions to which he is subjected. The attempt to release the ruling class from the compulsions of the social order could only appear to them as a threat to the domination which they exercise over other classes. The opposition presents itself in a much sharper form here than in the case of psychoanalysis. The oppressed class not only doubts the ruling class's capacity for dialogue, but also has good reason to assume that every attempt on its part to enter into a dialogue with the ruling class could only serve as an opportunity for the latter to secure its domination. For this reason, the oppressed class may not, on pain of a set-back to their emancipatory efforts, follow the psychoanalytic path.[18]

The issues involved in these criticisms deal with the practical and political implications of Habermas's formulation. These criticisms are basically unlike the two earlier theoretical objections. They attack Habermas's purported link between theory and practice not from the theoretical side but from the side of practice. They call into question the practical and political application of Habermas's theory; an application which is, of course, a constitutive component of the theory itself.

At least two other criticisms of importance have been raised against Habermas's early formulation of critical theory (objections to the labour and interaction distinction and objections to the seemingly pragmatic criterion of truth).[19] The three criticisms discussed above (dealing with the notion of 'reflection', the status of a 'quasi-transcendental' theory of knowledge and the use of psychoanalysis as a model for critical theory) are, however, the most significant in at least one respect. They have led Habermas to make three fundamental revisions in his project. A discussion of these revisions will pave the way for an account of Habermas's later reformulation of the basis of critical theory.

Revisions in the project

The first (and perhaps the most important) revision in Habermas's project resulting from the above criticisms concerns the central idea of 'reflection'. In 'A Postscript to *Knowledge and Human Interests*' (1973), he states that:

> It occurred to me only after completing the book that the traditional use of the term 'reflection', which goes back to German Idealism, covers (and confuses) two things: on the one hand, it denotes the reflection upon the conditions of potential abilities of a knowing, speaking and acting subject as such; on the other hand, it denotes the reflection upon unconsciously produced constraints to which a determinate subject (or a determinate group of subjects, or a determinate species subject) succumbs in its process of self-reflection.[20]

Habermas introduces a distinction between 'reflection' in the first sense (what he calls 'rational reconstruction') and 'reflection' in the second sense (what he calls 'critical self-reflection'). While critical self-reflection is brought to bear on something particular in a manner 'rich with practical consequences', rational reconstructions address anonymous and general rule systems governing basic human competencies without involving practical consequences. While critical self-reflection is a historically situated and context-bound reflection on the particulars of a self-formative process aimed at transforming the specific socially situated determinants of ideological distortion, rational reconstructions are not context-bound in this way in as much as they explicate the general and unavoidable (in this sense 'transcendental') conditions of cognition, speech and action. They proceed by making explicit our 'know-how' (that is, our implicit and intuitive knowledge acquired with a competence). Rational reconstructions may aid critical self-reflection by making subjects aware of the general and unavoidable conditions which make human cognition, speech and action possible and also limit their scope. Rational reconstructions represent the 'purest' form of theoretical knowledge since they are not derived from either the technical, the practical or the emancipatory interest. They arise only in the context of a theoretical discourse which suspends the ordinary imperatives of action and communication in order to examine what they always implicitly presuppose. Although rational reconstructions represent Habermas's reformulation of the Kantian component of his project, unlike their transcendental ancestor they are subject to empirical conditions in so far as they attempt to explain the empirical competencies of empirical subjects.

The above distinction changes Habermas's conception of critical theory in a fundamental way. Critical theory is no longer viewed as contributing directly to the self-reflection of the human species, but rather to the elaboration of general human competences. Rational reconstructions, however, must direct themselves not only at the 'deep structure' of human competencies but also at the processes under which these structures change. They must be connected with 'developmental logics' which explicate the stages through which these competencies develop. This is the case, at least, if one wants to avoid an ahistorical approach as Habermas certainly does. Just as the work of Chomsky is the model for rational reconstruction, Piaget's work serves Habermas as the model for developmental logics. The latter represent Habermas's reformulation of the Hegelian component of his project. Unlike their phenomenological ancestor, these 'logics' are also subject to empirical conditions in so far as they attempt to explain the development of empirical competencies in empirical subjects.

The distinction between rational reconstruction and critical self-reflection is also important for the second major revision in Habermas's project. The early Habermas attempted to reconstruct

Marx's 'philosophy of history with a practical intent'. But Habermas came to see that the philosophy of history itself had been tied to the notion of the progress of a 'collective subject'. Not only criticisms such as Theunissen's above, but also the theoretical responses to historical developments themselves traced in the rationality problematic (see Chapter 2) render the notion of collective subject questionable. Habermas thus shifts from the notion of collective subject to 'universal competences' in order to free historical material-ism from a reliance on a Hegelian–Marxist philosophy of history. His 'reconstruction of historical materialism' (which represents his reformulation of the Marxian component of his project) is thus developed as a theory of social evolution that will explicate the evolution of universal competences rather than the history of a collective subject. It will provide not a 'philosophy of history with practical intent', but a theory of social evolution.

Finally, critical self-reflection itself, in as much as it aims at a justified critique of ideology as systematically distorted communica-tion, must rely upon a theory of normal communication. A rational reconstruction of what is presupposed in communication, of its general and unavoidable conditions, could direct itself at the problem of providing a normative foundation for critical theory capable of answering the question, 'why is the critique of ideology not itself ideological?' This is the third major revision in Habermas's project, his turn from a materialistically transformed phenomenological self-reflection to a materialistically transformed transcendental reflection. This is also a turn from the early attempt to ground critical theory in a theory of knowledge to an attempt to ground critical theory in a theory of communication. And, ultimately, this turn will require a theory of communicative rationality.

These revisions by no means answer all of the objections above. In particular, the dilemma of granting priority to nature or to history remains, as Habermas recognises, unresolved. But further, while the distinction between rational reconstruction and critical self-reflection seems to meet the core of the theoretical objections by adequately separating the Kantian and the Marxian moments in the argument, it exacts a price. McCarthy states the problem as follows: 'in trying to do justice to the theoretical character of theory (rational reconstruction as "pure" knowledge) and the practical character of practice (critique as bound to the system of action and experience), he seems to have reintroduced the gap between theory and practice, between reason and emancipation that *Knowledge and Human Interests* tried to close'.[21] This problem is best addressed after examining Habermas's response to the third criticism of his early statement of critical theory, namely, the practical objections to his use of the psychoanalytical model.

Habermas responds to the objections of Gadamer and Giegel by separating out the tasks of critical theory. Therapeutic dialogue is not intended as a model for the conflict between opposing groups and classes. Instead it is intended for the organisation of enlightenment. The critical theory seeks to legitimise the activity of enlightenment. It cannot, however, legitimise the dangerous political decisions made by actors in concrete cases. At this level, justification lies in a consensus attained among the participants themselves. Thus, no theory, not even critical theory, can 'assure from the outset a world-historical mission in return for potential sacrifices'. Both these levels (organisation of enlightenment and political action) should be distinguished from theory construction, a level at which the critical theory must stand the test of dialogue as well as empirical falsification. Finally, 'there is no privileged access to truth' at any level. The unavoidable claim of superiority of the enlighteners over those to be enlightened is a fiction – 'in a process of enlightenment there can be only participants'.[22] This separation of tasks once again meets much of the force of the criticisms, but again at the cost of separating theory (theory construction focused on rational reconstructions) from practice (political action aided by critical self-reflection).

In summary, Habermas's later work centres on the notion of rational reconstruction. His project of reconstruction develops at the level of both the individual and society. On the individual level, reconstructions are pursued in three areas: cognition, communication and action. On the social level, reconstructions are pursued in two areas: productive forces (in terms of the technical knowledge embodied in them) and forms of social integration (in terms of the practical knowledge embodied in them). Hypotheses advanced in these reconstructive enterprises are viewed as subject to test in discourse as well as empirical falsification. Although Habermas's later focus on reconstruction does seem to break the link between theory and practice, he continues to maintain that such a link exists. Further, Habermas continues to recognise that some conception of ideology critique is still a necessity if the 'practical intentions' central to the whole enterprise are to be saved. His later conception of the link between theory and practice can be uncovered only in his theory of communication, which is also to provide a new normative basis for critical theory.

I will now trace the major stages in the development of Habermas's communication theory, beginning with his account of communicative competence and ending with his central concept of communicative rationality. This will complete my account of Habermas's reformulation of the basis of critical theory in response to the two basic problems of the Frankfurt School (normative justification and the relationship between theory and practice), as they mutated in the course of the development of what I have called the problematic of rationality.

The reconstruction of critical theory: stages in the development of Habermas's communication theory

As McCarthy has argued, 'Habermas's entire project, from the critique of contemporary scientism to the reconstruction of historical materialism, rests on the possibility of providing an account of communication that is both theoretical and normative, that goes beyond a pure hermeneutics without being reducible to a strictly empirical–analytic science'.[23] Habermas's theory of communication is an attempt to provide a normative foundation for critical social theory. It is a new approach to the problem of defending an expanded conception of reason. The Frankfurt School theorists first defended such a conception in their polemic with the positivists who limited rationality to technical rationality and knowledge to scientific knowledge. As discussed above (see Chapter 2), the Frankfurt School developed criticisms of positivism as a technocratic ideology from the standpoint of a philosphical conception of reason and a philosophy of history that included the normative, critical dimension. These criticisms were carried out largely in isolation from developments in the philosophy of language, which was viewed as a part of positivism and technocratic ideology.[24] Habermas, however, sees the developments in the philosophy of language as a point of departure for social theory. For Habermas, this new direction is necessary since 'the problem of language has today replaced the problem of consciousness'.[25] Further, an expanded conception of reason which includes the normative and critical dimension requires a theory of language which justifies the 'insight that the truth of statements is linked in the last analysis to the intention of the good and true life'.[26] The 'linguistic turn' taken by Habermas began as an attempt to meet this requirement by showing that the normative goal of critical theory (a society free from all unnecessary domination) is anticipated in every act of communication.

The development of Habermas's theory of communication may be divided into four stages, each of which finds expression in important theoretical texts: (i) the theory of communicative competence, systematically distorted communication and the ideal speech situation; (ii) the theory of discourse and the consensus theory of truth; (iii) the theory of universal pragmatics and the theory of social evolution; (iv) the theory of communicative action and rationality. The logic of development of Habermas's theory through these various stages exemplifies his synthetic method of theory construction (see Chapter 1). Important difficulties in each stage of the theory require correction at a subsequent stage. First, problems concerning the notion of 'reflection', the status of a 'quasi-transcendental' theory of knowledge and the use of psychoanalysis as a model for critical theory drove Habermas to communication theory. Problems with the initial formulation of the theory of communicative competence and its central notion of the ideal speech situation required the development of a theory of discourse and a consensus theory of truth. The systematic development of this enterprise required a theory of universal pragmatics which in turn led Haberamas to develop a theory of social evolution. Finally, these theories required support and correction from a theory of communicative action and rationality. In what follows, I will briefly discuss Habermas's main line of argument at each stage, indicating the problems that led to the next stage. This critical account of the development of Habermas's communication theory will culminate in his latest formulation of the basis of critical theory in *The Theory of Communicative Action* (1981) to be examined in Chapter 4.

1. Communicative competence, systematically distorted communication and the ideal speech situation (1970)

Habermas's work on communicative competence begins with an account of Chomsky. The aim of linguistic theory as expounded by Chomsky in *Syntactic Structures* (1957) is to describe syntax by specifying the rules underlying the construction of sentences.[27] Chomsky's generative grammar is a system of rules that operate on a set of elements. It defines a subset of the total set of possible combinations of the elements to be well formed and the complement of the subset to be not well formed. The concern of linguistic theory is with linguistic competence (the ability of an ideal speaker to master the system of rules) in abstraction from linguistic performance (the actual use of the system by speakers under the limiting conditions of memory, attention and error). Against behaviourist accounts of language, Chomsky argued that the creativity of the speaker of a language (the speaker's ability to produce an infinite number of grammatical sentences) could only be explained in terms of an innate language mechanism. Chomsky's difficulty in ascertaining the system of rules by traditional methods of classification lead him to postulate further that the well-formed combinations are surface structures resulting from the transformation of deep structures. Chomsky's basic research programme thus became the reconstruction of linguistic competence understood as the mastery of a system of rules based in an innate language mechanism.

Later proposals for the integration of semantics and syntax within this framework were made by Katz and Fodor (1963) and Katz and Postal (1964). These proposals were adopted in Chomsky's later theory (*Aspects of the Theory of Syntax*, 1965).[28] The aim was to provide the complete 'grammar' (in Chomsky's sense) of a language. This was to be achieved in three parts: (i) a syntactical component that generates and describes the sentences; (ii) a phonological component that describes the sound structure of the generated sentences; (iii) a semantic component that describes the meaning structure of the generated sentences. The heart of his programme is the syntactic component. The phonology and semantics only describe the sentences it generates, they do not themselves generate sentences. The extension to semantics involved the addition of a dictionary providing semantic information for each of the words, and rules for providing a semantic interpretation for each of the sentences. All information required for the interpretation was viewed as being contained in the deep structure and, ultimately, capable of being associated with a universal inventory of lexical components.

Habermas's criticisms of this programme are directed at the semantic extension in as much as he attends primarily to theses concerning meaning. In particular, he is concerned with the linguistic universals postulated in the semantic extension which he misleadingly calls 'universal meanings' or 'semantic universals'. For Habermas, linguistic universals 'arise in all natural languages'.[29] They cannot be understood, however, only in terms of a universal inventory of lexical components based in the equipment of the individual human organism. They must also be understood as arising in the socio-cultural contexts studied by ethno-linguistics.

Habermas discusses three theses of the Chomskyan programme to which he objects: (i) the thesis of monologism – linguistic universals belong solely 'to the basic equipment of the solitary organism of the speaking subject', (ii) the thesis of a priorism – linguistic universals 'precede all experience', and (iii) the thesis of elementarism – meaning can be adequately analysed in terms of 'combinations of a finite number' of lexical components.[30] Against (i) and (ii), Habermas argues that linguistic universals neither automatically precede all experience nor are they all rooted in the equipment of the human organism prior to socialisation. Some linguistic universals are a priori 'in as much as they establish the conditions of potential communication and general schemes of interpretation'. Other linguistic universals are a posteriori 'in the sense that they represent invariant features of contingent scopes of experience . . . common to all cultures'.[31] A posteriori linguistic universals process experience, while a priori linguistic universals make such processing possible. For Habermas, linguistic universals may also be distinguished depending upon whether they are inter-subjective (socio-culturally based) or monological (based in the equipment of the individual human organism). This yields the following classification of linguistic universals:[32]

	a priori	*a posteriori*
intersubjective	dialogue-constitutive universals (for example, personal pronouns)	cultural universals (for example, kinship and colour terms)
monological	universal cognitive schemes of interpretation (for example, deictic expressions of space and time)	universals of perceptive and motivational constitution (for example, vocabulary of basic drives and emotions)

Against (iii), Habermas argues that a consideration of linguistic universals such as kinship terms and colour words shows 'the dependence of semantic analysis upon the non-exceedable common context of the society to which the speakers belong'.[33] An adequate analysis of meaning cannot ignore this socio-cultural context. For Habermas, this points to the fundamental problem in the Chomskyan programme. The realisation that the lexicon disclosed in Chomskyan semantic analysis can change in accordance with culturally and historically changing worldviews (*Weltbilder*), shows the analysis to be valid only for 'a social system at a particular stage of development'.[34] Further, Habermas argues (in basic agreement with Gadamer's hermeneutics) that the Chomskyan programme itself is guided by a global pre-understanding rooted in a particular social system at a particular historical juncture.

For Habermas, what is needed is 'a frame of reference' for the 'analysis of all possible global interpretations of nature and society' developed systematically 'from the general theory of language itself'. Such a 'frame of reference' comes into view once we see that the competence of the speaker of a language does not involve simply the mastery of rules for the production of grammatical sentences, but also the capacity to communicate. The ability to produce 'a situation of potential ordinary-language communication is itself part of the general competence of the ideal speaker'. To be a participant in communication, the speaker must have (in addition to linguistic competence) 'basic qualifications of speech and symbolic interaction (role-behaviour), which we may call communicative competence'.[35] A theory of communicative competence is required which will reconstruct the competence of an ideal speaker to master an ideal speech situation. Just as linguistic competence can be 'rationally reconstructed' in terms of the mastery of a set of idealised formal procedures, so also communicative competence can be reconstructed formally in terms of the mastery of an 'ideal speech situation'.

Habermas attempts to elucidate the notion of an ideal speech situation by drawing on the theory of speech acts developed by Austin. According to Habermas, speech-act theory attempts to 'explain the meaning of certain idealized features of speech situations in general', including universal competencies the speaker must master in order to participate in any potential speech situation.[36] Following the work of Wunderlich, Habermas distinguishes five classes of 'dialogue-constitutive universals' that must be mastered by a speaker in order to enter into ordinary language communication:

(i) personal pronouns and their derivatives; (ii) forms of address and speech introduction; (iii) deictic expressions of space and time; (iv) performative verbs; (v) non-performative intentional verbs which expess the speaker's attitudes. Habermas directs his attention at the performatives (although a complete account of communicative competence must work out the logic behind the use of each). Habermas distinguishes four classes of performatives: (i) 'communicatives' which express the pragmatic meaning of utterances qua utterances; for example, 'say', 'express', 'speak', 'mention', 'ask'; (ii) 'constatives' which express the meaning of statements; for example, 'state', 'assent', 'explain', 'describe'; (iii) 'representatives' which express the meaning of the self-representation of the speaker; for example, 'admit', 'confess', 'deny'; (iv) 'regulatives' which express the speaker's relation to norms; for example, 'forbid', 'command', 'warn', 'allow'.[37]

Habermas claims that since every speech act involves either an explicit or implicit performative, the above classification represents a general classification of all speech acts. The mastery of these speech acts is fundamental to the ability to mark the distinctions basic to any speech situation: (i) constatives make possible the distinction between a public world (being) and a private world (appearance); (ii) representatives make possible the distinction between an individuated self and the speech and actions in which it appears; (iii) regulatives make possible the distinction between what is and what ought to be. Based on this classification, Habermas argues, one can arrive at three 'symmetry requirements' which characterise the ideal speech situation and ensure that it is free from 'systematic distortion'. These three requirements are the following: (i) 'unrestricted discussion' in which it is possible to 'develop strategies for reaching unconstrained consensus'; (ii) mutual 'unimpaired self-presentation' in which it is possible to 'achieve subtle nearness with inviolable distance among the partners and that means communication under conditions of extreme individuation'; (iii) 'full complementation of expectations' which makes possible 'the claim of universal understanding' and 'universalized norms'. For Habermas, 'these three symmetries represent . . . a linguistic conceptualization for that which we traditionally apprehend as the ideas of truth, freedom and justice'.[38]

The ideal speech situation is, of course, an idealisation. As Habermas admits, the mastery of 'dialogue-constitutive universals' is not the same as the ability actually to establish the ideal speech situation. Communicative competence means rather 'the mastery of the means of construction necessary for the establishment of the ideal speech situation'.[39] It provides a measure against which 'systematically distorted communication' (speech distorted either neurotically as analysed by Freud or ideologically as analysed by Marx) can be detected and criticised.[40] Regardless of the force of such distortions, 'the design of an ideal speech situation is necessarily implied with the structure of potential speech' . . . since all speech 'is oriented toward the idea of truth' which 'can only be analysed with regard to a consensus achieved in unrestrained and universal discourse'.[41] Thus, Habermas argues, in as much as we can master the means for constructing such an ideal situation, we are able to conceive the ideas of truth, justice and freedom as interdependent and mutually interpreting. But they remain 'ideals' which, at present, 'we can only anticipate'.[42] Finally, all speech 'anticipates' a form of life in which this ideal situation can be realised. To establish this point will require an account not only of truth as 'consensus' and an account of discourse, but also a 'universal pragmatics' which reconstructs the general and unavoidable conditions of all speech.

Before turning to Habermas's more recent work on these topics, it will be necessary to evaluate the above account in as much as it is the starting point for the later developments. The first problem with Habermas's account is his usage of the term 'semantics'. He uses it loosely to cover several different linguistic levels, for example in such formulations as 'general semantics'.[43] This usage tends to obscure the fact that Habermas's criticisms do not apply to the phonological and syntactic components of the Chomskyan programme. But even with the extension of this programme to semantics, only lexical meaning is a concern. The Chomskyan programme is simply not concerned with communication. Thus, it really makes no sense to criticise the programme for being 'monological', since the levels of linguistic analysis in question purposely abstract from the 'intersubjective'. Communication becomes a concern only at the pragmatic level. This level is never adequately distinguished from other levels of analysis in Habermas's early account.

The second problem with Habermas's account involves the notion of linguistic universals. This is a problematic and difficult notion in linguistic theory. Habermas, however, seems simply to adopt the term 'universals' and proceed. Although his own classification makes it clear that he does not accept the Chomskyan notion of linguistic universals (since some of his are a posteriori and intersubjective), no adequate account of his own is offered. A brief examination of his classification will show that such an account is required.

I will begin with Habermas's example of personal pronouns which are classified as a priori and intersubjective. Personal pronouns may be studied phonologically, syntactically, semantically or pragmatically. At which level of analysis, and in what sense, are they a priori? At which level of analysis, and in what sense, are they universals? Are they classified as intersubjective at all levels? And, if so, with what justification? Habermas's account does not even give us a way to begin to answer such questions. Various levels of analysis are confused in Habermas's classification and his account in general. This problem becomes particularly severe since it causes Habermas to lose sight of the fact that meaning may be analysed in different ways. Take, for example, the English personal pronoun 'I'. It has a lexical meaning, a context-dependent reference and a use in communication. Habermas's early account of communicative competence does not note these differences. Thus, the central issue of meaning is obscured.

Habermas wants to argue that the semantic extension of the Chomskyan programme does not provide an adequate analysis of meaning. But this argument can be made in a much clearer way. As Searle states, 'Any attempt to account for the meaning of sentences must take into account their role in communication, in the performance of speech acts, because an essential part of the meaning of any sentence is its potential for being used to perform a speech act.'[44] Habermas fails to see the radical difference between this account of meaning (for which communication is central) and Chomsky's account of meaning (for which communication is incidental). Further, for Chomsky, any analysis of communication is an analysis of performance. But, for Searle, the analysis of speech acts is an analysis of competence. On both these points Habermas is with Searle. However, Habermas fails to note these differences clearly at this stage in the development of his communication theory.

Hymes (1971) argued for the extension of the notion of competence from linguistic competence to communicative competence.[45] For Hymes, communicative competence referred to a person's ability to use all the sign systems available to him as a member of a given socio-cultural community. Linguistic competence then becomes only one part of communicative competence. The extension of the notion of competence in Hymes provides a useful direction for the study of utterances in social contexts. Habermas wants to revise this notion of communicative competence by retaining the Chomskyan notion of the reconstruction of a universal competence. Habermas seems to want his notion of competence to apply to all possible natural languages regardless of the contigent contexts of language use. At this stage, Habermas fails to distinguish adequately his own approach from that of Hymes. Further, one way of drawing this distinction is to say that the socio-linguistics of Hymes studies the meanings sentences have when uttered in particular classes of social contexts, while universal pragmatics studies what is, and must be, common to all the classes of contexts. In so far as universal pragmatics studies the meaning of sentences as they are used in utterance-units (speech acts), it belongs to the philosophy of language. Its findings, if they are true, 'should hold for any possible language capable of producing truths or statements or promises'.[46] Socio-linguistics belongs to the study of actually existing natural languages such as French, English and German while the philosophy of language studies what is, and must be, true of all languages. This distinction, however, will not work for Habermas in so far as he intends to develop a Chomskyan-type reconstruction. Again, his early account of communicative competence is not adequately developed.

For Habermas, 'communicative competence means the mastery of an ideal speech situation'.[47] But what is this ideal speech situation? It is true that in linguistic theory it is sometimes necessary as a heuristic device to postulate ideal-speaker hearers in an ideal speech situation in an ideal speech community under ideal conditions. But is this analysis really applicable to all speech? If so, in what sense? Habermas suggests that the ideal speech situation is immanent in all speech. But then, in what sense can it be 'counterfactual' as he also suggests?[48] Further, of what use can the ideal speech situation be in an account of what Habermas calls systematically distorted communication, since distortion is excluded by definition from the ideal? It is obvious that what is needed is a much clearer and more comprehensive formulation of the theory.

2. Discourse and truth as consensus (1973)

The second stage in the development of Habermas's theory of communication is worked out primarily in the text

'Wahreheitstheorin' which has yet to be published in English translation. In this text, Habermas introduces his crucial distinction between communicative action and discourse, his consensus theory of truth and an improved formulation of his central notion of the ideal speech situation. I will begin with a discussion of the distinction between communicative action and discourse. 'Communicative action' refers to those forms of social interaction in which individuals tacitly and uncritically accept the norms, social practices and belief systems of everyday life. 'Discourse', on the other hand, explicitly thematises and criticises the background consensus concerning belief systems, norms, values and ideologies taken for granted in everyday life. During everyday communicative interaction, situations arise in which validity claims concerning beliefs and values become problematic; through discourse one questions their validity and engages in argumentation 'in which validity claims which have become problematic are made the topic and are examined for their justification'.[49] Discourses attempt to resolve disputes over truth claims through discursive vindication or redemption (*Einlosung*) of problematic claims, that is, through argumentation.[50]

Discourses thus mark a break with normal contexts of social action and put in question and critically thematise dominant belief systems, ideologies, norms and values. Entering discourse ideally involves putting aside all motives except the willingness to reach an agreement free from the constraints of action and guided only by the 'unforced force of the better argument'.[51] Habermas locates four presuppositions involved in discourse: (i) genuine discourse aims at agreement or what he calls a rational consensus; (ii) attaining a rational consensus is possible; (iii) a true consensus can be distinguished from a false consensus; and (iv) only such a rational consensus can serve to ground truth claims and norms as 'objective', (that is, valid and binding for all possible participants). Without these presuppositions, Habermas believes, rational communication could not take place. Consequently, he believes that these presuppositions are embedded in the very structure and telos of speech and that his theory is thus explicating what is always already involved in communication.

This account of discourse implies a practical hypothesis which is crucial for Habermas's reformulation of the normative foundations of critical theory, namely, that the truth of statements and the correctness of norms depends upon a form of life free from domination.

Habermas conceptualises this form of life in terms of the 'ideal speech situation' which requires equality and freedom from inner and outer constraints for all participants. He argues that this ideal, although counterfactual, is 'anticipated' in all communication and as such it is also 'effective'.[52] Thus, the ideal speech situation can serve as a critical standard against which 'systematically distorted communication' may be measured. 'Theories of Truth' contains Habermas's most sustained analysis of the ideal speech situation and the conceptual relations between truth, freedom, non-distorted communication and a future form of an emancipated society. In the following discussion, I shall first highlight the central theses in Habermas's 'Theories of Truth' and then cite some criticisms of his position which lead to the third stage in the development of his communication theory.

'Theories of Truth' is primarily devoted to a defence of Habermas's version of the consensus theory of truth which is of independent philosophical interest apart from its implications for his own version of critical theory. He begins his inquiry into theories of truth with a discussion of the Austin–Strawson debate. In agreement with both, Habermas argues that truth is properly ascribed to assertions and not to sentences; he argues that truth cannot be explicated solely at the semantic level in abstraction from the pragmatic level. In agreement with Strawson and against Austin, Habermas maintains that truth is properly ascribed to assertions not as particular utterance events or episodes, but rather in the sense of what is said in speech acts. For Habermas, however, what is said (the propositional content) must be viewed in connection with its performative aspect – a proposition gains its 'assertive force' through being asserted.[53] In the cognitive use of language, the propositional content so asserted rests on a validity claim that can be made good, if at all, only in dialogue. Truth is the validity claim we attach to propositions by asserting them and thus, at least implicitly, offering them up for discursive vindication. For Habermas, any adequate theory of truth must address itself to the 'pragmatics of assertions' which should explain not only under what conditions statements are true, but also under what conditions we are justified in holding statements to be true. Criteria for truth cannot be established in separation from the notion of warranted assertability.

To support this latter contention, Habermas engages in an extended critique of theories of truth that maintain a separation between criteria of truth and criteria of warranted assertion. In particular, Habermas argues against correspondence theories of truth. Basing himself on Ramsey and Strawson, he points out that 'facts' have a different status from 'objects'. Facts are asserted; objects are experienced. Facts are not 'something in world' in the same sense that objects of our experience are, yet 'the correspondence theory must maintain . . . this or an equivalent assertion'. The correspondence between statements and reality that we call 'facts' can only be ascertained through statements, thus 'the correspondence theory tries in vain to break out of the sphere of language'.[54] However, after drawing our attention to this familiar 'circle of words', Habermas points out that the correspondence theory is based on the correct insight that our statements should agree with the facts and that these facts must be 'given' in perceptual experience. To escape the problems in the correspondence theory of truth in explaining the relationship between facts and the world, Habermas appeals to his theory of discourse. It is only in discourse, he claims, that 'facts' can be certified as 'facts' and this is 'always only at that time when the validity claim connected with statements becomes thematized'.[55] In his view, both what we mean by 'facts' and what the 'facts' actually are can only be clarified by referring to discourse in which problematical validity claims are examined.

Habermas distinguishes three experiences of certainty: (i) perceptual certainty (*sinnlichen Gewissheit*) based on experiences of things and events; (ii) non-perceptual certainty (*nichtssinnliche Gewissheit*) based on the recognition of signs; and (iii) belief-certainty (*Glaubensgewissheit*) based on experience with persons and their utterances.[56] Habermas argues that each of these experiences of certainty gives rise to a misleading model of truth. Truth cannot be understood in terms of experiences of certainty at all because truth belongs to validity claims that are capable of producing a consensus through argumentation. Habermas states: 'Experiences support the truth claim of assertions . . . But a truth claim can be made good (*einlosen*) only through argumentation. A claim founded (*fundiert*) in experience is by no means a grounded (*begrundet*) claim.'[57] Thus, the notion of truth necessarily involves an analysis of the discursive justification of validity claims. And this will require a logic of discourse at the pragmatic level.

The logic of discourse, and the consensus theory of truth which it supports, must account not only for the truth of statements, but also for the correctness of norms. It will be a 'logic' not only of 'theoretical', but also of 'practical' discourse. As Habermas argues, the very notion of 'discursive justification' is normative. If every case of an actually achieved agreement were to count as 'consensus', the latter obviously could not serve as the criterion of truth. Habermas states: 'Truth is not the fact that a consensus is realized, but rather that at all times and in any place, if we enter into a discourse a consensus can be realized under conditions which identify this as a founded consensus.'[58] Truth means 'warranted assertability', the promise to achieve a 'rational' consensus. But under what conditions is a consensus a founded or 'rational' consensus? The very notion of discourse depends upon our ability to distinguish a rational from an irrational agreement, thus we cannot avoid this question.

To answer this question, Habermas returns to the notion of the ideal speech situation. By participating in discourse, by attempting to come to an agreement on questions of truth or questions of norms, we unavoidably presuppose that a genuine agreement is at least possible. We unavoidably presuppose that such an agreement, in so far as it is to count as rational, is the outcome only of the force of the better argument and not of accidental or systematic constraints on the discussion. The absence of such constraints, in particular the constraints of systematically distorted communication, can be characterised formally in terms of the ideal speech situation. The idea of truth as consensus, as well as a consideration of our communicative competence, requires the anticipation of such an ideal situation. Habermas is thus able to characterise the ideal speech situation not only in terms of the 'symmetry requirement' discussed above (that is, generally stated, for participants in a discourse there is an equal chance to select and employ each class of speech acts), but also in terms of the condition for the possibility of discourse and of truth.

Habermas's theory of truth and his concept of the ideal speech situation have been subjected to severe criticism. In 'Theories of Truth', Habermas notes Walter Schulz's objections concerning the 'startling irreality' of his claims for the ideal speech situation.[59] Anglo-American philosophers have made similar criticisms of Habermas's theory of truth and discourse. David Held has argued that 'the ideal speech situation itself is not a sufficient condition for a fully open discourse, nor, by extension, for the critical assessment of barriers to this type of discourse in society. The conditions of the ideal speech situation fail to cover a range of phenomena, from the nature (content) of cultural traditions to the distribution of material resources, which are obviously important determinants of the possibility of discourse and, more generally, of a rational, free and just society'.[60] Further, one could argue that Habermas severely underestimates material constraints in communicative action and the roles of ideology, false consciousness, inequality and force.

Alvin Gouldner has argued, on the other hand, that Habermas's model of an ideal speech situation is too strict. By placing unrealistic demands on the conditions of a rational consensus, it actually provides barriers to agreement and consensus.[61] Raymond Geuss has claimed that Habermas is simply generalising his own mode of interaction with other philosophers and that most of the language games of everyday life do not contain features that would lead its participants to engage in discourse.[62] Others have doubted whether speech is oriented towards reaching consensus, and whether average individuals are in fact capable of adopting an open and unbiased attitude and engaging in the sort of rational argumentation that Habermas is calling for. Richard Bernstein, for example, argues that 'any illumination on the problem of human agency and motivation' is lacking which would specify why individuals would be motivated to enter into discourse, to submit to the force of the better argument and to aim at rational consensus.[63] Finally, it is not clear what constitutes a 'better argument' in terms of evidence and agreement with the facts.

Habermas is open to Bernstein's objection. No account of 'agency' or motivation has been supplied to make the ideal speech situation something more than 'ideal'. An account of communicative action will represent Habermas's attempt to deal with this problem at a later stage in his project. Even at this stage in his work, however, it can be shown that some of the above objections rest on misunderstandings of Habermas's main point. In 'Theories of Truth', more sharply and in more detail than in his earlier work, he makes it clear that his concept of the ideal speech situation (and its condition of undistorted communication) is idealised and counterfactual. It has, in part, the status of a normative ideal. He also specifies its similarities (and differences) from Kant's notion of a regulative ideal and he even suggests that it could be seen as a 'transcendental illusion' except that it expresses the immanent telos of all communication and 'anticipates' the form of an ideal society.[64]

Habermas's theory of communication depends upon a concept of discourse that attempts to explicate what is involved in an ideally open, non-coercive and non-manipulative theoretical discussion where participants do aim at truth and rational consensus. This ideal is indeed a version of the traditional ideal of philosophical discussion.[65] The analysis takes as given that theoretical discourse aims at truth and tries to unpack what is involved in ascertaining and establishing what is true. His analysis has normative implications as well, implying that rational discourse *should* attempt to realise the ideal of non-distorted communication and rational consensus. But this is no mere *ought* as opposed to an *is*, as Habermas hopes to show by arguing that his notion of ideal speech is embedded in the very structure of communicative action (interaction) itself.

Even if one grants, however, that Habermas has a plausible account of what should take place in rational discourse, one could still question whether his theory of discourse, rational consensus and the ideal speech situation has a more limited sphere of validity and plausible application than he allows. He is aware, however, that discourse is a rather limited and special form of argumentative reasoning and that it is rarely found in everyday life. Habermas maintains that his theory of discourse and the ideal speech situation can be used as critical standards to disclose distortions in a wide range of forms of communicative action. He also stresses that his programme requires much more analysis to develop a fully realised theory of communicative action (an analysis he later supplies). At this stage in his programme, though, many difficulties of formulation (discussed above) also remain. In particular, his theory of communicative competence needs correction and extension in terms of a theory of universal pragmatics. It is to this stage in the development of his communication theory that I will now turn.

3. *Universal pragmatics and social evolution (1976)*

(a) Universal pragmatics. Habermas's work on universal pragmatics refines the attempt to provide a foundation for the justification of the normative dimension of critical theory. To this end, he attempts to defend a cognitive ethical theory. Against non-cognitivist ethical theories (such as Stevenson's), Habermas argues that the binding character of norms can only be explained if they have a rational foundation. Habermas maintains that such a foundation may be

developed through a communicative ethics. In communication, we attempt to arrive at a rationally motivated consensus concerning both what is and what ought to be. The binding character of norms can be explained only upon the supposition that the consensus arrived at is constraint free and represents the common good. Habermas's position is basically Kantian in as much as such norms always make a claim to universality and are the product of a 'rational will'. However, for Habermas, the rational will is the outcome of the communication process itself. As McCarthy has noted, here the emphasis shifts from what each individual can will without contradiction to be universal to what all can will together to be universal.[66] For Habermas, universalisation must be possible both on the level of universalisation of the common good and universal access to participation in communication. Thus, the normative principle of universalisation also points in the direction of social criticism. But how can the principle of universalisation itself be justified? How can the norm used to justify all other norms itself be justified, except in a circular way? Habermas's answer is that the principle is immanent in the very structure of language.

He attempts to establish his position through an account of the general presuppositions of communication. The analysis is directed at what Habermas calls (communicative) 'action oriented to reaching an understanding' (*verstandigungsorientiert*) in as much as he takes such action to be fundamental. This type of communicative action is selected for analysis because it aims at securing a rational consensus. Universal pragmatics is thus an attempt 'to identify and reconstruct universal conditions of possible understanding' (*Verstandigung*). Again taking a basically Kantian direction, Habermas claims that the development of a universal pragmatics will show 'that the general and unavoidable – in this sense transcendental – conditions of possible understanding have a normative content' when one considers 'the validity basis of speech across its entire spectrum'.[67]

For Habermas, communication aimed at reaching an understanding always involves (either implicitly or explicitly) the raising of validity claims. In performing any such speech action, the speaker cannot avoid raising the following four claims. He claims to be: (i) 'uttering something understandable', (ii) 'giving (the hearer) something to understand', (iii) 'making himself thereby understandable', and (iv) 'coming to an understanding with another person'.[68]

These validity claims are of the four following types: (1) comprehensibility (*Verstandlichkeit*), (2) truth (*Wahrheit*), (3) rightness (*Richtigkeit*), and (4) sincerity (*Wahrhaftigkeit*). According to Habermas, communication oriented to reaching an understanding can be continued only to the degree to which participants credibly sustain these four types of validity claims: (a) the utterance is comprehensible; (b) its propositional content is true; (c) it is appropriate; and (d) it is sincerely spoken. Communication depends upon the presupposition that each participant can justify the validity claims he raises. Although this presupposition may prove false, Habermas holds that it is unavoidable. For him, the goal of communication is coming to an understanding in regard to each of the types of validity claims that culminates in 'reciprocal understanding, shared knowledge, mutual trust, and accord with one another'.[69] Universal pragmatics aims 'at reconstructing the universal validity basis of speech' at all four levels.[70]

Habermas attempts to specify the level of linguistic analysis involved in his approach to universal pragmatics. He argues that the pragmatic level of analysis should not be left to a strictly empirical approach as in socio-linguistics and psycho-linguistics. The separation of language (what Saussure called *langue*, the syntactic and semantic levels that study the language system) from speech (what Saussure called *parole*, the pragmatic level that studies the use of the language system in actual speech) does not justify the restriction of formal analysis to the former. Habermas defends 'the thesis that not only language but speech too – that is, the employment of sentences in utterances – is accessible to formal analysis. Like the elementary units of language (sentences), the elementary units of speech (utterances) can be analyzed in the methodological attitude of a reconstructive science'.[71] The goal of reconstructive analysis of the Chomskyan type is to develop an explicit description of the rules a competent speaker must master in order to produce grammatical sentences. Universal pragmatic analysis aims at an explicit descritpion of the rules a competent speaker must master in order to use these sentences in utterances in an acceptable way. Assuming that communicative competence is as universal as linguistic competence, what is needed is a general theory of speech actions which describes the rules competent speakers must master so 'they can fulfill the conditions for a happy employment of sentences in utterances, no matter to which individual language the sentences may belong and in which accidental contexts the utterances may be embedded'.[72]

For Habermas, the theory of speech acts initiated by Austin and developed by Searle is the most satisfactory point of departure for universal pragmatics. Austin began by drawing a distinction between constative and performative utterances. Constative utterances say something that can be true or false. Performative utterances say something in order to do something, to perform some act. They are not true and false, but rather happy or unhappy. Austin's point was that constative utterances (or statements) were only one class of meaningful utterances and that performative utterances also deserve analysis. Austin's distinction implied a criticism of the positivistic focus on the descriptive function of language.

Austin drew a further distinction between primary and explicit performatives. For example, we can perform the act of promising in English in the following two ways: (i) I shall be there, (ii) I promise that I shall be there. (i) is a primary performative, while (ii) is an explicit performative. Explicit performatives are characteristically declarative sentences with a first-person subject and a performative verb in the simple present tense. Not all performatives are of this form, but we can generally tell if we have a performative by seeing if we can insert the word 'hereby' [as in: 'Passengers are (hereby) requested to stop smoking'].

Austin later abandoned the constative–performative distinction when he realised that constatives also involved performing some act, such as stating or asserting or telling. A constative utterance such as 'It is cold' may be viewed as a primary performative whose explicit form is, 'I (hereby) state that it is cold'. Austin found many such primary performatives that could be rewritten in explicit form, such as questioning or commanding. He thus introduced a threefold distinction for the analysis of all performatives as follows: (1) a locutionary act – the act of saying something semantically meaningful; (2) an illocutionary act – an act performed in saying something, such as making a promise or a statement; (3) a perlocutionary act – an act performed by means of saying something, such as persuading someone or getting someone to believe something. For Austin, the illocutionary force of an utterance is its status as a promise or a statement. The perlocutionary effect of the utterance is its effect on the hearer (either intended or incidental). Thus, if I warn someone to stop smoking, I may succeed in getting him to stop (intended effect) and I may frighten him (incidental effect). The perlocutionary effect may be distinguished from illocutionary uptake – the hearer's recognition that a particular illocutionary act has been performed. Illocutionary uptake is a necessary, not a sufficient condition, for the hearer's understanding of the utterance. It is not a sufficient condition because the hearer's knowledge of the grammatical and lexical structure of the language is involved. There is a sense in which this may be described as a cognitive response on the part of the hearer. This cognitive response may be distinguished from the intended (or the incidental) perlocutionary effect.[73]

Austin's discussion of speech acts included the various felicity conditions which an illocutionary act must fulfil if it is to be happy or successful. In Searle's extension of speech-act theory, he states these felicity conditions in the form of three rules as follows: (i) preparatory rule – the speaker must have the necessary authority to do the act, the circumstances must be appropriate and the conventions surrounding the act must be obeyed (otherwise we have a 'misfire'); (ii) sincerity rule – the speaker must be sincere in performing the act (otherwise we have an 'abuse'); (iii) essential rule – the speaker must be committed to certain beliefs and intentions, and be willing to follow through on the commitment (otherwise we have a 'breach of commitment').[74] On the basis of these various distinctions, speech-act theory attempts to explicate the speaking of a language as a rule-governed activity that depends upon social as well as linguistic conventions. As Lyons has pointed out, what such an approach offers 'is, in principle, a unified theory of the meaning of utterances within the framework of a general theory of social activity'.[75]

In view of the above, it is clear why Habermas finds speech-act theory so promising as a starting point for a universal pragmatics that intends to provide a foundation for social theory. Habermas begins his account of speech acts (most often he uses the term 'speech actions') by delimiting the class of such actions to be analysed. First, Habermas wants to confine his attention to explicit speech acts in standard form. They have both an illocutionary component and a propositional component. Also, the propositional component may be held invariant across changes in the illocutionary component. The standard form is as follows:

'I (hereby) (performative verb) you   that ___

illocutionary component   propositional component

Habermas calls such speech acts 'propositionally differentiated speech actions'. Secondly, based on a distinction drawn by Strawson, Habermas wants to confine his attention to what he calls 'institutionally unbound speech actions' (such as asserting, questioning and commanding) as opposed to 'institutionally bound speech actions' (such as christening).[76] The distinction is between speech acts that depend upon a single institution (or a narrowly circumscribed group of institutions) and those that are not essentially fixed to any institution.[77] Finally, Habermas wants to exclude speech acts which appear in contexts that produce shifts of meaning. This is accomplished by Searle's principle of expressibility which Habermas modifies as follows: 'in a given language, for every interpersonal relation that a speaker wants to take up explicitly with another member of his language community, a suitable performative expression is either available or, if necessary, can be introduced through a specification of available expressions'.[78] Thus, Habermas's units of analysis are verbal and explicit, propositionally differentiated, institutionally unbound, context independent speech acts.

For Habermas, an important feature of communication is revealed in the double structure (illocutionary component/propositional component) that can be read off the surface structure of speech acts in standard form. The possibility of holding the propositional component invariable across changes in the illocutionary component appears as an 'uncoupling of illocutionary and propositional components'. This uncoupling is a condition for the separation 'of two communicative levels on which speaker and hearer must simultaneously come to an understanding if they want to communicate'. These two levels are as follows: '(1) the level of intersubjectivity on which speaker and hearer, through illocutionary acts, establish the relations that permit them to come to an understanding with one another; and (2) the level of the propositional content which is communicated'.[79] Further, the double structure of speech acts reveals the inherent reflexivity of language. In a speech act, we communicate a content and communicate about the role in which the communicated content is to be used. Thus, we may always embed a previous speech act in a new speech act as follows: 'I (hereby) state that I promise you that I will be there.' The previous speech act becomes the propositional component of the new speech act. And there is no logical reason why this process of embedding cannot continue infinitely.

Habermas discusses the impact of speech act theory on the theory of meaning. He argues that Austin's distinction between the locutionary act (which has semantic meaning – sense and reference) and the illocutionary act (which has force) is unsatisfactory. The illocutionary component has a lexical meaning. The performative sentence as a whole also has a semantic meaning. Because of this one might conclude that the illocutionary force of an utterance is simply that aspect of its meaning conveyed by its explicitly performative component (or that might be so conveyed if the component is missing).[80] However, this neglects the fact that force belongs only to utterances and not to sentences. Habermas holds that it is possible to distinguish sentence meaning from the meaning 'that comes about through the employment of a sentence in an utterance'. Thus, we can distinguish between the semantic meaning of a sentence and the pragmatic meaning of an utterance. Moreover, the fact that the same speech acts can be performed with different sentences has led some philosophers of language to grant priority to pragmatic meaning by holding 'that sentence (and word) meanings are a function of the meaning of the speech acts in which they are principally used'. However, for Habermas, this use theory of meaning does not adequately account for the relative independence of semantic meaning in relation to the changes in pragmatic meaning produced by different contexts. Further, semantic meaning is 'apparantly less dependent on the intention of the speaker' than is pragmatic meaning.[81]

Habermas contends that a purely semantic analysis of sentence meaning 'abstracts from the relations to reality into which a sentence is put as soon as it is uttered and from the validity claims under which it is thereby placed'.[82] Thus, a complete analysis of meaning requires a pragmatic analysis that takes these factors into account. Based on his distinction between the communicative level of intersubjectivity and the level of propositional content, Habermas reinterprets Austin's distinction between meaning and force. Force 'stands for the meaning of expressions

that are originally used in illocutionary acts, and 'meaning' for
the meaning of expressions originally used in connection with
propositions'.[83] For Habermas, 'force' and 'meaning' are two
categories of meaning that correspond to the pragmatic functions
of establishing interpersonal relations (force) and representing
facts (meaning). To these two categories of meaning, he adds a
third which has the pragmatic function of expressing the speaker's
intention.

Based on his account of meaning, Habermas also 'reconstructs'
Austin's original distinction between constatives and performatives.
For Habermas, speech acts can be in order with respect to
typically restricted contexts (this is the focus of the speech act
theory of Austin and Searle), 'but they can be valid only with
respect to the 'fundamental claim' raised by the speaker. In this
latter respect, constative speech acts do have a special status in
as much as they raise an 'unmistakable validity claim, the claim
to truth'. The possibility of transforming the propositional
component of even a non-constative speech act (that p) into a
proposition (p) shows that the claim to truth is 'built into the
very structure of possible speech in general. Truth is a universal
validity claim; its universality is reflected in the double structure
of speech'.[84] However, truth is not the only universal validity
claim reflected in the formal structure of speech. Again based on
his distinction between the level of propositional content and the
level of intersubjectivity, Habermas distinguishes two uses of
language as follows: (i) the 'interactive use of language' which
thematises the interpersonal relations into which speaker and
hearer must enter, while only mentioning propositional content; (ii)
the 'cognitive use of language' which thematises the propositional
content, while only indirectly expressing the interpersonal relations.[85]
Thus, Habermas distinguishes between constative speech acts and
regulative speech acts.

Just as the assertion is a paradigm of constative speech acts,
so the authorised command is a paradigm of regulative speech
acts. Habermas argues that in all speech acts, the illocutionary
force 'is borrowed from the force of recognized norms' and
involves the '(at least) de facto recognition of the claim that these
norms rightfully exist'.[86] He maintains that the normative validity
claim to rightness revealed by illocutionary force is just as
universal as the claim to truth. In constative speech acts, the

claim to truth is explicit and the claim to rightness implicit. In regulative speech acts, the claim to rightness is explicit and the claim to truth implicit. Habermas claims that this distinction captures what Austin intended in the constative–performative distinction, but failed to develop because of a failure to recognise the two implicitly raised general validity claims.

Habermas also distinguishes a third type of speech action. The paradigms here are first-person sentences in which the speaker discloses his wishes, feelings, intentions (such as 'I wish that . . .' and 'I long for you'). These sentences express the truthfulness of the speaker by disclosing his intentions. They belong to the 'expressive use of language'. Such sentences are not usually expressed in standard speech act form unless the truthfulness of the speaker is not taken for granted. What Habermas calls 'avowals' are the paradigm for this (such as 'I must confess to you that . . .' and 'I don't want to conceal from you that . . . ').[87] Although these speech acts cannot be correlated with the expressive use of language in the way that constatives can be correlated with the cognitive use and regulatives with the interactive, Habermas still wants to argue that truthfulness also is a universal validity claim implicit in all speech.

After distinguishing the above three types of speech acts, Habermas returns to the question of illocutionary force. Austin and Searle analysed illocutionary force by examining conditions for the success or failure of speech acts. Habermas wants to extend this analysis by examining the 'acceptability' of speech acts. This means that the hearer 'not only understands the meaning of the sentence uttered but also actually enters into the relationship intended by the speaker'.[88] For this purpose, Habermas begins with Searle's three rules. He accepts Searle's account of the preparatory rule. However, Habermas argues that 'the peculiar force of the illocutionary' cannot be explained by these 'speech-act-typical context restrictions'. Illocutionary force requires the essential rule which shows that 'the success of an illocutionary act consists in the speaker's entering into a specific engagement, so that the hearer can rely on him'. The content of the speaker's engagement should be distinguished from the sincerity of the engagement. The sincerity rule 'must always be fulfilled in the case of communicative action oriented to reaching an understanding'.[89]

For Habermas, previous analyses of speech acts have not paid enough attention to the engagement of the speaker on which the acceptability of the speech act depends. When a speaker performs an illocutionary act, he enters into a bond which guarantees he will meet certain conditions such as the following: drop assertions that prove false, act in accordance with his disclosed intentions, follow his own advice when he is in the same situation, and so on. Thus, for Habermas, 'the illocutionary force of an acceptable speech act consists in the fact that it can move a hearer to rely on the speech-act-typical commitments of the speaker'. But on what is this reliance based? For institutionally bound speech acts, this reliance can be understood in terms of the binding force of established norms. For institutionally unbound speech acts, however, Habermas maintains that this reliance must be understood in terms of the 'reciprocal recognition of validity claims'. But this recognition need not be irrational in as much as 'validity claims have a cognitive character and can be checked'. Thus, for Habermas, illocutionary force has a rational basis because the 'speech-act-typical commitments are connected with cognitively testable validity claims'.[90]

By appealing to validity claims, the speaker assumes the obligation to support his claims. For the cognitive use of language, this is an obligation to provide grounds based on experiential data. For the interactive use of language, this is an obligation to provide justification based on norms. For the expressive use of language, this is an obligation to prove trustworthy based on subsequent actions. For Habermas, the acceptability of a speech act depends not only upon Searle's three rules. It also depends upon the speaker's willingness to assume the appropriate obligations and to defend, if necessary, the validity claims he raises.

Habermas places his discussion of the validity basis of speech in the context of what he calls 'a model of linguistic communication'. Each of the universal validity claims (comprehensibility, truth, rightness, sincerity) comes into play in every instance of communication, although generally only one is thematic. Finally, Habermas argues that the universality of these validity claims can be clarified in relation to 'the systematic place of language'. Through the medium of language, speakers and hearers 'realize certain fundamental demarcations'. The subject demarcates himself from external nature, society, internal nature and language. According to this model, language is the medium that interrelates three 'worlds': the world of existing states of affairs, the world of normatively regulated social relations and the inner world of the individual's intentional experiences. In every successful communicative action, our utterances enter into this threefold relationship. For Habermas, language itself 'remains in a peculiar half-transcedence in the performance of communicative actions . . . it presents itself to the speaker and the actor (preconsciously) as a segment of reality sui generis'.[91]

Habermas's account may be summarised by means of the following chart:[92]

Universal pragmatics

Mode of communication	Cognitive	Interactive	Expressive
Thematic validity claim	Truth	Rightness	Sincerity
Theme	Propositional content	Interpersonal relation	Speaker's intention
Type of speech act	Constatives	Regulatives	Avowals
Domains of reality	'The' world of external nature	'Our' world of society	'My' world of internal nature
General function:	Representation of facts	Establishment of legitimate interpersonal relationships	Disclosure of speaker's subjectivity
Universal pragmatic subtheories	Theory of elementary sentences	The theory of illocutionary acts	The theory of intentional expressions

Habermas's work on universal pragmatics is clearer and more carefully formulated than his earlier work on communicative competence. The later work removes much of the confusion over levels of linguistic analysis. It represents a much stronger attempt to provide a normative foundation for social theory through an examination of communicative competence, understood in terms of the ability of a speaker to master the rules for embedding utterances in speech acts. Such an examination, in the form of a universal pragmatics, attempts to uncover the general and unavoidable presuppositions of communication by identifying and reconstructing the universal conditions of possible understanding. Habermas attempts to synthesise the work of Chomsky, Hymes, Austin and Searle in the framework of a general theory of social action. As even Bar-Hillel admits, some such synthesis is needed.[93] I will now outline some basic criticisms of this stage of his account.

First, Habermas's analysis of communication is directed at communicative action (specifically, action oriented to reaching an understanding) as distinguished from strategic action. Only in a brief and cryptic note is any attempt made to clarify what is an important distinction for Habermas.[94] McCarthy's clarification of Habermas's distinction between labour and interaction characterises strategic action as social and means–end oriented.[95] If this is what Habermas intends in the context of his theory of universal pragmatics, then it seems unfortunate. Speech acts are certainly both social and means–end oriented in as much as they use a means (speech) for an end (to do something) in a social context. Further, it is arguable that strategic action is more basic to communication than 'communicative action oriented to reaching an understanding'. In any case, at this stage in the development of Habermas's communication theory, he gives no adequate justification for taking 'communicative action oriented to understanding' as basic – either for speech or action. Ironically, the practical political point Habermas is attempting to make concerning equal access to communicating roles and constraint free communication suggests that his own account might itself be construed as an example of strategic action. Both the distinction between strategic and communicative action, and the practical political conclusions drawn from the distinction, need to be developed in terms, first of all, of social *action* and not *speech*. Habermas turns to this task later in his theory of communicative action.

Habermas's theory of universal pragmatics briefly glosses many complex and controversial issues in the philosophy of language and linguistic theory. This is to be expected in a work that attempts to synthesise so many approaches in a short compass. However, this practice frequently leads Habermas into serious problems. I will briefly mention only two.

First, Habermas gives an entirely inadequate account of meaning. It is not clear whether he accepts a Gricean–Searlean account of meaning in terms of intention, or something closer to Chomsky's account. His remarks concerning categories of meaning based on pragmatic function (whatever theory of meaning is operative in the background) is clearly misguided. Habermas equates Austin's notion of illocutionary force with one of these categories, but illocutionary force is a much more specific notion. It fixes meaning in a certain sense (that itself requires analysis), but it is not itself some special 'type' of meaning. Again, Habermas pays insufficient attention to the distinction between semantic and pragmatic levels. If we examine a line of poetry by Dylan Thomas we need to know not only the lexical meaning of the words, but also what the line means poetically. In as much as this involves effects on hearers and a consideration of values, this belongs to the pragmatic level. And since Habermas is centrally concerned with values, it is particularly unfortunate that his account of meaning pays insufficient attention to the distinction between these two levels of analysis.

Secondly, the double structure of speech that figures so prominently in Habermas's account is inadequately explained. It is not clear, for one thing, to what extent he accepts a performative analysis of sentences using the deep structure–surface structure account developed by Lakoff (1969). At least some of what he says seems to presuppose some such account. But such accounts face both semantic and logical difficulties ignored by Habermas.[96] Further, Habermas's account of the pragmatic 'universals' also relies on work in linguistics that has been subjected to important criticism which are not addressed.[97] This latter problem (to what extent are there pragmatic universals?) cannot be handled in summary fashion because it is central to Habermas's theory.

Finally, there is an unresolved tension running through Habermas's entire account between the Searlian side and the Chomskyan side that is parallel to tensions between the Marxian and Kantian sides in his early work. In many ways, Habermas is on the side of Searle. This is particularly true in regard to his emphasis on communication. But Habermas seems also to think universal pragmatics can be a rigorous science along Chomskyan lines. At this stage in the development of his communication theory, Habermas does not situate his enterprise adequately as either a contribution to the philosophy of language (to the extent that this is an a priori approach), or as a contribution to linguistics (to the extent that this is an empirical approach), or as some combination of the two. Specific problems, such as meaning and the status of the pragmatic 'universals', thus remain unclarified. Habermas attempts to explain further the nature of his communication theory, as well as addressing the problems raised above, in his latest work on communicative action. Before turning to his work, I will complete my account of the third stage in the development of Habermas's communication theory by examining his theory of social evolution.

(b) Social evolution. While Habermas's theory of universal pragmatics represents the reconstruction of the Kantian component of his earlier account of critical theory, his theory of social evolution represents the reconstruction of the Hegelian–Marxist component. The starting point for Habermas's theory of social evolution is a 'reconstruction of historical materialism'.[98] This 'reconstruction' begins with the anthropological hypothesis that labour and language are the irreducible presuppositions of any society. Only through labour and language does the material reproduction of societies and the socialisation of their members become possible. Social evolution cannot be treated on the model of biological evolution, since the criteria of biological selection do not allow us to formulate a 'reconstructed' history of the species. On the contrary, social evolution must be understood as the transformation and continuing reformation of social structures which are always in principle identifiable with action structures. The theory is 'evolutionary' because it views structural change as cumulative processes exhibiting direction. Drawing on Piaget, Habermas uses the term 'developmental logic' to describe the fact that changes are directed, and this can be claimed only when we can observe a factual development of discretely identifiable stages, each stage exhibiting an intrinsic structure, in an invariant order. By 'invariant order', Habermas means that no stage can be reached until a previous stage has been passed through (although stagnation and regression are possible) and that in the next stage new qualitative elements are integrated with elements from the previous stage to form a new structure.

For Habermas, social evolution can be understood (at least in part) in terms of the development of learning capacities. Such learning takes place in two central dimensions: moral–practical insight and empirical–analytic knowledge. The latter represents developments in the forces of production as an increasing mastery of nature and technological advance. The former dimension represents developments in the relations of production in which new levels of social–normative knowledge are achieved. The results of learning are passed down in cultural traditions which provide the essential resources for social movements. They provide a cognitive potential for dealing with disturbances and crises in the reproductive process of society, and serve as the basis for what Habermas calls the 'rationalisation of action'.

Habermas's account of the rationalisation of action may be outlined as follows. The rationalisation of action takes place in the two learning dimensions distinguished above: the empirical–analytic and the moral–practical. A basic action type belongs to each, purposive–rational action to the empirical–analytic and communicative action to the moral–practical. Purposive–rational actions are 'rationalised' in terms of empirical efficiency and success, while communicative actions are 'rationalised' in terms of the moral responsibility of the acting subject and the justification of the rightness of norms. Effects of the 'rationalisation of action' can be located in the productive forces for purposive–rational action, and in forms of social integration (including the relations of production) for communicative action. Purposive–rationality is embodied in technology and in social subsystems such as the economy, while communicative rationality is embodied in worldviews and in mechanisms for resolving conflict (law and morality). 'Rationalisation' in the purposive–rational sense refers to the growing capacity to control nature (development of the productive forces), while 'rationalisation' in the communicative sense refers to the expansion of the realm of consensual action based on agreement. The 'rationalisation process' refers to learning levels achieved in both dimensions, the empirical–analytic and the moral–practical.

Although Habermas insists on the importance of both dimensions, he maintains that the development of normative structures 'is the pacemaker of social evolution, for new principles of social organization mean new forms of social integration; and the latter, in turn, first make it possible to implement available productive forces or to generate new ones'.[99] Habermas, however, admits that his description of patterns of normative structures (and of the development of productive forces) is not in itself a theory of social evolution. It is rather a 'developmental logic' which says nothing about the actual empirical 'mechanisms of development'. It tells us only 'something about the range of variations within which cultural values, moral representations, norms and the like – at a given level of social organization – can be organized'. The real developmental dynamics of normative structures remain dependent upon systems problems conditioned by the economy and the learning processes that emerge in reaction to them. Thus, culture remains 'a superstructural phenomenon', for Habermas, although 'it does seem to play a more prominent role in the transition to new developmental levels than many Marxists have heretofore supposed'.[100]

Habermas claims that his approach remains both historical and materialist:

> The analysis of developmental dynamics is 'materialist' in so far as it makes reference to crisis-producing systems problems in the domain of production and reproduction; and the analysis remains 'historically oriented' in so far as it has to seek the causes of evolutionary changes in the whole range of . . . contingent circumstances. Only after rationalization processes (which require explanations that are both historical and materialist) have been historically completed can we specify the patterns of development for the normative structures of society. These developmental logics betoken the independence and to this extent the internal history – of the spirit.[101]

For Habermas, social evolution proceeds at two levels: 'in processes of learning and adaptation at each given level of learning (until its structural possibilities are exhausted) and in those unlikely evolutionary thrusts that lead to new learning levels'.[102] The emergence of problems that overload the 'adaptive capacity' of society is largely a contingent matter. If such problems arise, how they will be settled depends upon 'access to new stages of learning'. Solutions to crises require both attempts to alter existent forms of social integration, and a social environment and social movements which can sustain such attempts. The movement to a new evolutionary stage is subject, for Habermas, to at least two initial conditions: (i) 'unresolved system problems that represent challenges' to the status quo; (ii) 'new levels of learning that have already been achieved in world-views'.[103]

For Habermas, the history of the species can be reconstructed as the species' increasing capacity for freedom both from material want and distorted communication. True freedom and autonomy means success along both dimensions. History, however, is also the history of crises. And there is never a metaphysical or scientific guarantee that a crisis will be overcome, that there will be progress. Advances in the forces of production do remove certain crucial burdens, however, new problems can arise and even increase in intensity. Habermas discusses this point in terms of the 'dialectic of progress':

> The dialectic of progress can be seen in the fact that with the acquisition of problem solving abilities new problem situations come to consciousness . . . suffering from the contingencies of an uncontrolled process gains a new quality to the extent that we believe ourselves capable of rationally intervening in it. This suffering is the negative form of a new need . . . At every stage of development the social–evolutionary learning process itself generates new resources, which means new dimensions of scarcity and thus new historical needs.[104]

In *Legitimation Crisis* (1975), Habermas applied this general scheme to the analysis of contemporary society, what he calls 'late capitalism'.[105] Stated briefly, Habermas's argument is that late capitalist societies are endangered from at least four possible crisis tendencies: (i) economic crisis – the 'requisite quantity' of consumable goods is not produced; (ii) rationality crisis – the 'requisite quantity' of rational administrative decisions is not forthcoming; (iii) legitimation crisis – the 'requisite quantity' of motivations is not generated; (iv) motivational crisis – the 'requisite quantity' of meaning which motivates action is not created. By 'requisite quantity', Habermas means the required amount of the respective subsystems's (economic, political–administrative, socio-cultural) products (goods, decisions, legitimations, meaning) to maintain social production and reproduction and thus 'system identity'.[106]

Without following out the details of this analysis, it is important to point out at least one application of Habermas's theory of universal pragmatics in distinguishing particular and general interests for purposes of developing a critique of late capitalist society based on 'the suppression of generalisable interests'. A social theory critical of ideology can start from the model of the suppression of generalisable interests by comparing our current system of norms with a hypothetical system of norms formed discursively. As Habermas states:

> Such a conterfactually projected reconstruction . . . can be guided by the question (justified, in my opinion, by

considerations from universal pragmatics): how would the members of a social system, at a given stage in the development of productive forces, have collectively and bindingly interpreted their needs (and which norms would they have accepted as justified) if they could and would have decided on the organization of social intercourse through discursive will-formation, with adequate knowledge of the limiting conditions and functional imperatives of their society?[107]

The ideal speech situation represents such a counterfactual ideal in which no force but the better argument is exercised, and no motives but the shared search for truth and rightness accepted. In such a situation of equal access and participation in discussion, rational consensus can be established which represents and expresses a 'rational will'. It is 'rational' in so far as the formal properties of discourse guarantee that 'a common interest' may be ascertained without deception.[108] Present society can become the object of critique for failing to measure up (in so far as possible) to this model. Once again, Habermas returns to the idea of the 'public sphere' central to his first book. Now, however, he feels he is in a position to justify this standard and argue for the objective possibility of its (at least partial) realisation through a consideration of social evolution that is, once again, a 'critical prologue' to the actual practice required for realising it.

A whole series of objections have been raised against Habermas's theory of social evolution and his reconstruction of historical materialism.[109] I will mention only two of them here. The first, and crucial, objection relates to the very idea of 'developmental logic' and the concept of 'invariant stages'. As Habermas admits, these ideas have yet to be adequately worked out and made consistent with the remainder of his programme. The research projects upon which he bases his theory of social evolution (Piaget and Kohlberg) have been subjected to severe criticisms concerning ethnocentric research bias and other problems.[110] Against other research projects (functionalism, positivism, systems theory, and so on) Habermas has himself raised the problem of ethnocentrism and pointed out the historical contextuality of modes of research.[111] How is he to avoid having the same arguments raised against his own position with what seems to be its own scientistic and rationalistic bias? To answer this question will require Habermas to develop systematically a comprehensive and complete theory of rationality.

The second objection relates to the adequacy of Habermas's 'reconstruction of historical materialism'. Does it really represent an advance over Marx and, if so, in what respects? Habermas seems, at least, to dismiss the revolutionary core of Marx's theory. The very contrast 'evolutionary' versus 'revolutionary' indicates a decisive shift. How do such crucial notions as 'class struggle' fit into Habermas's theory? And, if they do not, in what sense is Habermas's 'Marxism' Marxist? These questions will have to await an account of the fourth stage in the development of Habermas's communication theory of society in his latest work on the theory of communicative action and rationality. I will develop this account in detail in Chapter 4.

4

Habermas on Communicative Action and Rationality

'That communicative rationality, precisely as suppressed, is already embodied in the existing forms of interaction and does not first have to be postulated as something that ought to be is shown by the causality of fate which Hegel and Marx, each in his own way, illustrated in connection with phenomena of ruptured morality – the reactions of those who are put to flight or roused to resistance by fateful conflicts, who are driven to sickness, to suicide, crime, or to rebellion and revolutionary struggle ... Communicative reason operates in history as an avenging force.'—Jürgen Habermas

Habermas's complex and far-ranging work, *Theorie des kommunikativen Handelns* (1981, two volumes), addresses four major themes: (i) the theory of rationality; (ii) the theory of communicative action; (iii) the dialectic of social rationalisation; (iv) the critique of functional reason.[1] In what follows, I will attempt a summary of the main lines of argument developed for the first three of the above themes. In particular, I will focus on the two themes that are of central importance for Habermas's attempt to provide a normative foundation for critical social theory: communicative action and rationality. For this purpose, I will draw not only upon Habermas's magnum opus (volume one published in English translation), but also upon recent (1980–3) articles and interviews which serve to clarify or support important elements in my account.[2] After providing an account of this fourth (and latest) stage in the development of Habermas's communication theory of society, I will raise critical issues concerning the theory as a whole. These issues will be addressed in Chapter 5, where I conclude by discussing Habermas and the prospects of critical theory.

Habermas begins *The Theory of Communicative Action* by attempting to clarify its status *vis-à-vis* philosophy. For him, 'philosophical thought originates in reflection on the reason embodied in cognition, speech, and action: and reason remains its basic theme . . . from the beginning . . . If there is anything common to philosophical theories, it is the intention of thinking being or the unity of the world by way of explicating reason's experience of itself'. Today, however, the very possibility of a philosophical worldview has become questionable. In Habermas's view, 'Philosophy can no longer refer to the whole of the world, of nature, of history, of society, in the sense of totalising knowledge' . . . philosophy has lost its 'self-sufficiency', its 'ontological hopes for material theories of nature, history, society' as well as its 'transcendental–philosophical hopes for an aprioristic reconstruction of the equipment of a non-empirical species subject, of consciousness in general'. In short, 'All attempts at discovering ultimate foundations, in which the intentions of First Philosophy live on, have broken down'. Philosophical worldviews have been undercut not only by the progress of science, but even more so through the activity of philosophical consciousness itself which has become radically self-critical and moved to the level of 'metaphilosophy'. In spite of this, contemporary philosophy as developed in logic, the theory of science, the theory of language and action, continues to direct its interest at 'the formal conditions of rationality in knowing, in reaching understanding through language, and in acting, both in everyday contexts and at the level of methodically organized experience or systematically organised discourse'. In all these areas, Habermas concludes that 'philosophy in its postmetaphysical, post-Hegelian currents is converging toward . . . a theory of rationality'.[3]

Habermas wants to take up this theme in the context of a 'reconstructive' social theory. But how can social theory 'claim any competence for the rationality problematic?' In answering this question, Habermas attempts to clarify the status of 'reconstructive' theories. In his view, the philosophical developments outlined above do not signal a relativistic collapse, but rather the occasion for the emergence of a 'new constellation in the relationship of philosophy and the sciences'. Modern theories of science, according to Habermas, raise 'normative' and 'universalistic' claims about scientific progress which can no longer be addressed in a purely 'ontological or transcendental–philosophical' way.[4] Establishing these claims requires instead both a formal explication of the conditions of scientific rationality, concerned with the context of justification (as in Hempel's theory of science), and an analysis of the social embodiment and historical development of scientific. rationality concerned with the context of discovery (as in Kuhn's theory of science). Such theories belong exclusively neither to traditional philosophy nor to the special empirical sciences. They 'can be tested only against the evidence of counterexamples, and . . . hold up in the end only if reconstructive theory proves itself capable of distilling internal aspects of the history of science and systematically explaining in connection with empirical analyses, the actual, narratively documented history of science in the context of social development'.[5] A 'reconstructive' social theory that follows this approach by linking a formal explication of rationality to an account of its social and historical development need not limit itself to scientific rationality, it could direct itself at moral–practical rationality and even aesthetic–practical rationality as well. This is the approach Habermas adopts for his own attempt to construct a comprehensive concept of rationality.

At this point we can see how Habermas's earlier thesis that 'the heritage of philosophy passes over to critical social theory' has been reformulated.[6] Now this 'passage' from philosophy to critical social theory does not depend upon the presuppositions of German idealism (as it did in *Knowledge and Human Interests*), but upon the success of Habermas's attempt to explicate a comprehensive concept of rationality linked to an account of its social embodiment and historical development. In *The Theory of Communicative Action*, this attempt takes the form of a systematic account of social theory from Marx to Parsons, as well as a formal explication of the 'reason' embodied in speech and action linked to a theory of 'social rationalisation'. Habermas's new approach, his effort to reconstruct a critical theory of society through a theory of rationality, has two basic advantages. First, a comprehensive theory of the reason embodied in speech and action grasps more adequately the importance of the problematic of rationality (discussed in Chapter 2) by making it a central and explicit theme. Secondly, the 'normative foundation' Habermas tried to establish for critical theory in his work on universal pragmatics (a 'reconstruction' of the reason embodied in speech) requires completion and correction in a theory of communicative action since society, understood as a 'communication community', must be approached 'in the first place as a community of (social) interaction and not of argumentation, ,as action and not discourse'.[7]

Habermas's account of communicative action makes possible an important reformulation of his earlier distinction between labour and interaction. Drawing on his account of the communicative competence of social actors, Habermas distinguishes between 'action oriented to success' and 'action oriented to understanding' and between the social and nonsocial contexts of action. 'Action oriented to success' is called 'instrumental' by Habermas when the action can be understood as following technical rules and can be evaluated in terms of efficiency in dealing with the physical world (a nonsocial context). 'Action oriented to success' is called 'strategic' by Habermas when the action can be understood as following rules of rational choice and can be evaluated in terms of efficiency in influencing the decisions of other social actors viewed as potential opponents (a social context). 'Action oriented to understanding' which can only take place in a social context Habermas calls 'communicative action'. 'Communicative action' occurs when social intercourse is co-ordinated not through the egocentric calculations of the success of the actor as an individual, but through the mutual and co-operative achievement of understanding among participants. This yields the following schema of action types:[8]

TYPES OF ACTION

Actor

Action	Oriented to success	Oriented to reaching understanding
Non-social	Instrumental action	
Social	Strategic action	Communicative action

By drawing these distinctions in terms of the 'competencies' of social actors rather than in terms of 'quasi-transcendental interests' (the fundamental level of the labour and interaction distinction), Habermas is able to make a much stronger claim about their status. They are no longer simply 'analytic' distinctions, but rather distinctions that we can expect any competent social actor to be able to make. As Habermas states: 'I am in fact supposing that the actors themselves, in every phase of interaction, can know – however vaguely and intuitively – whether they are adopting a strategic–objectivating attitude towards other participants or are oriented to consensus . . . [they] can by no means be understood only as different analytic aspects of the same behaviour'.[9]

Communicative action is linked internally to the reason embodied in speech 'reconstructed' by universal pragmatics, since it is directed towards achieving an agreement based on the intersubjective recognition of validity claims (truth, rightness, sincerity, comprehensibility), although this may be only implicitly present in any case of actual social interaction. A social actor can be mistaken about the nature of the agreement communicatively achieved. Communicative action rests on 'rationally motivated' agreement based on reasons and grounds rather than on coercion and force. Forced agreement can only count for the social actor as a subjectively acceptable and genuine agreement to the extent that the force goes unrecognised. This takes place either because the actor deceives herself or himself (systematically distorted communication) or because the actor is deceived by others (manipulation). Finally, although social actors can in fact be wrong about their motives in the above ways, and thus behave strategically instead of communicatively, they always remain capable in principle of making the requisite distinction and orienting themselves to genuine and unforced agreement and mutual understanding.

Further distinctions are drawn by Habermas within the sphere of communicative action itself. Social actors as members of a communication community have the competency to distinguish between external nature, society and internal nature.[10] Competent speakers have the ability to relate these different 'worlds'. They are able to take different attitudes to these 'worlds' and to evaluate the different validity claims raised within these attitudes. In communication directed at external nature, speakers take up an 'objectivating' attitude and raise a validity claim to offer a *true* representation of the facts. In communication directed at society, speakers take up an 'interactive' attitude and raise a validity claim to offer an evaluation of the *rightness* of rules governing relations between social actors. In communication directed at internal nature, speakers take up an 'expressive' attitude and raise a validity claim to give a *sincere* disclosure of their desires, wishes and needs. Beyond this, speakers are able to direct attention to language itself in an attempt

to clarify the validity claims offered in any of the three dimensions. *ie discursive*
Interpretations of communication raise and thematise a specific
validity claim, a claim to *comprehensibility*, which must be met in
all effective communication.[11]

The analysis of communicative competence carried out by
Habermas in his work on universal pragmatics takes an important
turn when applied to social action. Habermas's communication
community is also, fundamentally, a community of social interactions. Speech acts are themselves social actions. His theory of
communicative action is thus based on an analysis of the social use
of language oriented to reaching understanding, which focuses on
the action co-ordinating effects of the validity claims offered in
speech acts. Participants in communication can, through offering
validity claims, establish intersubjective relations which make possible the socially binding recognition of these claims. This social
mechanism for reaching understanding and building agreement and
consensus depends upon the 'rational motivation' to accept the
offers made in speech acts to the extent that speakers are able to
provide grounds and reasons to support their claims. What
underlies the reciprocally raised validity claims and action
expectations raised in communicative action 'are potential reasons
as a (kind of) security reserve, rather than sanctions or gratifications,
force or money'.[12] Thus, communicative action (and this is a
central point Habermas hopes to defend) is internally connected
to communicative rationality.

Communicative rationality is the central concept in Habermas's
latest attempt to provide a normative foundation for critical social
theory. This attempt at normative jusification moves even farther
away from the 'foundationalism' (discussed in Chapter 1) which
many critics found in Habermas's theory of universal pragmatics,
particularly in regard to the 'transcendental' notion of an ideal
speech situation. Habermas no longer claims that the ideal speech
situation, or any other feature of communicative rationality, directly
represents the 'image' or the 'anticipation' of a concrete form of
life. The perfectly rational society *is* an illusion. Thus, communicative
rationality represents neither a resurrected transcendental deduction
of a utopian critical standard capable of judging concrete forms of
life as a whole, nor a telos for a resurrected philosophy of history.
Understood formally as a procedural concept, communicative
rationality involves an attempt to characterise universal features of —

communication in their structure and development that remains open to empirical–reconstructive test and refutation. Understood concretely as a sociological concept, communicative rationality involves an attempt to identify empirically the actual social embodiment and historical development of rationality structures, as well as the objective possibilities for extending rationality to more spheres of social life. The critical thrust of the concept, its normative dimension, consists in its usefulness as an interpretive guide for locating social pathologies in modernity, and in suggesting remedies for these pathologies. The ultimate test of Habermas's account of communicative rationality is its empirical, theoretical and critical fruitfulness for social theory and research. I will question this characterisation of the status of Habermas's account of rationality later. For now, I will discuss the detailed development of the account itself.

Habermas begins his account with an analysis of the concept of rationality. For him, rationality can be predicated of both human beings and their symbolic expressions, and of both speech and action. The reason embodied in speech and action may be approached initially in terms of what Habermas calls 'cognitive–instrumental' rationality. He considers two paradigm cases of rationality from this perspective: (1) an assertion with which a speaker expresses a belief and (2) a goal-directed action with which a social actor pursues an end. Both (1) and (2) embody fallible knowlege and, thus, both can go wrong. Both (1) and (2) may be criticised in terms of the validity 'claims that the subjects necessarily attach to their expressions in so far as the latter are intended as assertions or as goal-directed actions'. In case (1), the speaker claims *truth* for his assertion. In case (2), the social actor claims prospects of success for his action or *effectiveness*. For Habermas, *truth* and *effectiveness* are internally related. *Truth* relates to the existence of states of affairs in the world, while *effectiveness* relates to interventions in the world through which states of affairs can be produced. In case (1), a speaker refers to something that occurs in the world through his assertion. In case (2), the social actor refers to something that should occur in the world through his purposive activity. In this way, both raise claims 'that can be criticised and argued for, that is, *grounded*'.[13] For Habermas, the possibility of grounding the claims raised (even if only implicitly) in the speech and the action is what constitutes their rationality. As he notes, this analysis suggest basing the rationality of speech and action on their ability to be criticised and grounded *in an objective way.* Such an objective evaluation is possible if it is undertaken on the basis of a transubjective validity claim that has the same meaning for observers and non-participants as it has for the acting subject himself'.[14] For Habermas, *truth* and efficiency (*effectiveness*) meet this condition.

The proposal to base the rationality of speech and action on the idea of criticisability and in terms of truth and efficiency, however, has two basic weaknesses according to Habermas. First, this characterisation 'does not capture important differentiations'. Secondly, 'it is too narrow, because we do not use the term 'rational' solely in connection with expressions that can be true or false, effective or ineffective'; instead, 'the rationality inherent in communicative practice extends over a broad spectrum'.[15] For Habermas, the cognitive–instrumental approach to rationality is proper but partial. Just as his concept of communicative action is intended to overcome a one-sided focus on instrumental action, so too the concept of communicative rationality is intended to overcome a one-sided focus on cognitive–instrumental rationality. The concept of communicative rationality is 'connected with ancient conceptions of logos' and 'carries with it connotations based ultimately on the central experience of the unconstrained, unifying, consensus-bringing force of argumentative speech, in which different participants overcome their merely subjective views and, owing to the mutuality of rationally motivated conviction, assure themselves of both the unity of the objective world and the intersubjectivity of their lifeworld'.[16] According to Habermas, such a conception comes into view against the background of the three 'worlds' that speakers are able to differentiate and co-ordinate in communicative action. Habermas states:

> Here we find the three dimensions contained in the concept of communicative rationality: first, the relation of the knowing subject to a world of events or facts; second, the relation to a social world of an acting, practical subject entwined in interaction with others; and finally, the relation of a suffering and passionate subject (in Feuerbach's sense) to its own internal nature, to its own subjectivity and the subjectivity of others.[17]

In each of these dimensions, validity claims are raised which are open to criticism and evaluation and which may be defended and rationally grounded. When challenged along any of these dimensions, speakers show their rationality to the extent that they are able to employ modes of 'argumentation' to support their claims. By 'argumentation' Habermas means that 'type of speech in which participants thematise contested validity claims and attempt to vindicate or criticise them through arguments'. An argument contains reasons or grounds that are connected in a systematic way with the validity claim of a problematic expression. The 'strength of an argument is measured. . . by the soundness of the reasons . . . whether or not an argument is able to convince the participants in a discourse . . . to motivate them to accept the validity claim in question'.[18] Habermas will use the term 'discourse' to apply 'only when the meaning of the problematic validity claim conceptually forces participants to suppose that a rationally motivated agreement could in principle be achieved . . . if only the argumentation could be conducted openly enough and continued long enough'. Habermas will use the term 'critique' to apply when the 'participants need not presuppose' that it must be possible in principle to bring about a consensus by means of grounds or reasons.[19] The concept of communicative rationality may be explicated formally in terms of the different modes of argumentation appropriate for evaluating the validity claims raised in connection with the three dimensions of communicative action: external nature, society, internal nature.

In communication directed at external nature (the cognitive–instrumental sphere), rationality consists in expressing grounded views and acting efficiently and includes the ability to learn from mistakes. The mode of argumentation proper to this dimension is *theoretical discourse* in which controversial truth claims are made thematic. In communication directed at society (the moral–practical sphere), rationality consists in justifying actions with reference to established norms, in acting prudently in situations of normative conflict, and in judging disputes from 'the moral point of view' oriented to consensus. The mode of argumentation proper to this dimension is *practical discourse* in which claims to normative rightness are thematised. In communication directed at internal nature (the evaluative and the expressive spheres), rationality consists in interpreting the nature of your own wants and needs (as well as those of others) in terms of culturally established standards of value, and even more so, in adopting a reflective attitude to the standards of value themselves. Here we cannot expect universal assent, so the mode of argumentation is not discourse but, prototypically, *aesthetic criticism* in which the adequacy of value standards is made thematic. For Habermas, the arguments reproduced in the psychoanalytic dialogue also belongs to this dimension (internal nature). In this context, rationality consists in being willing and able to free oneself from illusions due not to factual error, but to self-deception. The mode of argumentation here is *therapeutic critique* which serves to clarify systematic self-deception. Finally, in communication directed at language itself, rationality consists in overcoming disturbances to communication through a readiness to come to an understanding and reflection on linguistic rules. Both the comprehensibility of symbolic expressions and the meaning of these expressions may be reflectively examined. The mode of argumentation proper to this dimension is *explicative discourse* in which the comprehensibility and well-formedness of symbolic expression is no longer naively presupposed, but rather is explicitly thematised. Habermas's account yields the following schema:[20]

TYPES OF ARGUMENTATION

Modes of argumentation	*Problematic expressions*	*Controversial validity claims*
theoretical discourse	cognitive–instrumental	truth of propositions: efficacy of teleological actions
practical discourse	moral–practical	rightness of norms of action
aesthetic criticism	evaluative	adequacy of standards of value
therapeutic critique	expressive	truthfulness or sincerity of expressions
explicative discourse		comprehensibility or well-formedness of symbolic constructs

For Habermas, an adequate conceptual account of rationality cannot limit itself to a consideration of any one of these dimensions. A formal explication must be comprehensive enough to cover them all. On the other hand, he is not attempting a unified account of reason as in Hegel, but rather an account that seeks a harmony and balance between its separate spheres. As Habermas states, the question is whether individuals speak and act rationally *in general*,

> whether one may systematically expect that they have good reasons for their expressions and that these expressions are correct or successful in the cognitive dimension, reliable or insightful in the moral–practical dimension, discerning or illuminating in the evaluative dimension, or candid and self-critical in the expressive dimension; that they exhibit understanding in the hermeneutic dimension; or indeed whether they are 'reasonable' in all these dimensions. [21]

For Habermas, where we can see a systematic effect in all these respects and over a long period of time, we are entitled to speak of a rational 'conduct of life' (*Lebensfuhrung*). The socio-cultural conditions required for such a conduct of life reflect a rational 'form of life' (*Lebensform*). These latter questions of a rational conduct of life and a rational form of life cannot be addressed through a purely formal explication of the concept of rationality. To address these questions, Habermas must move from the formal account already discussed to an account of the social embodiment and historical development of rationality.

Habermas's social and developmental account of rationality attempts to show that the potentialities of communication elaborated in his formal account provide an interpretive guide which may be used to investigate the level of rationality (scientific, moral, aesthetic) achieved in different societies. The formal account of communicative rationality above relies 'on a preunderstanding anchored in modern orientations' of consciousness which implicitly attributes 'a claim to universality (to) our Occidental understanding of the world'. To evaluate the status of this latter claim requires moving from conceptual analysis to an anthropological and sociological perspective which addresses the question of a 'rational conduct of life' in an 'evolutionary perspective'. [22] From such a perspective, the claim to universality of the modern understanding of the world ('reconstructed' by Habermas in terms of the differentiation of theoretical, practical and aesthetic spheres of communication) may be more adequately evaluated. A discussion of the differences uncovered by anthropological investigation between 'mythical' and 'modern' worldviews initiates this second stage in Habermas's analysis of communicative rationality.

Using the work of Lévi-Strauss and Maurice Godelier, Habermas draws the contrast between 'mythical' and 'modern' worldviews as follows. He begins by arguing that 'the rationality of worldviews is not measured in terms of logical and semantic properties but in terms of formal–pragmatic basic concepts'.[23] Habermas draws the relevant contrasts in terms of these latter 'basic' concepts. First, the 'mythic' worldview reciprocally assimilates nature to culture and culture to nature. Secondly, the 'mythic' worldview fails to distinguish the social world, the external world and internal nature. Finally, the 'mythic' worldview fails to distinguish between language and world, between communication and what the communication is about. In contrast, these differentiations are constitutive of the 'modern' worldview. Any competent member of a modern society has the ability to make the relevant distinctions. Again, Habermas arrives at a concept of communicative rationality which characterises the modern understanding of the world. 'Of course', as Habermas realises, 'this does not yet prove that the supposed rationality expressed in our understanding of the world is more than a reflection of the particular features of a culture stamped by science, that it may rightfully raise a claim to universality.'[24] To address this question, Habermas turns to a consideration of the work of Peter Winch.

Habermas attempts to locate both the strengths and weaknesses in Winch's position. For Winch, 'each culture establishes in its language a relation to reality'.[25] 'True' and 'False', 'Real' and 'Unreal' may be concepts common to all languages, however, such conceptual distinctions are always drawn *within* a particular language system. Thus, to understand these concepts we must examine the use they have in a particular language system, and this means a particular culture and form of life. We cannot simply impose our standards of rationality on other cultures because both our standards and the standards of other cultures are based in particular language systems. There are no universal standards 'above' culture which can be appealed to in cases of conflict. Against this cultural relativism, Habermas argues that 'the context-dependence of the criteria by which the members of different cultures at different times judge differently the validity of expressions does not, however, mean that the ideas of truth, of normative rightness, of sincerity and of authenticity that underlie (only intuitively, to be sure) the choice of criteria are context-dependent in the same degree'.[26] Further, 'Whatever language system we choose, we always start intuitively from the presupposition that truth is a universal validity claim' which allows us to evaluate and understand other cultures 'from the standpoint of cognitive adequacy'.[27]

For Habermas, however, standards of rationality cannot be reduced to cognitive adequacy alone. The rationality of a worldview also depends upon its practical, aesthetic, expressive and, in general, meaning-conferring adequacy. From this perspective, Habermas maintains that Winch's argument is too weak to establish cultural relativism, but strong enough to warn us against imposing the scientific-technological rationality of our culture on others. Thus, Habermas uses Winch's argument to distinguish the 'universality' that 'gained expression in the modern understanding of the world' in the form of fundamental differentiations (that is, nature/culture, language/world, science/morality/art) from 'an uncritical self-interpretation of the modern world that is fixated on knowing and mastering external nature'. Habermas concludes: 'The modern understanding of the world is indeed based on general structures of rationality but . . . modern Western societies promote a distorted understanding of rationality which is fixed on cognitive–instrumental aspects and is to that extent particularistic'.[28]

As Habermas realises, the burden of proof is on the 'universalist' position to show that the rationality of the modern worldview is, in some sense, an advance over the mythic and the traditional worldviews. The 'universalist' must be able to trace, at least in broad outline, the systematic changes in worldviews in terms of an 'internally reconstructable growth of knowledge'. Thus, 'the universalistic position forces one to the assumption that the rationalisation of worldviews takes place through learning processes'.[29] Habermas attempts to clarify and support his position through a discussion of Piaget's evolutionary concept of learning. With Piaget, Habermas wants to distinguish between the learning of new *content* and higher levels of the *capacity* to learn. It is the latter that the 'universalist' must be able to 'internally reconstruct' without prejudicing the question of the actual *dynamics* of development and without assuming that such development is either *continuous* or *linear*. After making these conceptual clarifications, Habermas turns to Piaget's substantive thesis that higher levels of the cognitive development of individuals 'signifies in general the decentration of an egocentrically distorted understanding of the world'. 'Decentration' is understood by Paiget in terms of the child's ability to construct 'a reference system for the simultaneous demarcation of the objective and social worlds from the subjective world'.[30]

Extending Piaget's notion of 'decentration' from an individual to a social level, Habermas finds support for his concept of communicative rationality in terms of the growing rationalisation of worldviews. According to Habermas, Piaget himself suggests such an extension by: (i) regarding the development of intelligence as only one dimension of the process of decentration; (ii) understanding all transitions as progressive steps in decentration; and (iii) viewing the egocentric perspective of the child as a model for mythical thought. Worldviews represent a cultural store of knowledge that support cognition and action-orientations. If worldviews are not actualised by subjects in everyday interpretations, traditions break down. For Habermas, cultural tradition and its interpretive continuation cannot be adequately expessed in mythical, religious or metaphysical worldviews because the fundamental demarcations which allow for a critical and reflective appropriation of the past are missing. Only with the reflective concept of 'world' and the modern demarcation between external nature, society and internal nature can a truly critical appropriation of cultural tradition become possible. Access to the world can now be achieved through common interpretive efforts in which social actors can co-operatively and reflectively negotiate situation definitions capable of intersubjective recognition. Here the concept of the 'three worlds' serves 'as the commonly supposed system of co-ordinates' in which social actors can develop a definition of their situation 'ordered in such a way that agreement will be reached about what the participants may treat as a fact, or as a valid norm, or as a subjective experience'.[31]

At this point, Habermas introduces the concept of the 'lifeworld' (*Lebenswelt*). In the first place, Habermas defines the lifeworld as the context for language 'which stands behind the back of each participant in communication' and supports 'the process of understanding'. Every actual consensus is achieved against this 'uniquely pre-reflective form of background relations'. The lifeworld is a resource for what goes into explicit communication which can become subject to criticism. The lifeworld itself, however, always remains implicit, pre-reflexive and pre-critical. Its characteristics are 'certainty, background character, impossibility of being gone behind'.[32] This usage is close to Husserl's. Habermas, however, uses and extends the concept in other ways. As the unexceedable context for co-ordinating the three 'worlds', the lifeworld supports social collectives and cultural groups by providing a resource of meaning and situation definitions that are drawn upon for social reproduction. Thus, for Habermas, the lifeworld is crucial for the reproduction of culture, society and personality in so far as it is the carrier of personal, social and cultural tradition.

From this perspective, the lifeworld may be contrasted with the concept of 'system'. Social systems (particularly subsystems such as the economy and the state) follow functional imperatives and serve as 'formally organised systems of action based on media steering' (money and power).[33] The lifeworld is viewed in terms of communciative action, while social systems are viewed in terms of instrumental action. For Habermas, modern societies may be viewed developmentally from both of these perspectives. Mythical and, to a lesser extent, traditional societies rest upon an uncritical acceptance of meanings taken over from the lifeworld. Their worldviews are 'reified as the world order and cannot be seen as an interpretive system open to criticism'. Within such societies, 'actions cannot reach that critical zone in which communicatively achieved agreement depends upon autonomous yes/no responses to criticisable validity claims'. A 'rational conduct of life' is made possible to the extent that cultural tradition, as carried by lifeworld structures, allows for: (i) the articulation of the three formal 'world' concepts; (ii) a reflective attitude towards itself; (iii) a differentiation of cognitive, moral, evaluative and expressive components and institutionalisation of specialised forms of argumentation for each; and (iv) an at least partial uncoupling of the lifeworld and social system which allows systems of purposive–rational action to be institutionalised as 'rational' economics and administration.[34] Modern society is marked by this 'rationalisation of the lifeworld' and by the growing 'differentiation' of social systems. These last considerations lead back, for Habermas, to Weber's theory of social rationalisation.

By using Piaget's notion of 'decentration' as a guide, Habermas thus extends his concept of communicative rationality to cover the question of a rational conduct of life. Such an extension 'relates a decentered understanding of the world to the possibility of discursively redeeming criticisable validity claims'.[35] Habermas's defence of modernity rests upon the extent to which it allows crucial differentiations of validity claims, spheres of value and the institutionalisation of appropriate forms of argumentation for each, as well as the higher degree to which the lifeworld has been uncoupled from systems of purposive–rational action to allow for criticism and reflection on what was formerly simply taken for granted. For Habermas, it is not simply the scientific–technical superiority of modern society, but rather its 'decentered' worldview which, by allowing for the above differentiations, mark it as an advance in the level of learning of the species. This 'advance' is, however, 'accompanied by the shadow of systematic error' precisely to the degree that modernity becomes fixated upon science and technology and thus exludes 'the social and subjective worlds from the domains of rationally motivated agreement'.[36] Habermas wants to distinguish the 'advance' represented by modernity from its deformations. This leads him to address the problem of 'social rationalisation' (that is, the process through which rationality comes to be embodied in society) in the transition from traditional to modern society.

Habermas's concept of communicative rationality is developed above: (i) in terms of a conceptual analysis of rationality; (ii) in confrontation with the relativistic position worked out in the rationality debate in analytic philosophy; (iii) through a review of the empirical argumentation of Lévi-Strauss and Piaget. All this, however, is still inadequate for the development of a comprehensive concept of rationality that can meet the relativist challenge without recourse to traditional philosophy. Habermas must also address the central problem of social rationalisation raised in the development of the problematic of rationality (discussed in Chapter 2). Thus, much of *The Theory of Communicative Action* is concerned with the transition from traditional to modern society as theorised by Marx, Weber, Lukács, Adorno and Horkheimer. Here Habermas connects his recent work to his earlier concerns by addressing the problem of the 'normative foundations' of critical theory at this fundamental level. For Habermas, the approach to the concept of communicative rationality through social theory is essential both to meet the relativistic challenge and to rehabilitate a critical theory of society drawing upon Marx and the Frankfurt School. Such an approach has a further significance for Habermas in that it allows him, in Hegelian fashion, to appropriate past achievements and reformulate them at a higher theoretical level. I will complete my account of Habermas's concept of communicative rationality by briefly discussing this appropriation and critique of the classical tradition of social theory, in its attempt to come to grips with the problematic of rationality and modernity.

Max Weber's work is the central critical focus for Habermas's interpretation and critique of the tradition of social theory, as well as contemporary social theory. Weber is central to Habermas's argument for three reasons: (i) Weber was the first social theorist to conceive the modernisation of traditional society as the result of a universal–historical process of rationalisation without relying on the premises of the philosophy of history (Hegel); (ii) Weber was the source out of which the best modern theoretical Marxism developed (Lukács, Horkheimer, Adorno, Marcuse); and (iii) Weber's theory of rationality is the focal point from which an alternative theory of modernity and social rationalisation can be developed. Habermas reads Weber in the context of the Marxist tradition and the Marxist tradition in the context of Weber, a reading within a reading. Habermas sketches the broad·outlines of his reading as follows:

> According to Marx, the rationalisation of society takes place directly in the development of productive forces, that is, in the expansion of empirical knowledge, the improvement of production techniques, and the increasingly effective mobilisation, qualification, and organisation of socially useful labour power. On the other hand, relations of production, the institutions that express the distribution of social power and regulate a differential access to the means of production, are revolutionised only under the pressure of rationalisation of productive forces. Max Weber views the institutional framework of the capitalist economy and the modern state in a different way – not as relations of production that fetter the potential for rationalisation, but as subsystems of purposive–rational action in which Occidental rationalism develops at a societal level. Of course, he is afraid that bureaucratisation will lead to a reification of social relationships, which will stifle

motivational incentive to a rational conduct of life. Horkheimer and Adorno, and later Marcuse, interpret Marx in this Weberian perspective. Under the sign of an instrumental rationality that has become autonomous, the rationality of mastering nature merges with the irrationality of class domination. Fettered forces of production stabilise alienated relations of production. The *Dialectic of Enlightenment* removes the ambivalence that Weber still entertained in relation to rationalisation processes, and it abruptly reverses Marx's positive assessment. Science and technology – for Marx an unambiguously emancipatory potential – themselves become the medium of social repression.[37]

Habermas begins by locating a basic weakness shared by all three of the above positions. First, Marx, Weber, Horkheimer and Adorno identify social rationalisation with the expansion of instrumental rationality. Secondly, they all share a 'vague' notion of a more comprehensive social rationality; Marx in 'the concept of an association of free producers', Weber in 'the historical model of an ethically rational conduct of life' and Adorno and Horkheimer in 'the idea of fraternal relations with a resurrected nature'.[38] Against this second, vague but more comprehensive notion of rationality, each measures the relative position of the empirical processes of social rationalisation examined in terms of the first concept. The weakness is that this more comprehensive concept of rationality is not developed and justified at the same level as 'forces of production', 'subsystems of purposive–rational action' or 'totalitarian carriers of instrumental reason'. The theory of communicative rationality is designed by Habermas precisely to overcome this weakness.

Habermas next locates specific strengths and weaknesses in each of the above positions using Weber as a starting point. On the positive side, Weber freed the analysis of social rationalisation from the presuppositions of both 'the philosophy of history' (Hegel) and 'the philosophy of consciousness' (the philosophical development from Descartes through Hegel centring on the acts and achievements of the conscious, knowing subject in relation to the object to be known). Weber also developed a concept of modernity based on a fundamental differentiation of value spheres. For Habermas, however, *Weber's error is to conceive the function, scope and goal of reason too narrowly.* Capitalist rationalisation introduced a selectivity favouring only the technical and instrumental use of reason which Weber did not adequately grasp. He did not see that capitalist development repressed the practical and ethical dimension of rationality that he himself analysed in terms of an 'ethics of brotherhood'. According to Habermas, these potentials of social rationalisation, embodied in the ethical and aesthetic value spheres excluded by capitalist development, point beyond Weber's pessimistic interpretation of the rise of scientific–technical rationality (formal rationality) as fating modern humans to live in an 'iron cage'.

For Habermas, the best theoretical Marxism from Lukács through the Frankfurt School took its point of departure from Weber's theory of social rationalisation. On Habermas's reading, Lukács' attempt to reconstruct Marx by extending the notion of commodity fetishism to the concept of the reification of bourgeois consciousness is based on the Weberian view that the dominant form of rationality in capitalist society is purposive (formal) rationality, which leads to an inevitable loss of meaning and freedom. Lukács criticised this process in terms drawn from Hegel and the philosophy of consciousness such as 'totality' and 'history as the realisation of reason'. Lukács opposed 'objective reason' (*Vernunft*) to the merely 'subjective reason' (*Verstand*) that dominate consciousness in capitalist society. For Habermas, Lukács' reconstruction of Marx actually fell behind the theoretical level achieved by Marx himself by returning to a reliance on classical German idealism and its speculative philosophy of history.

On Habermas's reading, Lukács' use of Weber's theory paved the way for Horkheimer and Adorno to replace purposive (formal) rationality with the concept of instrumental reason. Unlke Horkheimer's interdisciplinary 'materialism' of the 1930s, the work of Adorno and Horkheimer in the 1940s (in particular, *Dialectic of Enlightenment*) undertook a critical–revolutionary interpretation of philosophy and the whole of Western rationality. They located Lukács reification not simply in capitalist processes of rationalisation, but at the level of the history of the human species. For Habermas, this led them to devalue the special sciences and to postulate an unsupportable emancipatory role for nature. Further, Habermas maintains that their critical–revolutionary interpretation of philosophy is caught in the following dilemma: they must deal with the great tradition of philosophy to draw on its critical concept of reason, and yet their own interpretation of the history of the species reveals reason itself to be ideological. The irony, according to Habermas, is that they remain trapped by the problems of the philosophy of consciousness while rejecting it. In this subtle form, they too fell victim to the Weberian error of conceiving reason too narrowly.

In spite of the fact that Habermas attempts to reformulate the tradition of critical social theory stemming from Marx and the Frankfurt School, his account of that tradition in *The Theory of Communicative Action* is extremely critical (as the above suggests). This is particularly evident as Habermas returns once again to the critique of Marx. He argues that Marx is able, in *Capital*, to develop his scientific analysis of the law-like regularities of the capitalist economic system as, at the same time, a critique of bourgeois ideology because of the central role of the theory of value. For Habermas, the theory of value allows Marx 'to translate politico-economic statements concerning anonymous functional inter-connections of the economic cycle' (the systems level) which 'uncon-sciously penetrate and steer the action orientations of participants' into 'sociological–historical statements concerning the action contexts of which actors are intuitively aware' (the action level). This allows Marx to 'inconspicuously . . . implant the normative core of rational natural law, that is, the idea that things would go well in bourgeois society only so long as the equivalents exchanged represented not merely what was alleged to be equivalent, but what was in fact – according to the standard of the labour power expended – equivalent'.[39] Thus, for Habermas, Marx's analysis of capitalism understood as a science *and* as critique depends upon the labour theory of value.

Habermas discusses three weaknesses connected with the theory of value. First, by concentrating on the theory of value, Marx tends to see capitalism as a mystified totality of class relations. For Habermas, this model is too simple. It is unable to clarify the crucial distinctions between traditional and modern forms of life experiences. Further, this model lacks an adequate distinction between normal processes of identity formation and forms of alienation. In short, Marx's theory of crisis and his class analysis needs reformulation. Secondly, the centrality of the theory of value for Marx leads him to attempt to analyse the lifeworld under categories appropriate to system imperatives. Just as Habermas earlier criticised Marx for reducing interaction to labour, so Habermas now criticises Marx for understanding communicative action arising from the lifeworld exclusively in terms of systems functioning and purposive–rational (instrumental) action. The failure, in Habermas's view, of the theory of value leaves Marx with no explanation of revolutionary class consciousness or communicative action orientations in general. Such an explanation can be provided only if the two levels of analysis (action and system) are clearly distinguished. Thirdly, Habermas charges Marx with mixing the normative and descriptive dimension by following too closely in the footsteps of Hegel's philosophy of history. As Habermas states:

> Assumptions about a dialectical relation between productive forces and productive relations are pseudonormative statements about an objective teleology of history . . . This mixing of descriptive and normative contents was present in the basic concepts of historical materialism.[40]

For Habermas, the practical intentions of Marx's theory can be saved without confusing action and system or fact and value. But this will require a clean break with the 'historico-philosophical' presuppositions Marx took over from the philosophy of consciousness and within which the Frankfurt School theorists of the first generation remained trapped. It will require a turn from the inflated expectations of the philosophy of consciousness to the more modest claims of the philosophy of language. In this regard, Habermas views his own project of taking critical theory on the 'linguistic turn' as an attempt 'to free historical materialism from its historico-philosophical ballast'.[41]

Habermas's own theory of social rationalisation and modernity attempts to build on the great tradition of social theory without succumbing to the weaknesses criticised above. His basic strategy is to relocate what I have called the problematic of rationality in the sphere of communicative action, rather than in the historical development of Western consciousness. For Habermas, the limitation of a theory of social rationalisation to the emergence of scientific–technical, instrumental reason (understood as determined by advances in productive forces or in subsystems of purposive–rational action) is the common failure of the classical tradition of social theory. Although such analyses presupposed broader concepts of social rationality, they failed to develop them adequately. But the Marxian and Weberian insights into this process need not be totally rejected if they can be reconstructed in a more comprehensive and adequate framework. To supply the bridge towards such a framework, Habermas turns to the work of Mead and Durkheim in order to comprehend social rationalisation not only in terms of scientific-technical rationalisation, but also in terms of processes of moral–practical rationalisation.

Habermas uses an interpretation of Mead's theory of symbolically mediated interaction to support his own account (discussed above) of communicative action as normative behaviour, which depends upon a collective and linguistic context of social interaction distinguishable from contexts of purposive–rational action. Through this reading of Mead, Habermas wants to show that the American pragmatist tradition already contained an account of the social origin and collective nature of the competence for normative behaviour. Habermas uses an interpretation of Durkheim's theory of the sacred and the process of the secularisation of religious norms to take an evolutionary perspective on the development of this social and normative dimension. Through this reading of Durkheim, Habermas wants to show how the transformation from traditional to modern society involved a progressive secularisation of normatively regulated behaviour reconstructed in his own account of communicative action. Taken together, these two readings provide support for what Rasmussen calls 'a kind of double-edged theory of ethical behaviour, evolutionary and procedural'.[42]

Habermas makes use of his interpretations of Mead and Durkheim to add another dimension to his concept of the lifeworld. For Habermas, the lifeworld may be viewed as a collective linguistic context analogous to Durkheim's collective consciousness in which the socially constructed self (Mead) achieves its identity. What Habermas calls the progressive 'rationalisation of the lifeworld' can now be viewed, initially at least, as a normal process in which the material reproduction of the human species takes place at the level of culture, society and personality. These last three 'components of the lifeworld' that depend upon communicative action can be correlated with the reproduction process as in the following schema:[43]

1. Contributions of reproduction processes to maintaining the structural components of the lifeworld:

STRUCTURAL COMPONENTS

Reproduction processes	*Culture*	*Society*	*Personality*
Cultural reproduction	Interpretation schemata susceptible to consensus ('valid knowledge')	Legitimations	Behavioural patterns influential in self-formation, educational goals
Social integration	Obligations	Legitimately ordered interpersonal relations	Social memberships
Socialisation	Interpretive Accomplishments	Motivations for norm-conformative action	Capability for interaction ('personal identity')

These individual reproduction processes, for Habermas, can be evaluated 'according to standards of the rationality of knowledge, the solidarity of members, and the responsibility of the adult personality'.[44] Such standards, of course, vary within each domain according to the degree of what Habermas calls the 'structural differentiation of the lifeworld' (that is, the degree to which it has been 'rationalised'). The extent to which social actors require consensual knowledge, legitimate orders and personal autonomy is dependent upon the level of 'rationalisation' achieved in each of the above domains. Disturbances to the material reproduction of society from this lifeworld perspective manifest themselves in the domains of culture, society and personality as a loss of meaning, anomie or psychopathologies. For each domain there are corresponding withdrawal phenomena. Habermas summarises in the following schema:[45]

2. *Crisis phenomena connected with disturbances in reproduction:*

STRUCTURAL COMPONENTS

Disturbances in the domain of	*Culture*	*Society*	*Personality*	*Evaluative dimension*
Cultural reproduction	Loss of meaning	Withdrawal of legitimation	Crisis in orientation and education	Rationality of knowledge
Social integration	Insecurity of collective identity	Anomie	Alienation	Solidarity of members
Socialisation	Breakdown of tradition	Withdrawal of motivation	Psycho-pathologies	Account-ability of the person

In Habermas's extended sense, the lifeworld is at once a linguistic–phenomenological concept, a concept useful for the description of social evolution and a critical or normative concept. For Habermas, the 'rationalisation of the lifeworld' which is characteristic of modernity (that is, the differentiation of value spheres, the secularisation of norms, the institutionalisation of argumentation and so on) is a 'normal' function of the material reproduction of society. It may even be viewed as 'progressive' to the extent that the structural components of the lifeworld are maintained (see schema 1) in the process of social rationalisation. For Habermas, however, the rationalisation of the lifeworld in the transition from traditional to modern societies has also generated disturbances and crises (see schema 2). To explicate Habermas's view of social rationalisation as being both potentially 'progressive' and yet crisis ridden, it will be necessary to return to his distinction between lifeworld and social system.

Habermas's distinction here may be viewed as an attempt to reformulate Marx's distinction between base and superstructure in a more complex and adequate way.[46] From another perspective, it represents an extended application of concepts borrowed from two debate opponents, the concept of lifeworld drawn from the debate with Gadamer and the concept of system drawn from the debate with Luhmann. Habermas 'sharply distinguishes between the more or less differentiated or 'rationalised' lifeworlds that are reproduced by way of communicative action and, on the other hand, formally organised systems of action based on media steering' such as money (the economic subsystem) and power (the administrative, or state, subsystem) reproduced by way of purposive–rational action.[47] In modern societies in particular, two subsystems have been differentiated through the media of money and power, namely the capitalistic economic system and a 'rationalised' (in Weber's sense of formal rationality) state administration. Each forms a complementary environment for the other, and each is involved in processes of exchange with its environment through its medium. With the transition to the capitalist mode of production and the modern state, 'the material substratum of the lifeworld can be analysed from the standpoint of an action system that is stabilised through functional interconnections and has become independent in relation to the lifeworld'.[48] Following his earlier theory of crisis (*Legitimation Crisis*, 1973), Habermas traces 'economic crisis' and 'rationality crisis' to deficits in the production of economic values and legitimate decisions respectively (see my discussion above). Habermas, however, significantly reformulates his earlier account of 'motivation crisis' and 'legitimation crisis' and contrasts both with what he calls the 'colonisation of the lifeworld'.[49] This latter concept represents an attempt to reformulate earlier concepts of the tradition of critical social theory such as 'fetishism' and 'reification'.

For Habermas, the economic and the administrative systems are anchored in the lifeworld, just as, for Marx, the superstructure is 'anchored' in the base. The fundamental difference (one to which I will return) is that, for Marx, the base is to be understood in terms of the 'paradigm of production' (that is, forces and relations of production) while, for Habermas, the lifeworld is to be understood in terms of communication. On this latter account, the institutionalisation of the money and power media anchor the economic and administrative systems of action in the lifeworld. This connects the lifeworld with the functional system imperatives of the economy and state administration through private households (the family) and the legal system respectively. Thus, the symbolically structured lifeworld is subject to 'the limitations of material production within the framework of existing productive relations'. On the other hand, the economy (and its occupational system) and the state (and its administrative system of domination) are 'dependent on accomplishments of the symbolic reproduction of the lifeworld, namely on individual skills and motivations, as well as on mass loyalty'.[50] Marx's distinction may be (and has been) misunderstood as involving a strict 'determinism' where the base (economic 'reality') determines the superstructure (political, social and cultural formations; the sphere of 'ideology'). In contrast, Habermas's distinction involves a thoroughly interactive view of the relation between lifeworld and social system. For Habermas, the lifeworld depends upon the social system, both in terms of material production (the economy) and organisation (the state). The social system depends upon the lifeworld for both the reproduction of socialised individuals and the continuation of coherent cultural traditions. They are thus interdependent and interact in complex ways in the course of social development.

In the interaction between lifeworld and system, disturbances to the process of social rationalisation develop which may be characterised as disequilibriums or pathologies. The central such disturbance with which Habermas is concerned is what he calls the 'colonisation of the lifeworld'. Habermas makes a distinction (not present in *Legitimation Crisis*) between disturbances or crises that inflexible structures of the lifeworld (that is, those structures which absolutely depend on communicative action and consensus) can give rise to in maintaining the economic and political systems, and disturbances or crises that manifest themselves in the reproduction of the lifeworld itself. Although the two are empirically connected and interact with each other in actual cases, Habermas argues for an analytical separation between: (i) the withdrawal of motivation affecting the occupational system ('motivation crisis') and the withdrawal of legitimation affecting the system of administrative domination ('legitimation crisis'), and (ii) the colonisation of the lifeworld that is manifested in loss of meaning, anomie and psychopathologies. These latter disturbances or crises appear in modern societies 'as the destruction of traditional forms of life, as attacks on the communicative infrastructure of lifeworlds, as the rigidity of a one-sidedly rationalised everyday practice' which is expressed in 'impoverished cultural traditions and disturbed socialisation processes'.[51]

In order to examine the dynamics of the 'colonisation' process, Habermas turns to Marx's analysis of the dual character of labour in capitalist society. Considered concretely, labour is a human activity that belongs to the lifeworld of the labourer. Considered abstractly, labour is a function organised by the imperative of capital realisation that belongs to the economic system. The institutionalisation of the wage-labour relation which turns labour power into a commodity neutralises the lifeworld context of labour as a human activity, and thus renders it abstract. For Habermas, this 'real abstraction' analysed by Marx is a central but restricted case of the more general 'colonisation' phenomenon – the subordination of the lifeworld to systems imperatives. Habermas's model of the economy and state as two subsystems based on the media of money and power interacting with (and 'colonising') the lifeworld is designed to overcome the limitations of the restricted focus of orthodox Marxism on the economy and economic crises. In particular, Habermas believes his model is better able to account for important features of advanced capitalism such as the social welfare state, mass democracy and consumerism. According to Habermas, advanced capitalism has 'tamed' class struggle and 'pacified' the political realm. The cost of this 'taming' and 'pacificiation', however, has been the reduction of the role of citizen as active political participant to the role of client of the state and the role of active producer to passive consumer. The imposition of these abstract roles of client and consumer through system imperatives reaches its limit when it blocks the lifeworld processes of socialisation necessary for the reproduction of the system itself. Viewed in this way, Habermas's concept of 'colonisation' is an attempt to reformulate the earlier concepts of the tradition of critical social theory such as 'fetishism' and 'reification' in a broader framework that more adequately accounts for both the stability of advanced capitalism and the limits of that stability.

Habermas's account of social rationalisation developed in terms of the lifeworld and system distinction may now be summarised as follows. Social development takes place (in particular, the transformation from traditional to modern society) as a process of progressive differentiation and rationalisation. For Habermas, this means that the social system becomes ever more differentiated and complex, while the lifeworld becomes ever more rationalised. The growing complexity of the social system gives impetus to the rationalisation process of the lifeworld. New systems developments present new life possibilities. From this model, a complex theory of modernity can be outlined. The lifeworld, as a shared communicative context and as a carrier of tradition, makes possible the material reproduction of culture, society and personality. The differentiation of value spheres (science, morality, art) characteristic of modernity may be viewed as a normal, and even progressive, rationalisation of the lifeworld. This is the positive aspect of social rationalisation for Habermas because, to the extent that this process functions normally, it allows for a critical appropriation of tradition, argumentation and consensus. It also allows for the objective possibility of forming a more 'rational' (in the sense spelled out procedurally in the theory of communicative rationality above) political will, a more 'rational' conduct of life based on free and equal discussion and not on force. Thus, the rationalisation of the lifeworld as an expression of the growth of communicative rationality, and of the increase in the scope of communicative action, is the bright side of modernity. For Habermas, this is equally obscured by Marx, Weber, Lukács and the Frankfurt School through their emphasis on the complete triumph of purposive–rational action and (formal) instrumental reason, in spite of the different ways they interpret this 'triumph'.

Habermas, however, sees the dark side of modernity as well. Under the selective pressure of the system imperatives of capitalist modernisation, social rationalisation did in fact take place in a one-sided, distorted and crisis-ridden way. The capitalist economy and the modern administrative state privileged the value sphere of science for its functions of power and control, and thus they one-sidely imposed the hegemony of scientific–technological rationality over the other value spheres. This obscured the scope, role and goal of the more comprehensive concept of communicative rationality. For Habermas this process of rationalising the lifeworld under system imperatives crosses a crucial threshold when inherently communicative lifeworld structures are damaged. These communicative structures represent areas of life necessary for the material reproduction of social life such as cultural reproduction, social integration and the formation of the autonomous person through socialisation. These areas of life simply cannot be turned over to functional system imperatives and purposive–rational action without severe crises and disturbances. Primary among these are the loss of meaning, anomie and personality disorders which Habermas associates with the 'colonisation of the lifeworld'; although his framework is broad and complex enough to take into account other forms of crisis that distort modern society.

Finally, for Habermas, social rationality cannot be identified with a unified reason as in Hegel, or with the fate of a social class as in Marx. Instead, social rationality can only be understood as a balance and harmony between the various dimensions of rationality (scientific, moral, aesthetic). This latter idea, which Habermas spells out in terms of communicative rationality centred in the lifeworld, becomes the normative foundation necessary for the critique of the one-sided rationality of capitalist society. This criticism is balanced by Habermas's argument for the undeniable gains in the potential for human enlightenment that came with the rise of modern society. Perhaps the most important contribution of Habermas's theory of rationality is this defence of enlightenment based on an 'enlightened suspicion of enlightenment'.[52] Finally, Habermas's reconstruction of the foundations of critical social theory are provided by a theory of rationality developed at several levels: (i) a conceptual account of rationality; (ii) an empirically relevant account of the difference between traditional and modern forms of social rationality; (iii) a reconstructive account of the development of rational competencies; and (iv) an account of processes of social rationalisation developed in connection with the tradition of social theory from Weber and Marx through the Frankfurt School to Mead and Durkheim.

In *The Theory of Communicative Action*, Habermas also makes a brief and tentative attempt to address the second fundamental problem for a critical social theory, namely the relationship between the theory and the practice it hopes to engender. This problem of agency (that is, what actual social agents can realise the emancipatory–critical goals of the theory?) derives from the 'practical intentions' of the theory, intentions Habermas still refuses to relinquish completely. Thus, Habermas attempts to apply his latest reformulation of critical theory to the political struggles of today. He states:

> Today economic as well as administrative imperatives are encroaching upon territory that the lifeworld can no longer relinquish. . .it seems that the system's imperatives are attending areas of action which are demonstrably unable to perform their own tasks if they are removed from communicatively structured areas of action. This involves tasks such as cultural reproduction, social integration and socialisation.
>
> The battle lines between lifeworld and system thereby achieve a new relevance. Today economic and amdinistrative imperatives

embodied in the media of money and power encroach on areas that somehow collapse as soon as they are broken off from communication–oriented action and transferred to such interactions as are manipulated by these media. These are processes that no longer fit into the scheme of class analysis. But one can demonstrate a functional connection between the central conflicts of the lifeworld and the requirements of capitalist modernisation. I have shown this with examples from social, educational and family policy and also to a degree from the new protest movements.[53]

The new protest movements have a special significance for Habermas in regard to the problem of agency. The last chapter of *The Theory of Communicative Action* returns to this problem by attempting (in a tentative way and cautiously) to connect these movements to the crises located by the theory as well as to the emancipatory goal of the theory. Habermas argues that the nature of social conflict in advanced capitalist societies has changed in the last ten to twenty years. Conflict no longer centres on distribution, it is no longer channelled through official parties and organisations, and it cannot be resolved by compensations that conform to the system. The 'new conflicts arise in areas of cultural reproduction, social integration, and socialisation' and are 'manifested in sub-institutional, extra-parliamentary forms of protests'. These protests are directed at the question of how 'to defend or reinstate endangered life styles, or how to put reformed life styles into practice'. Thus, 'the new conflicts are not sparked by problems of distribution, but concern the grammar of forms of life'.[54] Unlike the 'old politics' which centres on questions of economic, social, domestic and military security, the 'new politics' centres on questions of equality, individual self-realisation, the quality of life, participation and human rights. For Habermas, the 'old politics' is supported by entrepreneurs, workers and the professional middle class, while the 'new politics' is supported by the new middle class, the young and those groups with higher levels of formal education. Habermas sees his theory as directed at the social movements associated with the new politics.

According to Habermas, there is a line of conflict between those social 'strata *directly* involved in the production process and interested in maintaining capital growth' and groups at the periphery. In advanced capitalist societies, it is the latter groups that are more sensitive to the self-destructive consequences of uncontrolled growth and technical–instrumental domination. These groups are the peace movement, the anti-nuclear and environmental movement, minority liberation movements, the movement for alternative lifestyles, the tax protest movement, religious fundamentalist protest groups and, finally, the women's movement. Habermas argues that these basically heterogenous movements are united in at least one respect, they all 'can be understood as resistance to tendencies to colonise the lifeworld'.[55] Of course, Habermas recognises that not all these groups are progressive or contain emancipatory potential. He distinguishes between those that take an 'offensive' posture which supports new forms of social life, co-operation and community and those that take a 'defensive' posture which supports traditional forms of life and property relations. Among the progressive, 'offensive' movements, Habermas distinguishes between those that remain at the level of particularistic demands and those that seek fundamental social change from a universalistic viewpoint. For Habermas, at the present time only the women's movement belongs to this latter category to the extent that it seeks not only a formal equality, but also a fundamental change in the social structure and in real concrete life situation.[56] Habermas sees the 'practical intentions' of a reformulated critical theory in terms of encouraging an 'offensive' and universalistic posture on the part of these heterogenous groups, as well as an aid in focusing the struggle against a one-sided capitalist rationality that denies the possibility of constructing a society of undistorted communication and free and equal participation.

In conclusion, *The Theory of Communicative Action* represents Habermas's mature reformulation of critical theory. This provides a sophisticated response to the problem of normative foundations by directly engaging what I have called the problematic of rationality. Further, by moving the focus of critical theory from production to communication, Habermas also attempts to re-establish a connection (however tentative) between the theory and actual social struggle in a new way. After placing Habermas's latest work in a theoretical and political context, I will turn to a critique of Habermas's theory intended to expose its limitations and highlight its strengths. I will then conclude by discussing the theoretical and practical prospects of critical social theory.

5

Habermas and the Prospects of Critical Theory

'Reason has always existed, only not always in reasonable form.' — Karl Marx

'Present talk of inadequate conditions is a cover for tolerance of repression. For the revolutionary, conditions have always appeared right. What appears in retrospect as a preliminary state or a premature situation was once, for the revolutionary, a last chance to change. A revolutionary is with the desperate people for whom everything is on the line, not with those that have time . . . Critical theory . . . rejects the kind of knowledge that one can bank on. It confronts history with that possibility which is always concretely visible within it . . . [Humanity] is not betrayed by the untimely attempts of the revolutionaries but by the timely attempts of the realists.' — Max Horkheimer

The account of Habermas's communication theory developed in Chapters 3 and 4 follows the various stages of his attempt to answer the two fundamental problems faced by the critical theory of society: the problem of normative foundations and the problem of the relation of theory to practice. These two problems arose in the context of what I have called the problematic of rationality outlined in Chapter 2. This problematic centres on the relationship between the concept of reason and the actual socially and historically embodied rationality characteristic of capitalist society. Habermas addresses this relationship directly in *The Theory of Communicative Action*. The basic strategy Habermas adopts in the name of a reconstruction of critical social theory is to move the problematic of rationality from the context of Marx's paradigm of production to the context of the paradigm of communication. Harbermas argues that the development of the problematic of rationality from Marx through Lukács to the Frankfurt School, which I discussed in Chapter 2, remains within the confines of what he calls 'the philosophy of consciousness'. He attempts to show how each of the above theorists relies, either implicitly or explicitly, on a philosophical concept of substantive reason, which includes the ideas of autonomy and freedom, for the norms in terms of which they are able to criticise the actual losses of autonomy and freedom entailed by the empirical and historical processes of capitalist rationalisation. For Habermas, however, the concept of substantive reason, and the philosophy of consciousness to which it belongs, can no longer be defended. Critical social theory can no longer draw on this source for normative support. Consequently, he argues for a turn in critical social theory from the philosophy of consciousness to the philosophy of language which corresponds to the 'linguistic turn' taken by contemporary philosophy.

In the first four chapters, I have attempted to do justice to the importance, the complexity and the plausibility of Habermas's project. As I argued in Chapter 1, an adequate criticism of Habermas requires such a full account in order to provide the framework for questioning the fundamental claims of what is perhaps the most discussed attempt to rehabilitate a critical social theory with ties to Marx. In this final chapter, I will develop a critique of the decisive paradigm shift in critical social theory from production to communication attempted by Habermas. I consider this critique, and the re-evaluation of the problems of normative foundations and the relation of theory to practice which it will entail, as the decisive level at which to confront Habermas's work. Thus, my critique will bypass many problems of detail involving Habermas's interpretation of the theories of other thinkers, as well as the use he makes of them. I will also bypass Habermas's various 'research programmes' where only empirical investigation can finally decide their usefulness and adequacy. I will focus instead on concepts such as the ideal speech situation, communicative action and communicative rationality which serve to guide and connect the various 'research programmes' and which are constitutive of Habermas's paradigm of communication. Further, my critique will include at least an indication of an alternative approach to radical theory based, or so I will argue, more closely on Marx. Finally, I will discuss the question of the possibility of critical social theory and, most importantly, its practical and political prospects.

Before developing my criticism of Habermas, I would like to indicate some strengths of his work that highlight what I take to be its importance. From his earliest essays to his latest work, Habermas has been engaged in a crucial attempt to salvage the potential for human liberation remaining in the Marxist tradition in the face of the widely recognised 'crisis of Marxism'.[1] This crisis is generated by failed predictions, disappointed expectations, theoretical uncertainties and interminable inter-Marxian divisions and debates. The Stalinisation of Russia and the rise of bureaucratic socialism, the failure of revolutionary movements in the advanced capitalist societies, the Sino-Soviet split and the continuing repressive character of most (if not all) nominally Marxist regimes are among the major anomalies for a theory which requires in its very structure to be judged historically.[2] Beyond this, the 'crisis of Marxism' is arguably a part of the larger crisis of Western civilisation, itself expressed in the fateful ambiguity of the Enlightenment project of which Marxism is a part. The attempt to free humanity through progress in knowledge and the overcoming of dogmatic authority and blind adherence to tradition is called into question by what it has engendered – a divided world on the brink of extinction faced with new forms of domination and control at least as powerful as the old.

In the face of this larger crisis, the question naturally arises: is Marxism not in fact obsolete. Perhaps it is as much a part of the crisis as capitalism itself? Many on the left have answered these questions in the affirmative. They have come to reject Marxism in favour of an ever increasing variety of neo-critical, post-structuralist, radical avant-garde viewpoints.[3] Such positions, however, are themselves caught in the paradox of favouring revolutionary change while opposing what remains, in much of the world, the only revolutionary force. Unable to connect their radicalism with social groups in their own countries or elsewhere, they reproduce rather than overcome many of the central anomalies of the Marxism they have rejected. Like their former conservative opponents, they become virulent critics not only of Marxism but of the project of enlightenment itself.

Habermas is keenly aware of these problems and paradoxes. He realises that, taken together, they call into question the very possibility of a critical theory of society with ties to the Marxian heritage. Is such a theory still possible at all? This is the question Habermas addresses directly. His own attempt to answer it by rehabilitating a Marxist approach developed in conjunction with a subtle defence of the Enlightenment and modernity, runs counter to powerful contemporary political and theoretical tendencies. Theoretically, Habermas's project represents a rejection of both what he sees as the relativism of post-modernist theories and the absolutism of defenders of the philosophical tradition, as well as revived forms of positivism. Politically, his project represents a rejection of both the neo-conservatives and the neo-radicals (as well as traditional liberal and conservative positions) which are supported by the theoretical currents mentioned above.[4] The theoretical strength of Habermas's project lies, as I argued in Chapter 1, in the attempt to go between the unacceptable alternatives of the various forms of relativism and absolutism without ignoring the power of either alternative. The political strength of Habermas's project lies in a parallel attempt to go between the unacceptable alternatives of a new and 'enlightened' commitment to technocratic control and stability at all costs, and a return to outdated liberal, conservative and orthodox Marxist positions. Habermas has been able to develop this middle ground with a critical social theory plausible enough to spur extensive theoretical discussion and a large number of adherents. Cornelius Disco has noted the practical effects of Habermas's work by calling it 'the ideology of the new class' (where, following Gouldner, 'ideology' means a relatively rational programme for social reconstruction and 'new class' refers to the growing stratum of intellectual and cultural workers) concerned with both the 'normative critique' and the democratisation of advanced capitalism.[5]

The undoubted influence Habermas has had among left intellectuals, particularly in Germany and America, makes it all the more important that his fundamental claims be questioned in the light of the Marxist tradition. Since, as I argued above, Habermas's basic strategy for contemporary radical theory is the move from the paradigm of production to the paradigm of communication, this strategy in particular needs examination. This will require a return to the discussion of Marx's paradigm of production and the subsequent development of two basic and opposed interpretations of that paradigm in the tradition of Marxism. How the problems of normative foundations and the relation of theory to practice have been handled in this tradition will serve as a context for, and alternatives to, Habermas's own attempted solutions.

Marx's paradigm of production: a brief recapitulation

As I argued earlier, Marx's social theory rests on the presupposition that material production is paradigmatic for the understanding of all the manifestations of human life. Marx uses the paradigm of production to distinguish Marxian 'materialism' both from its immediate tradition, from Hegelian philosophy in particular and from German classical philosophy in general, and from older, 'passive' forms of 'materialism'. The paradigm of production makes it possible to synthesise and surpass what Lenin called the three sources of Marxism: German Classical philosophy, British political economy and French revolutionary socialism.[6] Marx's paradigm of production, as I tried to show in Chapter 2, thus involved an implicit appeal to a broad notion of social rationality which encompasses not only theory and interpretation, but also criticism and practical activity. Social rationality is identified by Marx with the developing revolutionary workers' movement, with that practical activity of the association of socially conditioned and producing class-individuals, which can concretely abolish the irrationalities of their immediate material existence. This identification of social rationality with the workers' movement accomplished within the paradigm of production has at least two important consequences. First, it allows Marx to transform the basic problematic of philosophy from Descartes through Hegel (that is, a concern with the consciousness of the subject in relation to the object to be known) by viewing the constitution of the shared and meaningful world of human experiences, not in terms of 'consciousness', but as the social and historical result of material–practical activities understood in terms of 'production'. Marx's 'historicising' of this problematic also makes it possible for him not only to *describe* the productive relations of capitalism, but also to *criticise* their eternal hypostatisation in the problematic of political economy. Secondly, it allows Marx not only to construct a radical theoretical–critical model for the comprehension of social reality, but also to forge a practical weapon for use in the actual historical project of revolutionising social reality. Only from this second standpoint (the standpoint of the real possibility of socialist transformation, of a social organisation of production which invests the producers with the power to formulate and shape, with will and consciousness and collectively, their conditions of life) can history be viewed not as the irresistible march of an impersonal

Reason, but as the actual field of social struggle for the possibility of progressively bringing about social rationality as a qualitative increase in the freedom and meaning of individual human lives. That is why Marx's social theory, although resting on the paradigm of production, fundamentally relies on what I have called the linchpin of the proletariat (whose actual struggles are to bring about this social transformation) to hold the theoretical edifice together.

Today, of course, both Marx's paradigm of production and his reliance on the proletariat have become questionable. We can distinguish two kinds of anomalies faced by Marx's social theory. First, there are anomalies generated by historical events that do not 'fit' the predictions of the theory. Among these anomalies are, at least, the following: (i) socialist revolutions have not occurred in developed capitalist societies, but rather in 'backward' societies without a large industrial proletariat; (ii) the socialist societies actually established have not succeeded in meeting the emancipatory goals of the theory, they have not abolished exploitation or class divisions; and (iii) in advanced capitalist societies, the proletariat seems to be successfully integrated into the system and, thus, no longer to be a genuine revolutionary force. The second kind of anomalies faced by Marx's social theory are not based on 'newspaper events' such as the above, rather they are based on the interpretive work of Marxist theoreticians.[7] I will now turn to the central theoretical anomaly in the history of Marixist thought.

Interpretations of Marx's paradigm of production: scientific versus critical Marxism

Without developing Marx's 'paradigm of production' any further, one is able to see how two primary and fundamentally opposed interpretations of it are possible. On the one hand, 'production' can be understood narrowly and reduced to 'labour' in the economic sense of a technological process of exchange between humans and external nature. On the other hand, 'production' can be understood broadly and expanded to 'praxis' as an activity of unlimited human self-creativity. These two interpretations are elaborated in what Alvin Gouldner calls the 'two Marxisms' – 'scientific Marxism' (associated with the first interpretation) and 'critical Marxism' (associated with the second).[8] Although the history of Marx's theory has seen an amazing variety of 'Marxisms' bearing to each other what Wittgenstein might call a 'family resemblance', these two basic orientations have appeared and reappeared throughout nearly all the important subsequent theoretical developments. They reflect real tensions within Marx's 'paradigm of production' that cannot be removed simply by returning to the canonical texts. Both 'Marxisms' have complex theoretical traditions marked by uneven and contradictory developments closely associated with the historical fate of socialism and revolutionary action. Many individual Marxists do not fit neatly into either camp. An analytic distinction between the two, however, remains important for an adequate understanding of the problematic Habermas takes up from the Marxist tradition. Therefore, following Gouldner, I will briefly outline these two basic interpretations of Marx's paradigm of production in order to set the stage for my criticism of Habermas's turn away from that paradigm.

'Scientific Marxism', as the name implies, views Marx's theory as founding a science of society and history that is to be rigidly distinguished from 'ideological' (false) forms of thought such as philosophy, religion, myth and so on. It is deterministic, treating society and history as governed by 'iron laws' understood on the model of the natural sciences. The 'subjects' of these laws tend to 'disappear' under the weight of social structures. Scientific Marxists maintain a radical separation between Hegel and the young Marx, and the mature Marx, Engels and Lenin. Science is viewed as the ultimate form of rationality, while the 'ambiguous', 'philosophic', and 'idealistic' are rejected as 'humanism' in favour of a hard-headed 'materialism'. Scientific Marxists maintain rigid distinctions such as the base/superstructure model. They tend towards a structuralism which seeks decontextualised knowledge that holds of all social structures. They value technology and see themselves as belonging to the progressive scientific culture.[9]

'Critical Marxism', as the name implies, views Marx's theory as critique, a 'dialectical' theory that locates both the true and the false in 'ideological' forms of thought. It is voluntaristic, treating society and history as capable of change through the will and action of social actors. The 'subjects' in question tend to be viewed as a collective agent of social change. Critique is designed to motivate them to undertake the struggle. Critical Marxists maintain the continuity between Hegel, the young and the mature Marx, but they maintain the discontinuity between Marx and Engels and Lenin. Science is not viewed as the ultimate form of rationality, it itself becomes an object of critique. Technology and technological 'progress' are also among the most frequent targets of critical Marxists. They replace rigid distinctions such as the base/superstructure model with holistic concepts such as 'the social totality'. They tend towards a historicism which seeks contextualised knowledge that is grounded in specific historical situations. They tend to be viewed as belonging to the progressive humanistic culture.[10]

The two Marxisms also have different approaches to politics. Scientific Marxists tend to take a gradualist, evolutionary perspective that links Darwin to Marx. They are committed to patience and cultivating the 'objective conditions' necessary for change – usually understood as advancing the forces of production. They tend to rely on the party and organisation for these tasks. Thus, scientific Marxism is well suited for Marxists who are in positions of power. Critical Marxists tend to take a catastrophic perspective that links Marx with the radical interpretations of Hegel. They are impatient and tend to push for change even in the absence of the requisite 'objective conditions'. They believe in the efficacy of 'consciousness-raising' and the importance of 'ideological struggle'. Thus, critical Marxism is well suited for Marxists out of power.[11]

Each Marxism has complementary and important political limitations. Scientific Marxists tend to succumb to the cynical politics of power and bureaucracy, while critical Marxists tend to succumb to a revolutionary Messianism that is out of touch with political reality. Scientific Marxists, in their belief in the ultimate determinism of the economic, tend to be 'political utopians' who believe that the distortions of political power will disappear given the right economic conditions. Critical Marxists tend to be 'economic utopians' by underestimating the importance of prior economic developments for socialism.[12]

Finally, each Marxism takes a different approach to the problems of the relation of theory to practice and normative foundations. Scientific Marxists view theory as a body of scientific truth mastered by the 'vanguard' of the proletariat, the party, and brought to the actual struggle, the practice, of the proletariat from the 'outside'. The paradigmatic statement of this position is Lenin's contention that workers, left to struggle on their own, can only achieve a 'trade union consciousness' and, thus, it is the role of the party to impart 'socialist consciousness' to them based on a scientifically correct theory.[13] The obvious weakness of this conception of the relation of theory to practice is that it tends to introduce a hierarchical and élitist distinction between the party and the working class, a distinction that has in fact had the most disastrous practical consequences.[14]

Critical Marxism arose, in part, as a response to the failures of scientific Marxists to resolve this central problem. Critical Marxists view theory as a body of critical or practical truth uncovered by the progressive social critic. As such, it is not to be brought to the workers' movement 'monologically' (where the critic talks and the workers listen), but rather 'dialogically' (where critic and worker teach and learn from each other). In practice, however, critical Marxists have tended to view the workers, or other addressees of the theory, as not yet ready for a 'true' dialogue. First, the addressees must have their consciousness 'raised' through the dissemination of critical truth. The weakness of this conception was traced (at least in regard to Lukács and the Frankfurt School) in the problematic of rationality discussed in Chapter 2. Critical Marxism, in the course of its theoretical development, came to view the domination of capitalist forms of consciousness as such a seamless web that engaging in dialogue with the addressees of the theory, whether the proletariat or other possibly radical groups, became paradoxical. The 'disappearance of the proletariat' thesis left the social critic with no one to have dialogue *with*. Further, precisely how the social critic himself was capable of overcoming the all-pervasive 'distortion of consciousness' became a total mystery.

The problem of normative foundations is connected with these problems of the relation of theory to practice in scientific and critical Marxism. Scientific Marxists tend to separate fact and value. Values and norms are viewed as a part of 'ideology' as opposed to 'science'. As such, they are simply 'false'. The historical progress of the worker's movement is the only value, and is itself scientifically validated and inevitable. Criticism of the views of others is 'external' and rests on a simple opposition between the commitment to socialism and the commitment to capitalism. The obvious weakness of this conception is that it provides no justification whatsoever for a commitment to socialism. As Gouldner has remarked: 'Death is also inevitable and yet we commonly struggle against it.'[15] Only non-moral grounds are adduced for joining the struggle, yet these grounds cannot justify the practical commitments exemplified in Marx's (moral) exhortation to 'not only interpret the world, but also change it'. Again, this tendency to ignore values and norms, or to treat them as 'false', while criticising others from the external standpoint of the theorists' own scientifically validated commitment, has had disastrous practical consequences.[16] And again, critical Marxism arose, in part, as a response to the failures of scientific Marxists to resolve this central problem. Critical Marxists tend to reject a rigid separation of fact and value. All modes of thought (scientific, moral, aesthetic, religious) are, to some extent 'ideological'. For critical Marxists, this means they contain a historically and socially conditioned collection of 'true' and 'false' elements. Critical Marxists tend to engage in 'immanent' or 'internal' criticism (a method of criticism appealing only to those values actually found in a given social and historical context) that attempts to separate the 'true' from the 'false' by comparing concepts in their function of expressing social ideals with their social function and social preconditions. The weakness of this conception was also traced in the problematic of rationality discussed in Chapter 2.

The problematic of rationality began with the conflict between the philosophical concept of reason worked out in the course of the development of classical German idealism from Kant to Hegel, a concept of reason which includes the ideas of autonomy and substantive freedom, and the actual socially and historically embodied forms of reason characteristic of capitalist society. The early Marx expresses this conflict, and the method of internal criticism central to critical Marxism which it makes possible, quite clearly:

Reason has always existed, only not always in reasonable form. The critic can therefore start out by taking any form of theoretical and practical consciousness and develop from the unique forms of existing reality the true reality as its norm and final goal. Now so far as real life is concerned, precisely the political state in all its modern forms contains . . . the demands of reason. Nor does the state stop at that. The state everywhere presupposes that reason has been realized. But in just this way it everywhere comes into contradiction between its ideal mission and its real preconditions.[17]

This view of internal criticism which Marx took over from the left Hegelians and radicalised, and which exerted a continuing influence on the critical Marxism of Lukacs and the early Frankfurt School, led him to an extensive historical and empirical investigation of the 'real preconditions' of the modern political state. Marx located these 'real preconditions' in the capitalist mode of production. Within the capitalist mode of production, Marx located the proletariat as that embodiment of social rationality capable of concretely overcoming the irrationalities of capitalist production. Ironically, the proletariat was given the role of realising the highest values expressed by 'bourgeois' philosophy, namely reason as freedom, truth and meaning. Critical Marxists returned to the conception of 'critique' in general, and the method of internal criticism in particular, found most clearly in the early Marx. This method of internal criticism requires no scientific or transcendental 'external' standards, as I have argued. Like scientific Marxism, critical Marxism does not have a normative foundation. But, unlike scientific Marxism, it does not need such a foundation as long as it can rely on an embodied and developing social rationality which can be empowered by noting the conflict, *internal to the context of capitalism*, between social ideals required for the legitimation of the system and social practices necessary for the continuation of the system.

The method of internal criticism outlined above was basic both for Lukács and the early Frankfurt School. As I argued earlier, the method collapsed for two fundamental reasons. First, the thesis of the 'disappearance of the proletariat' as a revolutionary force left these critical Marxists with no actual embodiment of social rationality to be empowered by their internal criticism. Secondly, the thesis that capitalist legitimation no longer requires appeal to social ideals (norms and values), but only to a technologically secured rise in material well-being, left these critical Marxists with no effective internal values to which to appeal critically. The extreme outcome of these problems in the work of the later Frankfurt School found expression in Horkheimer and Adorno's *Dialectic of Enlightenment*. Here internal criticism goes 'into the abyss with its object' as Western reason itself is identified with domination, implicating both the Enlightenment and Marxism as participants in what they see as the general distortion and unfreedom.[18] How a criticism of reason itself could proceed except by means of reason left this negative form of total criticism in a position of extreme paradox – a paradox understood and embraced by Adorno. At this point, it is extremely doubtful whether this form of critical theory is still a critical *Marxism* at all.

Critical theory and critical Marxism

The 'two Marxisms' discussed above represent attempts to clarify Marx's paradigm of production by resolving the tensions between determinism and voluntarism, between science and critique, which it contained from the beginning. Both are, to some extent, one-sided and distorting interpretations. Both fail to resolve central problems, such as the relation of theory to practice and normative foundations, faced in the development of Marxist thought. In this situation, it is not surprising that contemporary radical theory has produced attempts to criticise, to revise, and even to reject Marx's paradigm of production itself, a point to which I will return. Habermas's reconstruction of the critical theory of society in terms of the paradigm of communication belongs to this development. Before discussing the paradigm change in radical theory from production to communication (and the criticism of Habermas I will develop from this perspective), I will examine the relationship between the critical theory of society of the Frankfurt School and critical Marxism in as much as this forms the immediate context for Habermas's project.

   The critical theory of society of the Frankfurt School (stemming primarily from the work of Horkheimer, Adorno and Marcuse) is perhaps the most important attempt to elaborate a critical Marxism. [19] In the discussion of the problematic of rationality in Chapter 2, I traced this elaboration from its beginnings in the interdisciplinary Marxism of Horkheimer in the 1930s to the stage of 'total critique' reached by critical theory in the 1940s under the influence of Adorno. I will not repeat that discussion here. Instead I want to make a few general points about this theoretical movement that will aid us later in understanding the strengths and weaknesses of Habermas's project. First, critical theory originated as the first entrance of Marxism into the university system in the West. This had a profound influence on its elaboration of critical Marxism. The very term 'critical theory' coined by Horkheimer signified both a commitment to a *critical* 'undogmatic' Marxism and a certain discretion in dropping the term 'Marxism' itself. Of course, it also signified a separation between 'critical theory' and the degeneration of scientific 'orthodox' Marxism.[20] In any case, critical theory from its beginnings faced not only the problems generated by the historical failures of Marx's paradigm, but also the problem of activating the revolutionary content of Marx's social theory (what Habermas calls its 'practical intentions') in a form that could withstand the pressures of the academic and scientific systems of knowledge of the time. An explicit awareness of this latter problem (that is, the need to develop a Marxism that could hold its own in the university system and raise claims relevant to the advancing and diversifying sciences) is characteristic, indeed almost constitutive, of Habermas's own reworking of the tradition.

My second general point is connected to the first. From its beginnings, critical theory saw the need to supplement a critical Marxist perspective with other viewpoints and with the findings of psychology and the social sciences. This is true in spite of the undeniably critical, and often hostile, approach that critical theory took towards competing traditions such as 'positivism' and 'existentialism'.[21] Thus, critical theory attempted a synthesis of Marx and Freud, engaged in sociological research on authority and the family, and developed theories of advanced capitalism (Pollock) and the authoritarian state (Horkheimer), as well as addressing cultural problems. Although they did not abandon a basically Marxist approach under Horkheimer's interdisciplinary model of critical theory, they felt free to extend and supplement this approach by drawing (even if implicitly) on Weber's theory of rationalisation and Freud's theory of instincts, as well as the findings of sociology, anthropology and psychology. The 'total critique' model of critical theory was forced to abandon such a positive approach both to other theoretical constructions and to the special sciences. An explicit return to the interdisciplinary method of the critical theory of the 1930s is a second characteristic of Habermas's approach. In this regard, he has literally opened the floodgates to a bewildering variety of competing approaches which, at times, threatens the very identity of his own theory as a Marxist approach.

My third point concerns the continuing interest critical theory took in problems of philosophy and methodology. The point is also connected to the first two. Critical theory dealt with philosophical and methodological topics from the beginning in order both to maintain the independence of critical theory as a theoretically justified undertaking, and to demarcate itself from traditional philosophy and the special sciences.[22] The lesson the critical theorists drew from the history of Marxism was that an inattention to philosophical and methodological questions had disastrous theoretical and practical effects.[23] In this context, they argued for the relative autonomy of theory. Habermas has continued and extended the concern with philosophical and methodological questions. This concern marks all Habermas's work and, to date, represents its main contribution to radical theory, as well as it main point of interest.

Finally, and most important, the relationship between critical theory and political practice was always problematic. With the exception of Marcuse at certain points in his career and the early Horkheimer, the critical theorists rejected any direct links between the elaboration of theory and participation in political struggles. The reasons for this separation, as I have already argued, can be found in their thesis of the disappearance of the proletariat as a revolutionary agent – a thesis they only slowly and reluctantly came to accept. With this 'disappearance', the search for other addressees of the theory began. No group of agents could be found to replace the proletariat. Critical theory, particularly in the 1940s, began to address itself more and more either to a handful of followers who could carry theory through the dark realities of the twentieth century or to humanity in general.[24] The implications of this change cannot be overestimated. At the extreme, it marks Horkheimer's and Adorno's abandoment of the attempt to elaborate a critical Marxism, an attempt that was to be replaced by a politically ineffective and theoretically paradoxical 'total critique' of Western reason that exposes the corruption of Marx's paradigm, along with everything else. Again, this problem has marked all Habermas's work. Early on, Habermas rejected the revolutionary role of the proletariat and generalised the addressee of critical theory to the whole of humanity. By so doing, he was carrying out a movement that has always been implicit in critical Marxism with its emphasis on the self-creation of the human species. Whether such a Marxism is still Marxist and, more crucially, whether it can provide a radical theory with practical and political prospects is a question I will turn to later. For now, I only want to suggest that the paradigm switch from production to communication that Habermas attempts was motivated in large part by the failure of the first generation of critical theorists to elaborate critical Marxism successfully within the confines of Marx's paradigm of production. What is called for then, in Habermas's view, is a fundamental reformulation of critical theory in terms of communication rather than production. After discussing the place of Habermas's work in this paradigm change in radical theory, I will turn to my critique of his position.

Production versus communication as paradigms for radical theory

As I argued earlier, the history of Marxist thought is marked by the decomposition of Marx's paradigm of production into what Gyorgy Márkus calls 'the "scientific" model of labour on the one hand, and the "philosophical" notion of praxis on the other'.[25] The tensions in Marx's original paradigm were held together by what I called the linchpin of the proletariat, as I tried to show in the interpretation of Marx developed in Chapter 2. I call the 'two Marxisms' a 'decomposition' because in *both* this linchpin is pulled and, thus, the theory falls apart in the two directions I have discussed. In scientific Marxism, of which Althusser's may serve as a contemporary model, the proletariat is submerged beneath the weight of social structures and treated as a passive, collective, and purely theoretical *role*. This may, in part, explain why Althusser has, throughout his work, paid so little attention to political struggle, and why the actual emergence of such struggles in Paris, in May 1968, took him by surprise.[26] In critical Marxism, of which I have suggested the critical theory of the Frankfurt School may serve as a model, the proletariat also 'disappears'. But this time, it is under the weight of a series of historical failures and the emergence of a conformist instrumental rationality which eclipses their revolutionary potential. With the exception of Marcuse, the Frankfurt School was also taken by surprise by the upheavals of the 1960s. It is ironic that Habermas, the theorist perhaps most widely influential among Western intellectuals radicalised during this period, went so far at one point as to call the protest movement a 'fascism of the left'.[27] In any case, the situation I have just outlined (the decomposition of Marx's paradigm of production) has lead to various attempts at a fundamental critique and explicit revision of the paradigm of production itself.

The most interesting of these attacks rejects Marx's paradigm of production altogether because it remains totally within the context of bourgeois thought and practice. From this perspective, Marx's 'productivist ideology' and the orthodox Marxist idea of history as progress do not challenge the current order of exploitation and alienation, but rather reinforce it. A truly radical theory will conceive of a socialist transformation as a total break with the inhuman continuity of history as 'progress', and not as a consummation of it. Socialism, on this view, is only possible if humans adopt a non-exploitative relation to nature (as well as to each other) and reign in the uncontrolled dynamism of their self-induced needs. Both the Marxist and the Enlightenment view of progress as involving human beings mastering and controlling nature (and thus, implicitly, also other human beings) stands in the way of a truly emancipatory theory and practice. Within the confines of the paradigm of production, no such theory and practice is possible; thus, it is replaced by the paradigm of communication.

The later Frankfurt School, in particular Horkheimer and Adorno, has already begun the shift in paradigm discussed above with their ideas of fraternal relations with nature and a renewed mimetic and non-instrumental use of language. Walter Benjamin also expressed these ideas with great force in his 'Theses on the Philosophy of History'.[28] In this work, Benjamin attacked the idea of history as 'progress' in the forces of production. Instead, he saw a revolutionary potential only in a total break with the vicious continuity of history. Benjamin conceived his work only as a critique of 'orthodox' Marxism, and not as a rejection of Marxism itself. Whether or not he was right in his self-assessment is a question I will not discuss here. In any case, the explicit formulation of the paradigm of communication in direct opposition to Marx's paradigm of production is not to be found in either the work of Horkheimer and Adorno, or in Benjamin. An attempt along this line *is* to be found in new radical French theory, in particular in the work of Jean Baudrillard. I will now turn to a brief discussion of this development.

Jean Baudrillard's *The Mirror of Production* is the first work to attempt to formulate explicitly the paradigm of communication as a direct opposition to Marx's paradigm of production.[29] In this work, Baudrillard gives expression to a broad tendency in new French theory that rejects Marxism because it is deeply implicated in a repressive and theoretically outmoded order of discourse.[30] Baudrillard's central argument is that Marx remains trapped within the very discourse of production of the bourgeois political economists that he attacks. By conceiving a socialist transformation in terms of the dialectic of forces and relations of production, Marx actually reinforces an oppressive view of human beings as workers. Marx's conception of the revolutionary movement as a consummation of production, rather than as the total overthrow of a life based on production, does not represent the end of exploitation and alienation, but rather their totalisation. A truly revolutionary theory would conceive capitalism not as a mode of production (based on the laws of the economy), but rather as a mode of discourse (based on what Baudrillard calls 'the terrorism of the code').[31] This latter conception of radical theory is the one Baudrillard attempts to spell out. I will not detail his theory here since it lies somewhat off the main lines of my argument. Instead, I will mention a few general points of comparison between this conception of radical theory and the conception of the later Frankfurt School and Habermas.

Like the later Frankfurt School, Baudrillard sees the 'ideology' of advanced capitalism as a seamless web of repression. The needs generated by the massive productive apparatus are false in their totality: 'Needs lose all their autonomy; they are coded.'[32] The code itself (the prevailing mode of discourse and discursive practice) is as powerful and ubiquitous as the instrumental reason criticised by the later Frankfurt School. And this generates a paradox very similar to the one faced by Horkheimer and Adorno in *Dialectic of Enlightenment*. Baudrillard states that 'whatever one does, one can only respond to the system in its own terms, according to its own rules, answering it with its own signs'.[33] How then is Baudrillard's own critique possible? What linguistic resources can he draw on except the code itself? And, if this is the case, how can he avoid reproducing the very code he attempts to disrupt? We have seen this problem before. And again it relates to the foundation of critical norms. Where distortion is total, then even the critic of distortion (who must, as a critic, rely on norms and values) cannot escape it. Baudrillard's rejection of Marx's paradigm of production, coupled with his rejection of all ties between radical theory and the Enlightenment, ends up in the same theoretical dead-end as the 'total critique' of the later Frankfurt School.

The problem of the relation of theory to practice faced by Baudrillard's critique is again a familiar one. Since the proletariat has been stupefied by a system which produces and satisfies 'false' needs and subjects all attempts to break out of the system to the 'terrorism' of a monolithic code, they are no longer a revolutionary force. What agent can replace them so that radical theory can remain practical and revolutionary? Baudrillard's answer in *The Mirror of Production* parallels the answer given by Marcuse in the 1960s. For Baudrillard, there is a collection of groups 'outside' the code such as women, youth, students, blacks and the elderly. They are 'relegated to a position of non-marked terms' and expelled to a 'non-place of the code'.[34] Here Baudrillard returns to Marx's earliest and most problematic argument for the revolutionary role of the proletariat – the myth of a class 'outside' society which can transform society.[35] The difference is that, for Baudrillard, this class appears in the plural as a collection of groups. But how can a class or group 'outside' society and, it seems to follow, reduced to powerlessness by this exclusion, transform society? Baudrillard seems to think this can be accomplished through 'refusal, pure and simple'.[36] Gyorgy Márkus summarises and criticises Baudrillard's position as follows:

> So the myth of a 'revolution', whose course is scientifically mapped and planned in all its essentials, is only replaced with the complementary myth of the 'revolt of the moment' ('refusal, pure and simple'). And no matter how wary one may be of the first ideology, there is no valid reason to forget the historical experience connected with an ideology of 'discharge, destruction, and death' and the dark rebellion of 'total irresponsibility'.[37]

The paradigm of communication, however, need not be used to break all ties with Marx and the Enlightenment. It can also be used to reinforce the link between Marx and the Enlightenment weakened by scientific Marxism. Thus, the paradigm of communication may be used to supplement Marx's paradigm of production where labour and communicative action are treated as complementary, but irreducible, models of human social action. Both the theoretical problem of normative foundations and the practical problem of agency requires, on this view, a clear distinction between their respective logics and an investigation of their interplay. This is the project Habermas began with the distinction between labour and communicative interaction. Whether, in working out the communicative side of the distinction, Habermas has not actually shifted to an almost exclusive reliance on the paradigm of communication that, in effect, rejects Marx's paradigm of production is a question I will turn to later. First, I want to make some critical points concerning Habermas's critique of Marx, to be followed by a critical examination of Habermas's own paradigm of communication.

In the first place, Habermas questions the critical and political potential of Marx's paradigm of production under the condition of advanced capitalism:

> Relative growth of the productive forces no longer represent eo ipso a potential that points beyond the existing framework with emancipatory consequences, in view of which legitimation of an existing power structure becomes enfeebled. For the leading productive force – controlled scientific–technical progress itself – has now become a basis for legitimation.[38]

On the other hand, Habermas is very hesistant to base the possibility of emancipation on the conscious demands of those groups which are marginal to the society itself. He is aware not only to the politically ineffective nature of such a radical strategy, but also of the authoritarian and terroristic dangers implicit in it. Perhaps the basic objective of Habermas's theory is to reconstruct the link between socialism and democracy. But if neither the productive forces nor the conscious demands of potentially radical groups can be counted on as the agents of such a democratic–socialist transformation (according to Habermas's own account), then the very possibility of critical theory becomes problematic. As I have argued, Habermas addresses this problem across its whole extent: in terms of epistemology and methodology, in terms of an analysis of legitimation problems in advanced capitalism and in terms of a new theory of communication. To answer the question about the 'possibility' of critical theory, Habermas believes it necessary to find a justification for the normative dimension of the theory and to reconstitute the relation between theory and practice. It is this attempt which I followed in detail in Chapters 2 and 3. Throughout, Habermas contrasted his project with a critical appraisal of Marx's exclusive focus on production as labour.

From Habermas's perspective, Marx's inattention to the question of the possibility of radical theory was already a basic defect in his work. Marx was able to avoid this question by identifying in a 'positivistic' manner (at least at the philosophical level, if not in his actual concrete historical analyses) technical evolution with social progress. Habermas argues that the 'positivism' in Marx is evident in his interpretation of the development of the human species in terms of labour as instrumental action alone. Habermas's remedy is to conceive the development of the human species also in terms of communication as communicative action.

But is this criticism of Marx's paradigm of production actually justified? I think not. Ironically, here Habermas actually engages in a scientific Marxist misinterpretation. Marx's paradigm of production does not reduce the concept of the development of the human species to the single dimension of growth in the technical–instrumental mastery of nature by human beings, except under the most limited scientific Marxist interpretation. The distinction between productive forces and productive relations serves, at least in part, to distinguish between the relation of humans to nature and the relation of humans to each other. Further, this dichotomy distinguishes the axes of continuity and discontinuity in history so as to make it possible to investigate concretely both the nature of progress, and the stops and catastrophic reversals it encounters. Marx's paradigm of production makes possible a subtle characterisation of the process of historical development which includes both the human mastery of nature and forms of human interaction. When not reduced to a scientific or a critical interpretation, Marx's paradigm of production makes possible an approach to the problem of normative foundations that can serve as an alternative to Habermas's own approach. The same may be said of Marx's approach to the problem of the relation of theory to practice. I will discuss these alternatives after my criticism of Habermas's communication theory. This will allow me to evaluate the shift in radical theory from the paradigm of production to the paradigm of communication.

Habermas's paradigm of communication: a critique

Initially, as I have said, Habermas conceived his paradigm of communication as a supplement to Marx's paradigm of production. This seems, at least, to be the major point of Habermas's early distinction between labour and communicative interaction. In the course of working out the communicative half of the distinction, however, the production half is eclipsed to the point that one can speak of Habermas's paradigm of communication more as a replacement than as a supplement to Marx's paradigm of production. In my view, the eclipsing of the production half of the distinction takes place through a double reduction. First, Habermas conceives production, specifically labour, only in terms of the relation between human beings and nature. Secondly, he conceives labour only in terms of instrumental action whereby human beings attempt to master nature. The first is a reduction because production and labour involve both the relation of human beings to other human beings and the relation of human beings to their own inner nature, as well as their relation to outer nature. Marx's analysis of alienated labour makes clear that each of these dimensions are present in the labour process.[39] The second is a reduction because human beings can, and do, adopt other relations to nature besides mastery and technological domination. Here even Marx speaks of the other attitudes to nature, such as the aesthetic, which might be freed from the narrow goals of capitalist production.[40] At the least, Habermas's criticism of Marx's paradigm of production seems to rest, as I have argued, on a one-sided scientific Marxist interpretation. It is clear that Habermas wants to shift radical theory from a concentration on production to a concentration on communication, finally, because he conceives social relations as *paradigmatically* relations of communication. This justifies us in speaking of Habermas's 'communication theory of society' and of his 'paradigm of communication'.

Three concepts developed by Habermas are constitutive of his paradigm of communication and connect his entire communication theory of society, in particular in so far as the latter is directed at the problems of normative foundations and the relation of theory to practice. These three concepts are: the ideal speech situation, communicative action and communicative rationality. I will now proceed to raise questions concerning each of these concepts and the arguments that support them.

Habermas's initial attempt to provide a normative foundation for critical social theory in terms of communication was carried out through the concept of the ideal speech situation. Critical social theory traditionally has been concerned with identifying and dissolving relations of power masked by ideology, so as to make it possible for human beings to make their own history with 'will and consciousness' and achieve social arrangements based, not on unreflected and hidden power, but on open and equal discussion and real consensus. But how can this critique of ideology escape the suspicion that it is itself ideological? Habermas's response is that the critical norms of the theory are implicit in the structure of language. Conceiving ideology as 'systematically distorted communication', Habermas attempts to explicate what is involved in 'undistorted communication' by investigating the conditions for the possibility of reaching understanding/agreement (*Verstandigung*) in ordinary language. His argument may be reconstructed as follows:[41]

1. The ability to communicate in ordinary language (communicative competence) presupposes that it is possible for at least two subjects to reach an understanding/agreement.

2. 'Reaching an understanding/agreement' presupposes that it is possible to distinguish between a genuine and a deceptive understanding/agreement.

3. A 'genuine understanding/agreement' is an agreement based on the force of the better argument alone.

4. 'The force of the better argument' can prevail if and only if communication is free of hidden constraints.

5. Communication is 'free of hidden constraints' if and only if for all participants there is a symmetrical distribution of chances to select and employ speech acts.

6. A situation in which this 'symmetry requirement' is met is an ideal speech situation. Thus, –

7. The 'ideal speech situation' (as a communicative characterisation of the ideas of freedom, truth, and justice) contains a 'practical hypothesis' (namely, that such a situation *ought* to be brought about) upon which the critique of ideology (as 'systematically distorted communication') can be based.

Although the point is not brought out clearly enough in his early formulation of the argument, Habermas is concerned with both speech and action, as his concept of communicative action makes clear. I will examine this concept later. For now, I will direct my attention to Habermas's argument in so far as it concerns the structure of language and, thus, involves the conditions for the possibility of speech.

The first step of Habermas's argument rests upon the centrality of what he calls *verstandigungsorientierten Handelns* (action oriented to reaching an understanding/agreement), exploiting the ambiguity between 'understanding' and 'agreement' conveyed by the word *Verstandigung*. Before addressing the question of the centrality of the idea of reaching an 'understanding/agreement' for the structure of language, I will discuss the difference between 'understanding' and 'agreement' obscured by Habermas's formulation. The fact that it makes sense to say 'I understand you, but I don't agree with you' shows there is a difference between the two. On the other hand, the fact that it doesn't make sense to say 'I agree with you, but I don't understand what you say' shows there is a connection between the two. What is this connection? Here one might plausibly argue that 'agreement' *presupposes* 'understanding'. But the reverse is clearly not the case. I can understand what you say at the grammatical level, at the semantic level and at the pragmatic level without agreeing with you. Thus, 'understanding' does not *presuppose* 'agreement' since, for example, one might have a genuine understanding of racism without agreeing with racism, or being a racist. Even a genuine understanding does not guarantee a genuine agreement. Habermas's failure to distinguish these two cases weakens both the first and the second steps in his argument.

His assumption that the idea of reaching an understanding/ agreement is central to language and, thus, that misunderstanding and deception are derivative, is also problematic. This assumption is also shared by speech–act theory and, perhaps, by the philosophical tradition generally.[42] Nevertheless, it can be challenged. If understanding and agreement belong to the structure of language, if they are conditions for the possibility of speech, then misunderstanding and disagreement must also belong to the structure of language and be conditions for the possibility of speech. The words 'understanding' and 'agreement' would be meaningless if misunderstanding and disagreement were impossible. If they are possible, then they also belong to the structure of language, to the conditions for the possibility of speech. In Louis Mackey's phrase, 'a possibility once is a necessity forever'.[43] Since both understanding and misunderstanding, agreement and disagreement, belong to the conceptual–transcendental structure of language, no basis remains for privileging the 'positive' terms over their 'negative' counterparts. In order to question Habermas's assumption of priority, it is not necessary to argue that the 'negative' terms are themselves central, prior, basic. It is sufficient to show that, on the same conceptual–transcendental grounds appealed to by Habermas, they are not derivative and secondary. Whether or not one accepts this criticism, it is clear that Habermas's argument depends upon his ability to show (and not simply to assume) the priority of 'reaching an understanding/ agreement'.

Habermas could respond to the above criticism by claiming that the priority of understanding/agreement is not conceptual– transcendental, but empirical–reconstructive. This response depends upon his extention of Chomsky's research approach from grammatical competence to communicative competence, from a search for linguistic universals to a search for pragmatic universals which I questioned in Chapter 3. As an empirical research programme, this extension should not be prejudged. Nevertheless, Habermas's assumption of the priority of understanding/agreement is so basic to this research programme that it is at least questionable whether or not the assumption can be proven by the programme. How can an empirical–reconstructive approach be used to prove the very assumption on which it is based without circularity? In any case, steps one and two of Habermas's argument require a more detailed elaboration than he has yet provided.

Even if we grant Habermas his assumption concerning the priority of understanding/agreement and, along with it, the first two steps of his argument, the third step is open to criticism. Why is a genuine understanding/agreement based only on the force of the better argument? Couldn't it also be based on love, compassion, solidarity or sympathy? Here, as elsewhere, Habermas seems to base his argument on one particular kind of speech – theoretical discussion. Habermas's focus on critical, scientific and philosophical discussion is what gives plausibility to steps five and six of his argument as well. Freedom from internal and external constraints and the 'symmetry requirement' do belong, at least ideally, to this kind of discussion. But again, Habermas has not shown that they belong to speech fundamentally, or across its whole spectrum. There are many uses of language, many speech acts, to which they do not belong such as 'commanding', 'joking', 'telling a story' and so on. In spite of the undeniable importance of theoretical discussion in the Western tradition, an importance Habermas rightly emphasises, it is questionable whether this kind of speech really has the centrality and world–historical importance he believes. It is perhaps true that, as Joan Robinson has argued, 'for the most part the human race, even today, does not attach importance to the distinction between a thing being the case and not being the case'.[44] Habermas tries to meet this objection in his work on communicative rationality to which I will turn later.

Finally, Habermas's move from stage six to stage seven of his argument is questionable. This transition depends upon drawing certain *material* norms (stage seven) such as truth, freedom and justice from what seems to be a purely *formal*, or procedural, account of the presuppositions of speech (stages one through six). Here the problems of Kant's practical philosophy seem to return in Habermas's communicative account, at least in the early formulations of that account. Habermas has recognised this problem, and it has led him to alter the status of the concept of the ideal speech situation. He no longer believes that the ideal speech situation represents 'the ideal of a form of life which has become perfectly rational – there can be no such ideal'.[45] As Habermas states: 'The attempt to provide an equivalent for what was once intended by the ideal of the good life should not mislead us into deriving this idea from the formal concept of reason with which modernity's decentered understanding of the world has left us.'[46] With this detranscendentalising alteration, the argument seems to lose its critical power, since the concept of the ideal speech situation no longer represents an ideal in terms of which we can judge concrete forms of life as a whole. And Habermas in fact concedes this point.[47] By so doing, he realised he must look elsewhere besides the formal concept of the ideal speech situation for the normative foundation of his critical social theory. By giving up the attempt to formulate the idea of a rational form of life in the substantive sense, as Habermas states, 'there remains only the critique of deformations inflicted, in two ways, on the life forms of capitalistically modernized societies, through devaluation of their traditional substance and through subjection to the imperatives of a one-sided rationality limited to the cognitive–instrumental'.[48] Habermas attempts to provide a foundation for this more limited conception of critique in his work on communicative action and communicative rationality, to which I will now turn.

I will not linger on Habermas's concept of communicative action, since it also involves the assumption of the priority of 'action oriented to reaching understanding/agreement' already criticised in detail. Here I will briefly criticise the concept of communicative *action* which is a type of action that is based on the mutual and co-operative achievement of understanding and agreement. Social actors, as participants in a communication community comprised of speech and actions, have the competence to distinguish between action oriented to understanding/agreement (*communicative action*) and action oriented to success (*instrumental action* in the non-social context of subjects interacting with nature and *strategic action* in social contexts of influencing other subjects). The first question I wish to raise concerns the competency to make these distinctions. Precisely because there exist internal constraints on speech and action and 'systematic distortion' of even the inner nature of social actors, it is questionable whether social actors actually have this competency now, or whether further social changes might not completely eclipse it. Drawing the distinction between acting communicatively and strategically is, in many actual cases, an extremely difficult and subtle matter. But, on Habermas's account, it is a distinction of which social actors are always aware (as a universal species competence it is one of which they *will* always be aware), even if only intuitively and vaguely. Is this a conceptual point or an empirical point? Or again, is it subject to what Habermas calls empirical–reconstructive research strategies? Here the same points I made in connection with ideal speech apply to communicative action. In any case, it seems even more questionable to extend the idea of 'reaching understanding/agreement' to action than it was in the case of speech in terms of universal species' competencies. In the case of speech, Habermas could draw on our presuppositions concerning theoretical discussion. In the case of action, theoretical discussion itself in the modern period serves primarily the ends of instrumental action. If humans have, as a species, a universal competence, it might be more plausible to assume that it is the competence to 'instrumentalise' the whole of our world, and ourselves as well.

Finally, the same general tension between the transcendental perspective and the historical perspective in Habermas's work reappears here again. On the one hand, his account of competence should provide a replacement for the decontextualised knowledge provided by Kantian conceptual–transcendental argument. On the other hand, his account of the historical embodiment and social development of these competencies should provide a replacement for the contextualised knowledge provided by Marxian historical and social critical–empirical argument. From the latter perspective, the competency for communicative action (involving both speech and action) is obviously the product of a certain specific historical development and social situation. How do the two kinds of accounts relate to each other? Which has priority? The 'transcendental' or the 'empirical' or something in between? I will return to this point in connection with Habermas's account of communicative rationality.

I will conclude my account of Habermas's paradigm of communication by examining his concept of communicative rationality. As I have argued throughout, Habermas is seeking a normative foundation for critical–social theory, which is not simply external (transcendental) or internal (immanent) in order to avoid both absolutism and relativism. I have pointed to the tensions between the Kantian and the Marxian poles in his project generated by this attempt. Further, I have argued that the 'ideal speech situation' cannot provide such a normative foundation, and here it seems Habermas now agrees that it cannot. Does the concept of communicative rationality represent a renewed attempt at solving the problem of normative foundations? Or has Habermas abandoned a foundationalist approach entirely? Thomas McCarthy seems to argue for the latter alternative in his introduction to *The Theory of Communicative Action*. McCarthy states that 'the notion of communicative rationality does not serve Habermas as the telos of a philosophy of history, or as the equivalent of progress, or as the standard for the good life'.[49] In other words, communicative reason is not an immanent standard or a transcendental standard; it is not, one seems forced to conclude, a normative and critical concept at all. This suggests it is a simple empirical concept. McCarthy seems to agree. He states: 'Habermas is not seeking to demonstrate conceptually that what is rational is (or will be) real and what is real is (or will be) rational, but to identify empirically the actually existing possibilities for embodying rationality structures in concrete forms of life.'[50]

This interpretation of the concept of communicative rationality cannot be the whole story. The concept has clear normative implications, both in regard to the idea of progress and to the idea of the good life. Entirely abandoning the attempt to provide a foundation for this normative dimension would leave Habermas with no way to avoid the ethical scepticism of Weber's 'Gods and

Demons'. And this would seem to reduce Habermas's project to a mere academic sociology without practical and political implications. I believe it *is* true that Habermas has moved further away from a transcendental approach to the problem of normative foundations in his latest work in communication theory. But he has not abandoned the problem entirely, nor has he totally 'detranscendentalised' his project as McCarthy argues.[51] Rational reconstruction of universal competencies serves as a modern replacement for this transcendental pole in his thought. Such reconstructive-empirical approaches remain transcendental in the sense, at least, that they examine the conditions for the possibility of thought, speech and action. They continue to figure prominently in Habermas's account of rationality. On the other hand, Habermas also continues to address empirical–historical embodiments of rationality. Thus, the tension between the transcendental and empirical–historical also remains.

I will raise two final criticisms of Habermas's account of communicative rationality. The first is directed at this account in so far as it is intended, even in a weakened sense, as a 'normative foundation' for critical social theory. From his earliest attempts to justify the normative dimension of critical theory to his latest, Habermas has avoided an approach that treats norms as simply 'external' (conceptual–transcendental) or 'internal' (contextual or immanent). This attempt to go between the two approaches in order to avoid both absolutism and relativism produces a tension in his work that the concept of communicative rationality does not resolve. On the one hand, the orientation to understanding, agreement and consensus central to the concept is a 'universal and unavoidable – in this sense transcendental' presupposition of communication which belongs to the development of the 'communicative competence' of the human species.[52] On the other hand, communicative rationality is embodied in society and history, but only partially so that it can serve as a goal for action. Habermas's concept of communicative rationality as a critical standard that is both 'partially' transcendental and 'partially' immanent (both *in* and *not in* society and history) is a complex and subtle attempt to find a normative foundation for critical social theory of the kind he believes is required. In the end, however, Habermas remains trapped in the same dilemma he faced earlier in his theory of 'quasi-transcendental' interests. Once one has accepted the 'inside'/'outside' dichotomy, it is impossible to go down the middle. The 'foundation' is either external or internal, it is either in society and history, or it is not.

The external–internal problem is reflected in the way Habermas approaches the 'reconstruction' of communicative competence. Such a reconstruction should, by Habermas's own account, be tested in an analogous manner to Chomskyan reconstructions of grammatical competence. Habermas's use of reconstruction for communicative competence, however, appears to be a contribution to the philosophy of language (to the extent that it is an a priori enterprise) rather than to linguistics (to the extent that it is an empirical enterprise). Much the same could be said for Habermas's use of 'developmental logic' which he draws from Piaget. Again, the ambivalence between the a priori and the empirical marked by the earlier term 'quasi-transcendental' continues to be a feature of Habermas's work. This ambivalence cannot be removed, nor the external–internal problem solved, as long as Habermas continues to attempt to find a 'normative foundation' that is neither simply internal nor external, yet 'partially' both.

The second objection I would like to raise is directed at the use Habermas makes of the concept of communicative rationality for critical social theory. This objection relates to the problem of the relation of theory to practice. This 'normative foundation' would be unnecessary if Habermas did not accept the empirical thesis that advanced capitalist society no longer legitimates it power by appeal to norms. This thesis is coupled with the equally empirical thesis that social actors, in particular the working class, accept technologically secured gratification in place of the realisation of social ideals ('the proletariat as proletariat has been dissolved' in Habermas's phrase).[53] Both theses are open to serious questions as a number of studies suggest.[54] Accepting them has two serious consequences for Habermas's work. First, Habermas is led to present an overly harmonistic account of the capitalist social system which ignores the internal problems of both the state and the economy.[55] Virtually all the problems faced by capitalism on his account occur in the conflict of the life-world with the smoothly functioning system. Further, Habermas's approach turns our attention away from the kind of concrete social and political analysis capable of addressing the internal problems of the economy and the state through its focus on the 'general' interests of the species, instead of the particular interests that dominate in practical–political contexts. Secondly, Habermas is led to reject the possibility of internal criticsm in favour of a complex and abstract theory beset with the difficult task of finding critical standards that are both in, and not in, social and historical reality.

Habermas's communication theory of society compromises the 'practical intentions' of human liberation that characterise a critical theory of society based more closely on Marx, which must accept the social and historical contextuality of human thought, speech and action. From this latter perspective, Habermas's concept of communicative rationality cannot be defended against the charge that it too is the expression of a particular culture, society and period of history. To the extent that the critical standards of Habermas's theory stand abstractly above this context of human social practice, they cannot reclaim the 'practical intentions' which give critical social theory its point. Critical standards which are 'unavoidable' cannot help but impinge on the very freedom and autonomy Habermas wants to defend. In spite of all his precautions, Habermas's 'general and unavoidable' critical standards contain the implicit danger of being imposed upon social actors who do not have the 'competencies' of their leaders. This is a subtle form of the danger faced by all 'scientific' Marxism. A social theory based on a critical appropriation of Marx escapes this danger because internal criticism can only succeed if it clarifies to social actors the meaning of their *own* critical standards, standards which must unequivocally be *in* social and historical reality. My brief suggestion is that a critical theory of society, in its descriptive component, directs itself to a new investigation of class, power and political organisation. Perhaps then it could and should return to the only critical method appropriate to a theory that takes seriously the thesis of social and historical contextuality – namely the method of internal criticism. I will return to these latter points in the following, and final, section.

Habermas and Marx: the future of radical theory

If my critique of Habermas's paradigm of communication is correct, then the two central problems for a critical theory of society (that is, the problem of normative foundations and the problem of the relation of theory to practice) remain unsolved. This certainly does not mean that Habermas's entire project is without value or that it makes no contribution to radical theory. Habermas's latest work, in particular, provides a new and potentially fruitful approach to social rationalisation and modernity which allows for a distinction between the advance represented by modern forms of life and their deformations or pathologies. In this regard, Habermas's critical concept of the 'colonization of the lifeworld' as a communicative reformulation and extension of Marx's concept of 'fetishism' may prove particularly useful. Further, Habermas's articulation of the paradigm of communication is certainly superior to other attempts to use this paradigm for radical theory such as Baudrillard's. Nevertheless, in these final remarks, I will argue that the paradigm of communication itself does not represent an advance on the paradigm of production. In other words, I will argue that communication theory is most usefully construed as a supplement to the paradigm of production, and not as a replacement for it.

Marx's paradigm of production already represented a radical break with the 'philosophy of consciousness', as I have argued. Habermas's charge that Marx remains trapped in this 'outdated' philosophy applies, if at all, only to certain critical Marxist interpretations of his paradigm.[56] Even here the 'advance' represented by the philosophy of language in the twentieth century over the earlier philosophy of consciousness is overemphasised by Habermas. In many respects, as Richard Rorty has argued, the philosophy of language reproduces earlier philosophical dilemmas in an updated form without really solving them.[57] Marx anticipated this development in a fascinating passage in *The German Ideology* which I will quote at length:

> One of the most difficult tasks confronting philosophers is to descend from the world of thought to the actual world . . . Just as philosophers have given thought an independent existence, so they were bound to make language into an independent realm. This is the secret of philosophical language, in which thoughts in the form of words have their own content. The problem of descending from the world of thoughts to the actual world is turned into the problem of descending from language to life . . . thoughts and ideas acquire an independent existence in consequence of the personal circumstances and relations of individuals acquiring independent existence. We have shown that exclusive, systematic occupation with these thoughts on the part of ideologists and philosophers, and hence the systematisation of

these thoughts, is a consequence of the division of labour . . . The philosphers have only to dissolve their language into the ordinary language, from which it is abstracted, in order to recognise it as the distorted language of the actual world and to realise that neither thoughts nor language in themselves form a realm of their own, that they are only manifestations of actual life.[58]

In this passage, Marx shows an almost Wittgensteinian awareness of the way philosophers (whether of 'language' or of 'consciousness') distort the actual uses of language in the context of practical life. Unlike Wittgenstein and his followers, however, Marx actually has a plausible explanation for the source of philosophical puzzlement. Such puzzlement is an abstract expression of problems encountered in practical life, but not understood as such because of the philosopher's exclusive concern with 'thoughts' and 'ideas' (or 'words' and 'meaning') produced by the division of labour. The solution to philosophical problems, from this perspective, is not to 'dissolve' them with a kind of 'linguistic therapy', but rather to transform social life which is the source of these problems.

Marx's criticism of making language into a 'separate realm' from social practice applies less to Habermas than to radical new French theory. Nevertheless, Habermas radically underestimates the degree to which the contemporary concerns with language can be addressed *within* the paradigm of production. Frederick Will has argued for the contemporary relevance of Marx's view of language as a complex social institution.[59] Will shows how Marx's view provides a broad social and historical background against which linguistic practice may be understood. The detailed elaboration of this argument must wait for another occasion. For now, I would like to turn to the way problems of normative foundations and the relation of theory to practice can be handled by a non-reductive interpretation of Marx's paradigm of production.

I have already attempted to give the outline of a non-reductive interpretation of Marx's paradigm of production in Chapter 2, where I explicated the concept of social rationality implicit in his work. With that discussion as a background, I will examine an approach to the problem of the normative dimension of social theory that, as I will argue, is also implicit there. Marx rejects a 'foundationalist' approach to values and norms, whether such an approach is developed in terms of the philosophy of consciousness or the philosophy of language. His own approach may be characterised as a 'practical contextualism'. What is 'just' in an ancient slave society is not 'just' in a capitalist society, and what is 'just' in a capitalist society will not be 'just'in a socialist society. From Marx's perspective, there simply is no such thing as justice *in itself*; either as an ontological essence, or as a transcendental necessity, or as a universal competence. Values and norms are socially and historically contextual.

Marx's contextualism allows him to claim, without irony, that the wage-labour exchange is 'just' *within* capitalist society.[60] This exchange relation is 'unjust' only from the perspective of a socialist transformation of capitalist society. Marx emphatically does not 'implant the normative core of rational natural law, that is, the idea that things would go well in bourgeois society only so long as the equivalents exchanged represented not merely what was alleged to be equivalent, but, what was in fact . . . equivalent' into the labour theory of value, as Habermas claims.[61] The wage-labour exchange is *in fact* 'just' under capitalism. The 'freedom' to sell your labour to any capitalist that will buy is *in fact* 'freedom' under capitalism. This 'justice' and 'freedom' are *in fact* 'injustice' and 'wage slavery' from the *practical* standpoint of a potential socialist transformation. Marx's analysis of capitalism *as critique* is only made possible by his commitment to this practical and revolutionary standpoint. As Habermas rightly insists, such a standpoint can only be justified based on a theory of history which distinguishes between 'what men and things could be and what they actually are'.[62] He is wrong, however, to argue that Marx's theory of history involves the same commitment to strict logical necessity and finalism as Hegel's philosophy of history. As I have argued, Hegel's dialectic is fundamentally a logical dialectic, and quite consistently since he is concerned with ideas and the logical relations of ideas. Marx's dialectic is fundamentally a historical dialectic, and quite consistently since he is concerned with human beings and the social relations of human beings.

Marx's paradigm of production provides a categorical framework with the help of which a theory of history can be formulated that distinguishes, in each historical case, between necessary social objectivity and those social relations of 'pseudo-objectivity' which can (and should) be judged and changed by conscious collective activity. Marx's dialectic of the forces and relations of production makes possible the formulation of this distinction between human interaction with nature, driving back its limitations, as a necessary objective process and the human social relations which become fetters on this process by assuming a 'pseudo-objectivity'. Thus, Marx distinguishes the basic axes of continuity and discontinuity in history, so that it can be understood as progress through conflict, struggle, rupture. Marx's theory of history does more than provide an interpretation; it also indicates and delimits the field of radical social criticism, orients the direction and prospects of radical practical activity, and posits criteria both for the rationality of critiism and the desirability of change. And this is accomplished without reference to anything that either transcends history or ends it.

The very process of production, and social life in general, develops in the producers both manifest and latent needs which cannot be satisfied under existing social relations. The internal criticism of these social relations which make these needs conscious and active, and a demand for their fulfilment through a radical social transformation, is rational and justified in a double sense. First, it is rational in the sense of 'realistic' since it is an outcome of the real material life-processes of society. Secondly, it is rational in the sense of being normatively justified as a contribution to the expansion of human needs, abilities and potentialities, as emancipation from the barriers to the human development of real concrete social individuals as the true subjects of the actual historical process. Marx's revolutionary theory posits its historical objective not as a 'regulative ideal', nor as a mere 'ought' (*sollen*), nor as a predetermined inevitability. Through the paradigm of production, Marx justifies his normative commitment based on a fact, the unnecessary suffering present in a concrete historical context, and as a need conditioned by the real material production and reproduction of social life.

The split between 'is' and 'ought' (as well as the disintegration of reason into its aspects: science, morality, religion and art) are accepted by Habermas as a legitimate (and, in some respects, progressive) and unexceedable feature of modern life. From Marx's practical, historical and contextual perspective, these splits only ideologically express an empirically ascertainable and contradiction-ridden form of social life, a form that can be overcome. The split between 'is' and 'ought', 'facts' and 'values', does not constitute a riddle for speculative thinking that a metaphysical return to a concept of substantial reason could overcome. The present distance between what is and what ought to be does not pose a question to be answered theoretically, but rather a task to be solved by conscious collective practical activity.

The above interpretation of the normative dimension of Marx's paradigm of production (as well as my earlier discussion of his implicit concept of social rationality) makes it clear that the relation of Marx's *theory* to the *practice* of the workers' movement is constitutive for the entire construction. The proletariat, as embodiment of social rationality, as a class with radical needs and potentially universal interests, held the edifice together and gave it its practical and political thrust. This is why 'the disappearance of the proletariat' thesis has had such an impact on Marx's original paradigm and led to its subsequent degeneration into the 'two Marxisms' discussed above. This is why alternatives to the paradigm are being sought by radical theory in the paradigm of communication, the paradigm of the text, and so on. None of these alternatives, including Habermas's in my view, has nearly the theoretical, critical or political power of Marx's original. But what of the anomalies faced by Marx's original? In particular, what about the apparent 'disappearance' of the proletariat? If these questions make Marx obsolete, and no other radical theory has the practical potential contained in his project, then is radical theory still possible at all? Earlier I traced the dissolution of Marx's paradigm of production so as to present Habermas's project as an all but necessary consequence of this dissolution and (I can now add) of the entrance of Marxism into the university system in the West. If to be radical is 'to go to the roots', as Marx says, I will end by briefly discussing the 'disappearance' of the proletariat and sketching an alternative for radical theory.

The proletariat was not an a priori construct dreamed up by Marx to fill a theoretical need. It was a *class* composed of real human individuals, brought together as a class by common interests, needs and social life-situations. As E.P. Thompson has argued, and I believe demonstrated, in *The Making of the English Working Class*, 'class . . . (is) an historical phenomenon, unifying a number of disparate and seemingly unconnected events, both in the raw material of experience and in consciousness' . . . it is not a 'structure', nor even a 'category' . . . it is 'something which in fact happens (and can be shown to have happened) in human relationships'.[63] Marx's own historical investigations locate the industrial proletariat as the truly revolutionary class. If this class analysis had not been reified and eternalised by many subsequent Marxists, who expected it to apply in social and historical situations where Marx (with his practical–revolutionary contextualism and his dedication to detailed concrete and historical investigation) himself would have changed or extended it, then some of the grosser degenerations of his theory might have been unnecessary. What is important here is not a theological fidelity to Marx, but a commitment to a practical and emancipatory standpoint and a tradition of 'active reason'. As Thompson states: 'Marx is on our side; we are not on the side of Marx.'[64] And, as I have argued, his radical theory remains even today as our most important *theoretical* weapon. But what of the proletariat today?

Today, as I will suggest here, the proletariat has not 'disappeared'. Rather, it has been extended and fragmented. The equation of capital with the 'factory' which is characteristic of Marxist political economy is today clearly inadequate. Advanced capitalism has extended the 'factory' and thus the proletariat. A radical theory today that makes use of Marx must take this extension into account. Harry Cleaver summarises this development as follows: 'The reproduction of the working class involves not only work in the factory but also work in the home and in the community of homes . . . The "factory" where the working class works (is) society as a whole, a social factory. The working class (has) to be redefined to include nonfactory workers.'[65] This redefinition allows us to see the working class not simply as those who work for wages (the factory), but also as those who do unwaged work for capital (the social factory) such as housewives, students, peasants. The concept of the social factory makes it possible to use Marx's theoretical tools to advance new and concrete analyses of the working class that are sensitive to its autonomous struggles, as well as to the issues of sexism and racism.

The above use of Marx's paradigm for the purposes of contemporary radical theory certainly does not exhaust the important theoretical and historical work done since Marx's time. Marxist theoreticians have extended the analysis of the capitalist state (Gramsci, the early Horkheimer, O'Connor), the analysis of class and the capitalist economy (E.P. Thompson, C.L.R. James, Mario Tronti, Dalla Costa, Harry Cleaver), and the analysis of capitalist ideology and the culture industry (Lukács, Korsch, the Frankfurt School, the

Situationists, Douglas Kellner).[66] Habermas's own work, read as a supplement to Marx and not as a replacement, also contributes to this continuation of radical theory by forging a link between Marxism and a radical democracy in which all political decisions are subjected to the discussion of a reasoning public. These last remarks may seem to be no more than a listing of favourites. Instead, I wish to use this list to indicate the direction I think radical theory should take: new investigations of class, the state and economy, as well as the massive cultural apparatus. Such investigations might serve as the basis for internal criticisms of both advanced capitalism and bureaucratic socialism: the twin alternative that the élites of both societies believe to be the highest and final stage of world history. The latter may in fact be true, since both have wasted the labour and lives of millions of human beings to gain the power to obliterate the species. This fact alone should indicate that, while we cannot demonstrate with certainty the transcendental conditions for the possibility of radical theory, we can argue with good reasons for its necessity.

Notes and References

Chapter 1: Reading Habermas

1. Thomas McCarthy, *The Critical Theory of Jürgen Habermas* (Cambridge, Mass., 1978); David Held, *Introduction to Critical Theory* (Berkeley, 1980); Raymond Guess, *The Idea of a Critical Theory* (Cambridge, 1981); Garbis Kortian, *Metacritique* (Cambridge, 1980); Richard J. Bernstein, *The Restructuring of Social and Political Theory* (New York, 1976).
2. See James W. Goulding, Susan L. Kline, Cary J. Nederman, 'Jürgen Habermas: An International Bibliography', *Political Theory*, vol. 8 (1980), pp.259–85. For the 'positive' approach, see John B. Thompson and David Held (eds), *Habermas: Critical Debates* (Cambridge, Mass., 1982).
3. Thompson and Held, p.219.
4. Goran Therborn, 'The Frankfurt School' from *Western Marxism: A Critical Reader* (London, 1977); Axel van den Berg, 'Critical Theory: Is There Still Hope?', *American Journal of Sociology*, vol. 86 (1980), pp.449–78; Karl Popper, 'Reason or Revolution?' from *The Positivist Dispute in German Sociology* (London, 1976); Y. Bar-Hillel, 'On Habermas's Hermeneutic Philosophy of Language', *Synthese*, vol. 26 (1973), pp.1–12; Quentin Skinner', 'Habermas's Reformation', *The New York Review of Books* (7 October 1982); Murray Bookchin, 'Finding the Subject: Notes on Whitebook and 'Habermas LTD', *Telos*, vol. 52 (1982), pp.78–98; Rudiger Bubner, *Modern German Philosophy* (Cambridge, 1981), pp.182–94.
5. Alvin W. Gouldner, *The Future of Intellectuals and the Rise of the New Class* (New York, 1979). For the application of Gouldner's analysis of 'the new class' to Habermas, see Cornelius Disco, 'Critical Theory as Ideology of the New Class', *Theory and Society*, vol. 8 (1979), pp.159–214.
6. See *The Linguistic Turn*, introduced and edited by Richard Rorty (Chicago, 1967).
7 Frederick Will, *Induction and Justification* (Ithaca, 1974).
8. Richard Rorty, *Philosophy and the Mirror of Nature* (Princeton, 1979). This characterisation of Rorty's position is made by Richard J. Bernstein in 'Philosophy and the Conversation of Mankind', *The Review of Metaphysis*, vol. 33 (1980), p.772.
9. John Searle, 'Intentionality and Method', *The Journal of Philosophy*, vol. 78 (1981), p.720.
10. This criticism does not apply to American Pragmatism, Dewey and Mead in particular. The work of Charles Taylor, within the analytic tradition proper, is also a partial exception. Even in Taylor, however, no important connections are made between philosophical approaches

176   *Notes and References*

to action and sociological, economic and political dimensions of human action. See Charles Taylor, *The Explanation of Behavior* (New York, 1964), and 'Relations Between Cause and Action', *Proceedings of the Seventh Inter-American Congress of Philosophy* (1967).

11. Habermas explicates the 'practical intentions' of critical theory in the following: 'Literaturbericht Zur Philosophiscen Diskussion un Marx und den Marxismus', *Philosophische Rundschau*, vl. 5 (1957), pp.165–235, and 'Zwischen Philosophie und Wissenschaft. Marxismus als Kritik' from *Theorie und Praxis* (Neuwied-Belin, 1967), pp.228–90. For a complete bibliography of Habermas's work up to 1979, see René Gortzen and Frederik von Gelder, 'Jürgen Habermas: The Complete Oeuvre. A Bibliography of Primary Literature, Translations and Reviews', *Human Studies*, vol. 2 (1979), pp.285–300. Hereafter, I will refer primarily to the English translations of Habermas's major works.

12. Rorty, *Mirror of Nature*; Will, *Justification*.

13. Rorty, *Mirror of Nature*.

14. Richard Rorty, 'Pragmatism, Relativism, and Irrationalism', *Proceedings and Addresses of the American Philosophical Association*, vol. 53 (1980), p.728.

15. Jürgen Habermas, 'A Reply to my Critics', in Thompson and Held (eds), *Critical Debates*, p.238.

16. Joel Whitebook, 'The Problem of Nature in Habermas', *Telos*, vol. 40 (1979), p.48.

17. Ibid, p.51.

18. In particular, see 'Towards a Theory of Communicative Competence', *Inquiry*, vol. 13 (1970), pp.360–76, and 'What is Universal pragmatics?' from *Communication and the Evolution of Society* (Boston, 1979), pp.1–68.

19. McCarthy, *Habermas*, p.357.

20. This way of starting the point was made clear to me by Charles B. Guignon. See C. B. Guignon, 'Saving the Differences: Gadamer and Rorty', *Philosophy of Science Association*, vol. 2 (1982), pp.360–67.

21. Jürgen Habermas, 'Response to the Commentary of Bernstein and Dove', in D. P. Verene (ed.), *Hegel's Social and Political Thought* (New Jersey, 1980), pp.247–8.

22. I argue for these points in Douglas Kellner and Rick Roderick, 'Social Practice as Explanandum: McCarthy on Habermas', *Man and World*, vol. 15 (1982), pp, 417–26.

23. For an extended criticism of one-sided interpretations of Habermas, see Douglas Kellner and Rick Roderick, 'Recent Literature on Critical Theory', *New German Critique* vol. 23 (1981), pp.159–66.

24. Richard J. Bernstein and Kenley Dove, 'Comment on the Relationship of Habermas's Views to Hegel' in D. P. Verene (ed.), *Hegel's Social and Political Theory* (New Jersey, 1980), pp.233–46.

25. Habermas, 'Response to Bernstein and Dove', p.250.

26. For example, see Trent Schroyer, *The Critique of Domination: The*

Origins and Development of Critical Theory (New York, 1973), and Kortian, *Metacritique*.

27. Habermas, 'Reply', p.239.
28. Bernstein, 'Comment', p.238.
29. See Habermas's latest work: Jürgen Habermas, *Theorie des Kommunikativen Handelns*, 2 vols (Frankfurt, 1981). An English translation by Thomas McCarthy of volume one has appeared under the title: *The Theory of Communicative Action, Volume One, Reason and the Rationalisation of Society* (Boston, 1984).

Chapter 2: Habermas and the Heritage of Critical Theory

1. Jürgen Habermas, *Theory and Practice* (Boston, 1973), p.212.
2. David Held, *Introduction to Critical Theory* (Berkeley, 1980), p.398.
3. Jürgen Habermas, 'A Reply to my Critics', in J. B. Thompson and D. Held, *Habermas: Critical Debates* (Cambridge, Mass., 1982), p.221.
4. Gyorgy Márkus, 'Practical–Social Rationality in Marx: A Dialectical Critique', *Dalectical Anthropology*, vol. 4 (1979), p.257. The following interpretation of Marx owes much to this excellent article.
5. Karl Marx, *The Economic and Philosophic Manuscripts of 1844*, ed. Dirk J. Struik (New York, 1964), p.136.
6. Karl Marx and Frederick Engels, *The German Ideology* (Moscow, 1976), p.37.
7. Karl Marx, *A Contribution to the Critique of Political Economy* (New York, 1970), pp.20–1.
8. Márkus, 'Practical–social Rationality', p.256.
9. Ibid, p.258.
10. Immanuel Kant, 'What is enlightenment?' in H. Reiss (ed.), *Political Writings* (Cambridge, 1970).
11. Alasdair MacIntyre, *A Short History of Ethics* (New York, 1966), p.211.
12. Max, *Manuscripts of 1844*, p.181.
13. Marx and Engels, *German Ideology*, p.45.
14. Karl Marx, *Theses on Feuerbach*, addenda to *The German Ideology* (Moscow, 1976), p.616.
15. Marx and Engels, *German Ideology*, p.58.
16. Márkus, 'Practical–Social Rationality', p.259.
17. Ibid.
18. For a discussion of Marx's distinction between forces and relations of production, see John McMurtry, *The Structure of Marx's World-View* (Princeton, 1978), pp.54–99.
19. For a discussion of the differences between Marx's and Hegel's dialectic, see T. K. Seung, *Structuralism and Hermeneutics* (New York, 1982), pp.110–16.
20. Herbert Marcuse, *Reason and Revolution* (Boston, 1960), p.258.
21. Marcuse, *Reason*, p.261.
22. Marx, *Feuerbach*, p.617.

23. See Russell Jacoby, 'Towards a Critique of Automatic Marxism: The Politics of Philosophy from Lukács to the Frankfurt School', *Telos*, vol. 10 (1971), pp.119–46; and Paul Breines, 'Praxis and its Theorists: The Impact of Lukács and Korsch in the 1920s', *Telos*, vol. 11 (1972), pp.67–103. Also see my 'Ideology in Lukács, Korsch, and Gramsci' (unpublished). I am indebted to Douglas Kellner and James Schmidt for my understanding of this theoretical tradition.

24. On Russian Marxism as a 'legitimation science', see Oscar Negt, 'Marxismus als Legitimationswissenschaft', in Bukharin, Deborin *et al.*, *Die Kontroverse uber Mechanischen und dialektischen Materialismus* (Frankfurt, 1969).

25. For the history of the Frankfurt School, see Martin Jay, *The Dialectic Imagination* (Boston, 1973); and Helmut Dubiel, *Wissenschaftsorganisation und politische Erfahrung* (Frankfurt, 1978).

26. On the concept of reason in critical theory, see the discussion by Eike Gebhardt in, *A. Arato and E. Gebhardt (eds), The Essential Frankfurt School Reader* (New York, 1978), pp.390–6.

27. See Jürgen Habermas, *The Theory of Communicative Action* (Boston, 1984), pp.345–99.

28. See H. H. Gerth and C. Wright Mills (eds), *From Max Weber: Essays in Sociology* (New York, 1946).

29. Max Weber, *The Protestant Ethic and the Spirit of Capitalism* (New York, 1958), pp.180–3.

30. Georg Lukács, *History and Class Consciousness* (Cambridge, 1971). In particular, see 'Reification and the Consciousness of the Proletariat', pp.83–222.

31. Lukács, *History* (preface to the new edition), p.23.

32. Ibid, pp.95–103.

33. See Max Horkheimer, *Critique of Instrumental Reason* (New York, 1974); Herbert Marcuse, *One-Dimensional Man* (Boston, 1964); Max Horkheimer and Theodor W. Adorno, *Dialectic of Enlightenment* (New York, 1972). For an excellent discussion of this critique and its problems to which I am indebted, see Seyla Benhabib, 'Modernity and the Aporias of Critical Theory', *Telos* vol. 49 (1981), pp.39–59.

34. Thomas McCarthy, *The Critical Theory of Jürgen Habermas* (Cambridge, Mass, 1978), p.20.

35. Herbert Marcuse, 'Philosophy and Critical Theory', in *Negations* (Boston, 1968), pp.135, 147.

36. Max Horkheimer, *Eclipse of Reason* (New York, 1974), p.182.

37. Max Horkheimer, 'Traditional and Critical Theory', in *Critical Theory* (New York, 1972), pp.224, 227; and 'The Latest Attack on Metaphysics' from the same work, p.163.

38. Susan Buck-Morss, *The Origin of Negative Dialectics* (New York, 1977), p.66.

39. Theodor W. Adorno, *Negative Dialectics* (New York, 1973), p.146.

40. Benhabib, 'Modernity', p.40.

41. See Habermas, *Theory of Communicative Action*, pp.143–57.

42. Marcuse, *One-Dimensional Man*, pp.143–57.

43. Herbert Marcuse, 'Industrialisation and Capitalism in the Work of Max Weber' in *Negations*, pp.223–5.

44. Jürgen Habermas, 'Technology and Science as "Ideology" in *Towards a Rational Society* (Boston, 1970), p.82.

45. Jürgen Habermas, *Strukturwandel der Offenlichkeit* (Berlin, 1962).

46. Jürgen Habermas, *Theorie und Praxis*, pp.128–48.

47. Jürgen Habermas, 'Analytische Wissenschaftstheorie und Dialektik. Ein Nachtrag zur Kontroverse Zwischen Popper und Adorno', in Max Horkheimer (ed.) *Zeugnisse, Theodor W. Adorno zum sechzigsten Geburtstag*, (Frankfurt, 1963), pp.473–503.

48. Jürgen Habermas, 'Gegen einen positivistisch halbierten Rationalismus', in *Kolner Zeitschrift fur Soziologie und Sozialpsychologie*, vol. 16 (1964), pp.636–59.

49. Habermas, 'Reply', p.231.

50. Jürgen Habermas, *Erkenntnis und Interesse* (Frankfurt, 1968).

51. Habermas, 'Marx und den Marxismus', *Philosophische Rundschau*, vol. 15 (1957), pp.165–235.

52. Ibid, pp.425–8.

53. Habermas, *Theorie und Praxis*, pp.228–90. The English translation of this essay that appears as 'Between Philosophy and Science: Marxism as Critique', in *Theory and Practice*, pp.195–252, drops the phrase 'four facts against Marx' entirely.

54. Habermas, *Theory and Practice*, pp.195–8.

55. Jürgen Habermas, *Communication and the Evolution of Society* (Boston, 1979), p.97.

56. Theodor W. Adorno, 'Cultural Criticism and Society', in *Prisms* (London, 1967), p.34; and McCarthy, *Habermas*, p.108.

57. Jürgen Habermas, 'Technology', p.85.

58. Ibid, pp.85–7.

59. Benhabib, 'Modernity', p.49.

60. Jürgen Habermas, *Knowledge and Human Interests* (Boston, 1971), p.42; originally published as *Erkenntnis und Interesse* (Frankfurt, 1968).

61. Habermas, *Knowledge*, pp.25–63; and *Theory and Practice*, pp.195–252.

62. Habermas, *Theory and Practice*, pp.41–81.

63. See James Schmidt, 'Jürgen Habermas and the Difficulties of Enlightenement', *Social Research* vol. 49 (1982), p 188.

64. See McCarthy, *Habermas*, pp.1–16; and Held, *Critical Theory*, pp.260–7.

65. Habermas, *Theory and Practice*, p.44.

66. Jürgen Habermas, 'Arbeit und Interaktion. Bemerkungen zu Hegels Henenser Philosophie des geistes', in *Natur und Geschichte. Karl Lowith zum 70. Geburtstag.* (Stuttgart, 1967), pp.132–56; published in English as 'Labour and Interaction: Remarks on Hegel's Jena Philosophy of Mind', in *Theory and Practice*, pp.142–69.

67. See McCarthy, *Habermas*, pp.16–40.

68. Habermas, *Knowledge*, p.4.

69. Ibid, preface and pp.68–9.
70. Ibid, preface; and McCarthy, *Habermas*, pp.92–104.
71. Jürgen Habermas, *Zur Logik der Sozialwissenschaften*, in *Philosophische Rundschau*, vol. 14 (Tubingen, 1967).
72. Habermas, *Knowledge*, p.194.
73. Karl-Otto Apel, 'The a priori of Communication and the Foundation of the Humanities', *Man and World*, no. 5 (1972), p.10.
74. Habermas, *Knowledge*, p.195.
75. Ibid, p.193.
76. Habermas, *Theory and Practice*, pp.22–3.
77. Habermas, *Knowledge*, pp.197–8.
78. Jügen Habermas, 'A Postscript to *Knowledge and Human Interests*', *Philosophy of the Social Sciences*, vol. 3 (1975), p.176.
79. Habermas, *Knowledge*, p.214.
80. Ibid, p.269.
81. Habermas, *Theory and Practice*, p.9.
82. James Schmidt used this apt expression to characterise Habermas's position in a conversation with me.
83. See Steven Lukes, 'Of Gods and Demons: Habermas and Practical Reason', in Thompson and Held, *Critical Debates*, pp.134–48.

Chapter 3: Habermas and the Reconstruction of Critical Theory

1. See Fred R. Dallmayr, 'Critical Theory Criticised: Habermas' *Knowledge and Human Interests* and its Aftermath', *Philosophy of the Social Sciences*, vol. 2 (1972), pp.211–29.
2. See Theodor W. Adorno *et al.*, *Der Positivismusstreit in der deutschen Soziologie* (Berlin, 1969); Jürgen Habermas and Niklas Luhmann, *Theorie der Gesellschaft oder Sozialtechnologie: Was leistet die Systemforschung?* (Frankfurt, 1971); Karl-Otto Apel *et al.*, *Hermeneutik und Ideologiekritik* (Frankfurt, 1971).
3. See Garbis Kotian, *Metacritique* (Cambridge, 1980).
4. Karl-Otto Apel, 'Wissenschaft als Emanzipation? Eine Kritische Wurdigung der Wissenchaftskonzeption der "Kritischen Theorie"', in *Zeitschrift fur allgemeine Wissenschaftstheorie*, vol. 1 (1970), pp.173–95, reprinted in *Materialien zu Habermas' 'Erkenntnis und Interesse'*, ed. W. Dallmayr (Frankfurt, 1974), pp.341–2.
5. Apel, 'Wissenschaft als Emanzipaion?', pp.341–2.
6. Jürgen Habermas, *Knowledge, and Human Interests* (Boston, 1971), pp.62–3.
7. See Karl Marx, *The Economic and Philosophic Manuscripts of 1844* (New York, 1964) p.142.
8. Habermas, Knowledge, p.55.
9. Ibid, appendix, pp.314–5.
10. See Thomas McCarthy, *The Critical Theory of Jürgen Habermas* (Cambridge, Mass., 1978) pp.109–10; and Hans-Georg Gadamer,

'Replik', in K.-O. Apel *et al.*, *Hermeneutik und Ideologiekritik*, pp.283–317.
11. Dietrich Bohler, 'Zur Geltung des emanzipatorischen Interesses', in *Materialien zu Habermas' 'Erkenntnis und Interesse'*, pp.351–61.
12. McCarthy, *Habermas*, p..111.
13. Habermas, *Knowledge*, p.135.
14. Ibid, p.35, 39.
15. Michael Theunissen, *Gesellschaft und Geschichte: Zur Kritik der Kritischen Theorie* (Berlin, 1969).
16. Theunissen, *Gesellschaft*, p.13.
17. Gadamer, 'Replik', pp.294–5.
18. Hans Joachim Giegel, 'Reflexion und Emanzipation', in K.-O. Apel *et al.*, *Hermeneutik und Ideologiekritik*, pp.278–9.
19. On labour and interaction, see Goran Therborn, 'Jürgen Habermas: A New Eclecticism', *New Left Review*, vol. 67 (1971), pp.69–83. On the theory of truth, see McCarthy, *Habermas*, p.203.
20. Habermas, 'Postscript to *Knowledge and Human Interests, Philosophy of the Social Sciences*, vol. 3 (1975) p.182.
21. McCarthy, *Habermas*, p.101.
22. Jürgen Habermas, *Theory and Practice* (Boston, 1973), pp.33–40.
23. McCarthy, *Habermas*, p.272.
24. See Marcuse's critique of the philosophy of language, in Herbert Marcuse, *One-Dimensional Man* (Boston, 1964) pp.170–99.
25. Habermas, *Zur Logik der Sozialwissenschaften*, in *Philosophiche Rundschcau*, vol. 14 (Tubingen, 1967), p.220.
26. Habermas, *Knowledge*, p.317.
27. See John Searle, 'Chomsky's Revolution in Linguistics', in *On Noam Chomsky: Critical Essays* (Garden City, New York, 1974), pp.2–33.
28. See John Lyons, *Semantics*, 2 vols (Cambridge, 1977), pp.409–22.
29. Jürgen Habermas, 'Towards a Theory of Communicative Competence', *Inquiry*, vol. 13 (1970), p.363.
30. Ibid, p.363.
31. Ibid, p.363.
32. Ibid, p.364.
33. Ibid, p.365.
34. Ibid, p.366.
35. Ibid, pp.366–7.
36. Ibid, p.367.
37. Ibid, pp.368–70.
38. Ibid, p.370–2.
39. Ibid, p.372.
40. See Jürgen Habermas, 'On Systematically Distorted Communication', *Inquiry*, vol. 13 (1970), pp.205–18.
41. Habermas, 'Communicative Competence', p.372.
42. Ibid, p.372.
43. Ibid, p.362.
44. Searle, 'Chomsky's Revolution', p.30.
45. See Lyons, *Semantics*, pp.573–91.

46. John Searle, *Speech Acts* (Cambridge, 1969), p.4.
47. Habermas, 'Communicative Competence', p.367.
48. Habermas, 'Wahrheitstheorin', in *Wirklichkeit und Reflexion: Walter Schulz zum 60* (Neske, 1973), pp.211–65. See pages 258–9 for an account of 'the ideal speech situation' as 'counterfactual'.
49. Ibid, pp.214–15.
50. *Einlosung* may be translated as either 'vindication' or 'redemption'. In the context of critical theory, the term 'redemption' is associated with the work of Walter Benjamin. See Jürgen Habermas, 'Consciousness-raising or Redemptive Criticism – The Contemporaneity of Walter Benjamin', *New German Critique*, vol. 17 (1979), pp.30–59.
51. Habermas, 'Wahrheitstheorin', p.240.
52. Ibid, pp.252–60.
53. Ibid, pp.211–219.
54. Ibid, pp.215–16.
55. Ibid, pp.216–17.
56. Ibid, pp.219–31.
57. Ibid, p.218.
58. Ibid, pp.239–40.
59. Ibid, p.265.
60. David Held, *Introduction to Critical Theory* (Berkeley, 1980), p.396.
61. Alvin Gouldner, *The Idea of Ideology and Technology* (New York, 1976), pp.138–45.
62. Raymond Geuss, *The Dialectic of a Critical Theory* (Cambridge, 1981), pp.66–7.
63. Richard J. Bernstein, *The Restructuring of Social and Political Theory* (New York, 1976), pp.223–5.
64. Habermas, 'Wahrheitstheorin', p.259.
65. Richard Bernstein makes the intriguing observation that:

> Although based on contemporary philosophy of language and theoretical linguistics, Habermas's argument exhibits some striking parallels with the one that Socrates develops in the *Phaedrus*. Socrates too is concerned with the conditions for speech, and argues that the analysis of speech is oriented to the idea of truth – even when speech is intended to deceive. Further, the analysis of truth leads to the analysis of the conditions for ideal speech – the type of discourse characteristic of true philosophic friends. There is even a parallel with the four validity claims that Habermas specifies; when Socrates analyses the requirements for speech, he emphasises the importance of each of these features. Socrates' argument is intended to show that all speech – even the deceptive speech of Lysias – presupposes and anticipates ideal speech. And just as Habermas' line of argument leads him to recognise the reciprocal relation between ideal speech, which is essentially dialogue, and the ideal form of life, so the primary practical problem for Socrates becomes one of construction or reconstructing a polis in which such ideal speech can be realised. (Bernstein, *Restructuring*, pp.262–3.)

66. McCarthy. *Habermas*, p.326.
67. Jürgen Habermas, 'What is Universal Pragmatics?' in *Communication and the Evolution of Society* (Boston, 1979), p.1.
68. Ibid, p.2.
69. Ibid, p.3.
70. Ibid, p.5.
71. Ibid, p.6.
72. Ibid, p.26.
73. See J. L. Austin, *How To Do Things with Words* (Cambridge, 1962).
74. See John Searle, *Speech Acts* (Cambridge, 1969).
75. Lyons, *Semantics*, p.735.
76. Habermas, 'Universal Pragmatics', p.38–9.
77. See P. F. Strawson, *Logics-Linguistic Papers* (New York, 1971), pp.149–69.
78. Habermas, 'Universal Pragmatics', p.40.
79. Ibid, pp.41–2.
80. See L. J. Cohen, 'Do Illocutionary Forces Exist?', *Philosophical Quarterly*, vol. 14 (1964), pp.118–37.
81. Habermas, 'Universal Pragmatics', p.45.
82. Ibid, p.46.
83. Ibid, p.49.
84. Ibid, pp.51–2.
85. Ibid, p.53.
86. Ibid, p.54.
87. Ibid, pp.57–8.
88. Ibid, p.59.
89. Ibid, p.61.
90. Ibid, pp.62–3.
91. Ibid, pp.65–7.
92. Ibid, pp.58, 68.
93. Y. Bar-Hillel, 'On Habermas's Hermeneutic Philosophy of Language', *Synthese*, vol. 26 (1973), p.11.
94. Habermas, *Communication and the Evolution of Society*, p.209.
95. McCarthy, *Habermas*, p.25.
96. See Lyons, *Semantics*, pp.778–86.
97. See John B. Thompson, 'Universal Pragmatics', in J. B. Thompson and D. Held (eds) *Habermas: Critical Debates*, pp.127–128. Thompson points out that the volume of essays usually cited by Habermas (*Universals of Language*, edited by Greenburg (Cambridge, 1963)) has been severely and convincingly criticised.
98. Jürgen Habermas, *Zur Rekonstruktion des Historischen Materialismus* (Frankfurt, 1976). Four chapters of this work are translated in *Communication and the Evolution of Society*. A fifth, 'History and Evolution', is translated in *Telos*, vol. 39 (1979), pp.5–45.
99. Habermas, *Communication and the Evolution of Society*, p.120.
100. Ibid, p.98.
101. Ibid, p.123.
102. Habermas, *Zur Rekonstruktion*, p.235.

103. Habermas, *Communication and the Evolution of Society*, pp.121–2.
104. Ibid, pp.164–5.
105. Jürgen Habermas, *Legitimation Crisis* (Boston, 1975).
106. See Held, *Critical Theory*, p.287; and Habermas, *Legitmation Crisis*, p.49.
107. Habermas, *Legitimation Crisis*, p.113.
108. Ibid, pp.110–13.
109. For example, see Michael Schmid, 'Habermas's Theory of Social Evolution', in Thompson and Held (eds) *Habermas:. Critical Debates*, pp.162–80; and J. P. Arnason, 'J. Habermas, *Zur Rekonstruktion des Historischen Materialismus*', *Telos*, vol. 39 (1979), pp.201–18.
110. See McCarthy's discussion of these research projects: Thomas McCarthy, 'Rationality and Relativism', in *Critical Debates*, pp.69–75.
111. For example, see Habermas's comments concerning the historical contextuality of sociological concepts in *Zur Logik*, pp.121–2.

Chapter 4: Habermas on Communicative Action and Rationality

1. Habermas, *The Theory of Communicative Action*, vol. 1, *Reason and the Rationalisation of Society* (1984) has appeared in English translation. I will refer to this volume as *Communicative Action* hereafter. The original 2-volume German edition (1981) will be referred to as *Kommunikativen Handelns* 1 or 2. To my knowledge, two reviews of the book have appeared in English: David M. Rasmussen, 'Communicative Action and Philosophy: Reflections on Habermas's Theorie des kommunikativen Handelns', *Philosophy and Social Criticism*, vol. 9 (1982), pp.3–28; and a review by Johannes Berger, translated and published in *Telos*, vol. 57 (1983), pp.194–205.
2. See 'The Dialectics of Rationalization', an interview with Jürgen Habermas by Axel Honneth, Eberhard Knodler-Bunte and Arno Widmann, *Telos*, vol. 49 (1981), pp.5–31; Jürgen Habermas, 'New Social Movements' (a translation of part of the last chapter of *Kommunikativen Handelns* (2), *Telos*, vol. 49 (1981), pp.33–7; Habermas 'Reply' from *Critical Debates* (1982).
3. Habermas, *Communicative Action*, pp.1–2.
4. Ibid, p.2.
5. Ibid, pp.2–3
6. Jürgen Habermas, *Knowledge and Human Interests* (Boston, 1971), p.63.
7. Habermas, *Legitimation Crisis* (Boston, 1975), p.159.
8. Habermas, *Communicative Action*, p.285.
9. Jürgen Habermas, 'Reply to my Critics', in Thompson and Held (eds) *Habermas: Critical Debates* (Cambridge, Mass, 1982), p.266.
10. Habermas, *Communicative Action*, p.99–101.
11. Ibid, p.328–32.
12. Habermas, 'Reply', p.269.

13. Habermas, *Communicative Action*, pp.8–9.
14. Ibid, p.9.
15. Ibid, p.10.
16. Ibid, p.10.
17. Habermas, 'Dialectics of Rationalisation', p.16.
18. Habermas, *Communicative Action*, p.18.
19. Ibid, p.42.
20. Ibid, p.23.
21. Ibid, p.43.
22. Ibid, p.44.
23. Ibid, p.45.
24. Ibid, p.53.
25. Ibid, p.57.
26. Ibid, p.55.
27. Ibid, p.58.
28. Ibid, p.66.
29. Ibid, p.66–7.
30. Habermas, *Communicative Action*, p.69. McCarthy translates 'Dezentrierung' as 'decentration', although Piaget's concept is generally rendered in English as 'decentring'. For Piaget's own understanding of the concept, see Jean Piaget and Barbel Inhelder, *The Psychology of the Child* (New York, 1969), pp.94–8.
31. Habermas, *Communicative Action*, pp.68–72.
32. Habermas, 'Dialectics of Rationalization', p.16. See Habermas, *Communicative Action*, pp.70–1.
33. Habermas, 'Dialectics of Rationalization', p.18. On the distinction between 'lifeworld' and 'system', see Habermas, *Kommunikativen Handelns* (2), pp.173–293. Habermas summarises this account in 'Reply', pp. 278–81.
34. Habermas, *Communicative Action*, pp.71–2.
35. Ibid, p.72.
36. Ibid, p.73.
37. Ibid, p.144.
38. Ibid, p.144.
39. Habermas, 'Reply', p.230.
40. Ibid, p.253.
41. Ibid, p.253.
42. Rasmussen, 'Reflections', p.12.
43. Habermas, *Kommunikativen Handelns* (2), p.214.
44. Ibid, p.216.
45. Ibid, p.215.
46. See Rasmussen, 'Reflections', pp.12–13.
47. Habermas, 'Dialectics of Rationalization', p.18.
48. Habermas, 'Reply', p.279.
49. See Habermas, 'Reply', pp.280–1 and *Kommunikativen Handelns* (2), pp.489–547.
50. Habermas, 'Reply', p.280.

51. Ibid, p.281.
52. James Schmidt, 'Jürgen Habermas and the Difficulties of Enlightenment', *Social Research*, vol. 19, p.18.
53. Habermas, 'Dialectics of Rationalization', pp.18–19.
54. Habermas, 'New Social Movements', p.33.
55. Ibid, p.33–35.
56. Ibid, pp.34–35.

Chapter 5: Habermas and the Prospects of Critical Theory

1. On the 'Crisis of Marxism', see Alvin Gouldner, *The Two Marxisms* (New York, 1980), pp.26–29.
2. For attempts to deal with these anomalies from a Marxist perspective, see Herbert Marcuse, *Soviet Marxism: A Critical Analysis* (Boston, 1964); Frederick Pollock, *Stadien des Kapitalismus*, edited by Helmut Dubiel (München, 1975); Guy Debord, *Society of the Spectacle* (Detroit, 1970); E. P. Thompson, *The Poverty of Theory and Other Essays* (New York, 1978).
3. For example, see Jean Baudrillard, *The Mirror of Production* (St Louis, 1975). Habermas comments on these 'post-modern' viewpoints in Jürgen Habermas, 'Modernity versus Postmodernity', *New German Critique*, vol. 22 (1981), pp.3–14.
4. See Peter Steinfels, *The Neoconservatives* (New York, 1979). On Postmodern Liberalism, see Richard Rorty, 'Postmodernist Bourgeois Liberalism', *The Journal of Philosophy*, vol. 80 (1983), pp.583–9.
5. C. Disco, 'Critical Theory as Ideology of the New Class', *Theory and Society*, 8 (1979) pp.159–214.
6. V. I. Lenin, *On Marx and Engels* (Peking, 1975), pp.62–9. Originally published in March 1913 in *Prosveshcheniye*, no.3.
7. On the distinction between these two kinds of anomalies, see Gouldner, *Two Marxisms*, pp.15–16.
8. Ibid, pp.32–44.
9. Ibid, pp.36–44.
10. Ibid, pp.36–44.
11. Ibid, pp.44–8.
12. Ibid, pp.44–8.
13. See V. I. Lenin, *What is to be Done?*, in R. C. Tucker (ed.) *The Lenin Anthology* (New York, 1975) pp.12–144.
14. See the early warning contained in Rosa Luxemburg, *The Russian Revolution* and *Leninism or Marxism?* (Ann Arbor, 1961).
15. Gouldner, *Two Marxisms*, p.56.
16. See E. P. Thompson, *William Morris* (New York, 1976), pp.763–816, and *Poverty of Theory*.
17. Karl Marx, 'For a Ruthless Criticism of Everything Existing' (letter to Ruge, originally published in *Deutsch-Franzosische Jahrbucher*, 1844), in R. C. Tucker (ed.) *The Marx-Engels Reader* (New York, 1972), p.14.

18. M. Horkheimer and T. W. Adorno, *Dialectic of Enlightenment* (New York, 1972).
19. See D. Held, *Introduction to Critical Theory*; and M. Jay, *The Dialectical Imagination* (Boston, 1973).
20. See Jay, *Dialectical Imagination*, pp.4–85.
21. On 'existentialism', see Theodor W. Adorno, *Jargon of Authenticity* (London, 1973). On 'positivism', see Marx Horkheimer, *Eclipse of Reason* (New York, 1974).
22. On the problems of 'justification' and 'demarcation', see M. Horkheimer, 'Traditional and Critical Theory', in *Critical Theory* (New York, 1972); H. Marcuse, 'Philosophy and Critical Theory', in *Negations* (Boston, 1968).
23. See R. Jacoby, 'Towards a Critique of Automatic Marxism: The Politics of Philosophy', *Telos*, vol.10 (1971).
24. See Horkheimer and Adorno, 'Preface to the New Edition' and 'Introduction' to *Dialectic of Enlightenment*, and D. Held, *Introduction to Critical Theory*, pp.36–39, 254–5.
25. Gyorgy Márkus, 'Practical–Social Rationality in Marx: A Dialectical Critique – Part 2', *Dialectical Anthropology*, vol. 5 (1980), p.1.
26. See Vincent Descombes, *Modern French Philosophy* (Cambridge, 1980), pp.118–19. For a detailed account, see Jacques Ranciere, *Le leçon d'Althusser* (Paris, 1974).
27. Habermas refers to this remark in, Jürgen Habermas, 'A Test for Popular Justice: The Accusations Against the Intellectuals', *New German Critique*, vol. 12 (1977), pp.11–13. For an account of Habermas's reaction to the 'excesses' of the 1960s, see Rolf Ahlers, 'How Critical is Critical Theory?', *Cultural Hermeneutics*, vol. 3 (1975), pp.119–36.
28. Walter Benjamin, 'Theses on the Philosophy of History' in *Illuminations* (New York, 1968), pp. 253–64.
29. Baudrillard, *Mirror of Production*.
30. This tendency can be seen in Foucault, Lyotard and others.
31. Baudrillard, *Mirror of Production*, pp.130–1.
32. Ibid, p.128.
33. Ibid, p.127.
34. Ibid, p.134, 137.
35. See Karl Marx, *Critique of Hegel's 'Philosophy of Right'* (Cambridge, 1970), pp.141–2.
36. Baudrillard, *Mirror of Production*, p.141.
37. Márkus, 'Practical–Social Rationality – 2', p.3.
38. Habermas, 'Technology and Science as "Ideology"', in *Towards a Rational Society* (Boston, 1970), p.111.
39. See Marx, *The Economic and Philosophic Manuscripts of 1844* (New York, 1964) pp.106–19.
40. Ibid, pp.113–14.
41. See John B. Thompson, 'Universal Pragmatics', in Thompson and Held (eds), *Critical Debates*, pp.128–9.

42. See T. McCarthy, *The Critical Theory of Jürgen Habermas*, pp.292–3.

43. Louis Mackey, 'Slouching Toward Bethlehem: Deconstructive Strategies in Theology', *Anglican Theological Review*, vol. 65 (1983), p.257. I am indebted to Louis Mackey for this argument and for my understanding of the philosophy of language in general.

44. Joan Robinson, *Freedom and Necessity* (New York, 1970) p.60.

45. Albrecht Wellmer, 'Thesen uber Vernunft, Emanzipation und Utopie', unpublished manuscript (1979), quoted by Habermas in 'Reply' from *Critical Debates*, p.262.

46. Habermas, *The Theory of Communicative Action*, pp. 73–4.

47. Ibid.

48. Ibid, p.74.

49. Thomas McCarthy, 'Translator's Introduction' to *Communicative Action*, pp.5–37. This comment comes from a note to this introduction, note 12, p.405.

50. Ibid, pp.405–6.

51. McCarthy, 'Introduction' to *Communicative Action*, pp.6–7.

52. Habermas, *Communication and the Evolution of Society* (Boston, 1979) p.177.

53. Habermas, *Theory and Practice* (Boston, 1973), p.196.

54. See M. Burawoy and T. Skocpol (eds) *Marxist Inquiries* (Chicago, 1982), in particular, Erik Olin Wright and Joachim Singelmann, 'Proletarianization in the Changing American Class Structure', pp.176–209; E. P. Thompson, *The Poverty of Theory* and *The Making of the English Working Class* (New York, 1966), pp.2–14; Harry Cleaver, *Reading Capital Politically* (Austin, 1979); and Douglas Hibbs, *Economic Interest and the Politics of Macroeconomic Policy* (Cambridge, 1976). Also, see M. Bookchin, 'Finding the Subject', *Telos*, vol. 52, pp.92–5.

55. J. Berger, Review of *Kommunicative Handelns*, *Telos*, vol. 57, pp.198–205.

56. Habermas's charge might, for example, be plausibly brought against the Lukács of *History and Class Consciousness*. Even here it would require a much more detailed elaboration than any so far provided by Habermas.

57. See R. Rorty, *Philosophy and the Mirror of Nature* (Princeton, 1979); and R. J. Bernstein's review 'Philosophy and the Conversation of Mankind', *The Review of Metaphysics*, vol. 33 (1980).

58. Marx and Engels, *The German Ideology* (Moscow, 1976), pp.472–3.

59. See F. Will, *Induction and Justification* (Ithaca, 1974), pp.214–17.

60. See Karl Marx, *Capital*, vol. 1 (London, 1970–2), pp.194, 583.

61. Habermas, 'A Reply to my Critics', in Thompson and Held (eds) *Critical Debates*, p.230. For excellent defences of Marx's labour theory of value, see H. M. Cleaver, *Reading Capital Politically* (Brighton, 1979); and Marx W. Wartofsky, 'Is Marx's Labor Theory of Value Excess Metaphysical Baggage?' *The Journal of Philosophy*, vol. 80 (1983), pp.719–30.

62. Habermas, 'Reply', p.231.
63. E. P. Thompson, *English Working Class*, p.9.
64. E. P. Thompson, *The Poverty of Theory*, p.192.
65. Cleaver, *Reading Capital Politically*, p.57.
66. In addition to works already cited, see Antonio Gramsci, *Prison Notebooks*, selections (New York, 1971); Karl Korsch, *Marxism and Philosophy* (London, 1984); Douglas Kellner, *Karl Korsch: Revolutionary Theory* (Austin, 1977), and 'TV, Ideology, and Emancipatory Popular Culture', *Socialist Review*, vol. 45 (1979), and *Herbert Marcuse and the Crisis of Marxism* (London, 1964); Ken Knabb (ed.) *Situationist International Anthology* (Berkeley, 1981); James O'Connor, *The Fiscal Crisis of the State* (New York, 1973); C. L. R. James, *State Capitalism and World Revolution* (Detroit, 1950); Mario Tronti, 'Social Capital', *Telos*, vol. 14 (1972), pp.25–62; Mariarosa Dalla Costa and Selma James, *The Power of Women and the Subversion of the Community* (Bristol, 1972).

Index